PRAISE FOR

HOLLYWOOD TO THE HIMALAYAS

"Sadhvi Bhagawati Saraswati is a great teacher of spirituality and consciousness. Her inspiring wisdom illuminates the path to healing, happiness, and inner peace."

DEEPAK CHOPRA

"Courageous, Relatable, and Inspiring! Sadhvi's story will touch your heart and show you that the path to the divine is available to everyone."

PRINCE EA

"Sadhvi Bhagawati Saraswati describes in vivid and poetic prose the journey that took her, a Stanford graduate, from a life of privilege in America to a simple existence in an Indian ashram. She speaks of her transformation from a disturbed adolescent to a woman who has found spiritual enlightenment; and how she was able to renounce the pleasures of the material world and physical desire through the agency of an inspiring and inspired Guru, the beauty of nature, and a sacred river.

"Her journey is a river of love, compelling in its authenticity and unflinching honesty. Sadhvi transports the reader to a world and way of thinking that most will be unfamiliar with, and this book is a must for anyone who is interested in exploring different paths to fulfilment and to the Creator."

JANE GOODALL

"For so many of us, the road to the Divine sometimes begins with deep trauma. And, then Grace is bestowed upon us and we blossom in the holiness of love. Hollywood to the Himalayas *is filled with wisdom and truth about the powerful revelations that unfold on the path to a deeper relationship to the divine. This is a beautiful book."*

REV. IYANLA VANZANT,
EXECUTIVE PRODUCER OF *IYANLA, FIX MY LIFE*

"This is a book in which every sentence is a reflection of love and the wisdom of love. Sadhviji's journey is a lucid illustration of how her search for the Divine is taken with every step and every breath in a world ostensibly of the mundane. She speaks of her pain as a source of knowledge, as she shows how Divine love and light, ever present, leads her to an academically informed, humorously inspiring, inevitability of love as lived activism in the service of one and all."

DR. AZZA KARAM, SECRETARY GENERAL, RELIGIONS FOR PEACE;
FORMER SENIOR ADVISOR, UNFPA

"This true story shines a bright light on the path to becoming more deeply spiritual. Sadhvi courageously shares her life lessons, illustrating the infinite possibilities when we consciously seek connection to the divine."

JACK CANFIELD, COAUTHOR OF
CHICKEN SOUP FOR THE SOUL SERIES

"This very special book chronicles a unique transformational journey of an American woman who overcame childhood abuse and trauma to lead a life of service as a global spiritual leader. A beautifully written account of awakening that offers ancient wisdom for modern-day issues. I highly recommend this!"

MARCI SHIMOFF, AUTHOR OF *HAPPY FOR NO REASON, LOVE FOR NO REASON,* AND *CHICKEN SOUP FOR THE WOMAN'S SOUL*

"*In* Hollywood to the Himalayas, *Sadhvi unfolds deeply personal experiences that offer the reader most important and valuable insights on how to become resilient, self-empowered. Beyond the lessons offered, Sadhvi's wonderful writing style evoked a movie-like vision in my mind; it is a compelling story that made it hard to put this book down.*"

BRUCE H. LIPTON, PhD, STEM CELL BIOLOGIST, EPIGENETIC SCIENCE PIONEER, AND AUTHOR OF THE BESTSELLING BOOKS *THE BIOLOGY OF BELIEF, SPONTANEOUS EVOLUTION* (WITH JIM BHAERMAN), AND *THE HONEYMOON EFFECT*

"There is not one of us who hasn't suffered. For many, it is the suffering that gives one insight, wisdom and clarity. Sadhvi's journey is one such story that leads to India and her relationship with her Guru and with the Ganga. Yet, it is much more because it is also a story of the power of forgiveness, compassion, grace and love to set one free. Profound, engaging and ultimately liberating."

JAMES R. DOTY, MD, PROFESSOR AND AUTHOR OF *INTO THE MAGIC SHOP: A NEUROSURGEON'S QUEST TO DISCOVER THE MYSTERIES OF THE BRAIN AND THE SECRETS OF THE HEART*

"This inspiring and motivational book is a real page-turner. I believe it's the feminine version of the classic spiritual memoir, Autobiography of a Yogi."

JOHN GRAY, AUTHOR OF *MEN ARE FROM MARS, WOMEN ARE FROM VENUS*

"A compelling account and an inside look at a great ashram, offering a Western woman's remarkable odyssey of trust in Indian spiritual culture and her powerful healing journey."

JACK KORNFIELD, AUTHOR OF *A PATH WITH HEART*

"Sadhvi Bhagawati Saraswati was a student at Stanford seeking science-based solutions to her emotional wounds and childhood trauma, hoping to heal herself and then others. On a trip to India, in an unexpected twist of fate, she experienced a remarkable, divine healing, on the banks of the Ganges River. For those on a spiritual path, this book is a rare glimpse into connecting with the divine."

ARIELLE FORD,
AUTHOR OF *THE SOULMATE SECRET*

"While Dorothy had to go over the rainbow to discover there is no place like home, Sadhvi found her true home on the banks of the Ganges wrapped in the arms of the Divine. This enlightenment story will make your heart melt and your jaw drop."

JUSTIN MICHAEL WILLIAMS, AUTHOR OF *STAY WOKE*

"Hollywood to the Himalayas *is filled with soulful, deep insight and dynamic wisdom. Sadhvi Bhagawati Saraswati's honest, courageous, powerful story and resonant words radiate healing energy palpable to the heart and mind, borne of her authenticity and spiritual transformation. Study this book and allow your soul to sing."

MICHAEL BERNARD BECKWITH, FOUNDER AND SPIRITUAL DIRECTOR,
AGAPE INTERNATIONAL SPIRITUAL CENTER; AUTHOR OF *LIFE VISIONING* AND *SPIRITUAL LIBERATION*

"*What an extraordinary book!* Sadviji's *writing is personal, funny, wry, loving, earnest, self-reflective and incredibly engaging. And her story! Wow! The journey from being in pieces to being at peace, from being a brilliant student at Stanford to living a life of devotion in India with her beloved teacher is a teaching for us all. Although we may not move to India, we can move from being hooked on our personalities to realizing what is and has always been breathing through us, loving us, blazing us. If one person can do and be this, so can we all. Thank you, Sadhviji, for reminding us of what is always here, always possible. I won't be the same after reading your book.*"

GENEEN ROTH, AUTHOR OF THE #1 *NEW YORK TIMES* BESTSELLER
WOMEN FOOD AND GOD AND OTHER BOOKS INCLUDING HER LATEST,
THIS MESSY MAGNIFICENT LIFE

In Hollywood to the Himalayas *we join a journey of a borderless and courageous heart that learns three treasures: becoming closer to God everyday, serving humanity, and being happy. Sadhvi shares lessons of compassion and letting go learned from unflinchingly addressing abuse and suffering, lessons of extraordinary joy resulting from blessings of love and healing, insights of wisdom gained from modern and ancient disciplines of learning, guidance and transmission from an authentic teacher/disciple relationship, and inspiration to keep learning and serving. The integrity and clarity of her account (and ascent) is powerful and may rub off on the reader. If it does you will not be the same.*

JONATHAN GRANOFF
PRESIDENT, GLOBAL SECURITY INSTITUTE

HOLLYWOOD
to the
HIMALAYAS

HOLLYWOOD
to the
HIMALAYAS

A Journey of Healing
and Transformation

SADHVI BHAGAWATI SARASWATI

MANDALA

San Rafael Los Angeles London

"In the West, you sit around in a dark room discussing the details of the darkness. You measure every molecule of darkness. How many protons? How many neutrons? How many electrons make up these atoms? How long has it been dark? From whence did this darkness come? Is it darker than it was yesterday, or is it perhaps getting slightly less dark? You go around and discuss the way the darkness makes you feel. You encourage each other to express your frustration at sitting in a dark room. It goes on endlessly. In the East, we run our hands along the walls looking for the light switch. We know that once the switch is found and the light is turned on, it no longer matters how dark it was or what the molecules of darkness were made of, or where the darkness came from. What matters is now there is light."

PUJYA SWAMIJI

CONTENTS

FOREWORD

It was once said that people don't remember what you say to them, but they will always remember how you made them feel. From the first moment I was introduced to Sadhviji, she has always made me feel deeply loved and accepted.

We met in the garden of the Parmarth Niketan Ashram in Rishikesh, one of the holy cities of India. It was an early spring afternoon, five years ago, and we were surrounded by my traveling companions and a small film crew from UPLIFT, a conscious media organization I work with. We were making a documentary on the sacredness of water. At the time I did not yet know of the profound, life-changing impact the Ganges River had upon this American-born holy woman.

I will never forget the smile on her face when we met. Not only did her mouth and her eyes smile, if felt as if her heart was smiling directly at me.

Just before sunset, Sadhviji led our group to the steps on the banks of the river to participate in the daily aarti ceremony. With dozens of young boys in yellow robes surrounding her, Pujya Swamiji, her Guru, began to sing ancient Hindu chants with tablas and harmoniums providing the bass line. At one point, a few of the young boys began handing over large brass lamps containing small flames. Sadhviji made sure I was given one to slowly raise in circles as part of the ritual.

I was as humbled and in awe of this beautiful ceremony as I was wide eyed and open hearted. From that magical meeting, we quickly became good friends;

we continue to meet up when we can, whether it is in India, Los Angeles, or Boulder, Colorado, and we've done several video conference webinars together.

This book shares Sadhviji's remarkable story of leaving behind her privileged life in California to experiencing awakening, healing and transformation in the Ganges to becoming a world spiritual leader.

So often in spiritual circles there appears to be a certain priesthood or special type of person who is truly allowed in and accepted. In India, this is still mostly true. Even though she was once escorted off a stage for being the only female present among the religious leaders, Sadhviji generously and elegantly provides her wisdom and shakti to all who come in contact with her.

For me, *Hollywood to the Himalayas* is a spiritual "tell all." She tells everything: the ups, the downs, the stuff you never hear a person in her position express. From the dark details of her childhood abuse and trauma, to her feelings of desire, to her experience as a woman, even after taking vows of celibacy, Sadhviji shatters the myth that we need to be perfect and makes spirituality accessible, which is how it should be.

God's grace is available to all no matter what you look like, where you come from, or any thoughts or actions of your past. That is the healing message of this book: to understand and to know that there is no recipe or perfect formula to connect to the Divine.

Sadhviji models for us, at the deepest level, that in the true teaching of the spiritual traditions, healing and grace are always possible.

PRINCE EA

PROLOGUE

"Now There Is Light"

SUMMER 1996

I opened my eyes at the end of my first darshan in India to hear Pujya Swamiji saying, "Yes?" I was the last one in the room, and he addressed me in English: "Yes?" I rose quickly from my place, went in front of him, and bowed low, trying to remember the protocol. Then I sat back on the soles of my feet and saw him looking at me—or, rather, *into* me—with a love that seemed to permeate every cell of my body and every corner of my psyche. It was not a personal love, not directed at me, but a love so vast and available, it didn't matter how many others were swimming in it too—there was room for all. "Yes?" he repeated.

I had nothing to say. I could have sat forever in the ocean of his gaze, but his eyes were waiting for me to speak.

"Pujya Swamiji," I whispered. "Fear runs my life. I have a sense of anxiety all the time, even when I don't know what I'm afraid of."

"You fear because you don't trust," he said after a brief pause. I thought he would continue, but he didn't. Just that—lack of trust.

"Really horrible things have happened to me that have made me unable to trust." And I told him the full story of my twenty-five years: childhood sexual abuse and abandonment, struggles with bulimia, for which I was hospitalized several times. It was a story I'd told many times, and it never failed to elicit sympathy, open arms, and praise for how strong I am.

He just looked at me and asked, "Are you going to take this to the grave with you?" *Oh, God, no,* I thought—*of course not.*

"Are you going to let it go on your deathbed, just before you die?"

"No, of course," I replied. "I don't want to take this unbearable pain to my deathbed," which was surely six or seven decades away.

"Will you let it go a week before you die, a month before you die?" he continued to ask, never shifting his gaze from its lock on my heart.

"Swamiji, I don't want to take this to my grave or my deathbed. I don't want to hold onto it until a week or a month before I die. I want to be free of it as soon as possible. I'm in therapy with a wonderful psychologist. I'm processing it all so I can heal and move on with my life."

He continued to look at me calmly, with neither sympathy nor judgment. His presence stretched so wide, it was able to hold the love that poured from his eyes, the pain I'd experienced, and even the perpetrator, my biological father. In his gaze, there was room for everything.

Then he said, "You are waiting for someone to come and draw the line for you. You are waiting for someone to come and say, 'Now you are done.' But no one will do that. You must draw the line yourself. The choice is yours. You can carry this pain to the grave, you can give it up on your deathbed, you can give it up a week or a month before you die, or you can give it up tonight."

Tonight? Seriously? I didn't speak, but he must have heard my thoughts. "Yes, tonight," he said. "We have a beautiful ceremony at sunset called the *aarti*. I will tell the priest to give you the oil lamp so you can wave it and pray with it. Then go to Ganga and give her your pain. Take her water in your hands and give it all to her. Just give it to the river. If you give it, she will take it."

He patted me gently on the head as he stood and walked out of the room. Only as the door clicked shut behind him did I remember to bow.

"Just give it to the river?" I wrote over and over in my journal, smiling as I replayed in my mind the swami's touching yet nonsensical instructions. Fortunately,

I was being treated by doctors and psychologists who knew what to do. Abreactive therapy, extended trancelike regressions back to the abuse, behavior-modification techniques that made even the simple task of eating into "work," and the passage of time—these were answers to my pathology. I wasn't about to rely on a river to wash away my problems.

Afternoon became evening, and I sat on the cool marble steps lining the banks of the flowing Ganga River as the sun began its descent. As the final rays of light danced on the waters, the sound of Vedic mantras filled my ears. I stopped giggling long enough to remember my vow from the airplane—to keep my heart open, or leave India. To mock an instruction as seemingly useless as the one I had received today might be breaking my vow at the moment it was most needed—particularly as it had come from the mouth of someone revered as an enlightened master, particularly as my breath had stopped when he said it, particularly as I felt more comfortable and more at home in my own skin while sitting in his presence than I had ever felt before.

During the evening light ceremony called the aarti, I allowed myself to be swept away by the song, the music, the chanting, by the fire, the flowers, and the incense weaving in and out of and through each other in a dynamic tapestry of ecstatic prayer. A boy in yellow placed a flaming brass lamp in my hands. "Like this," he gestured in what looked like a clockwise movement. (Later, I learned that the motion for waving the lamp is in the shape of the Sanskrit symbol *Om*.) I faced the river, waving the lamp in clockwise circles until my time was up, and the boy took it away.

After the ceremony, as the guests began to disperse, I walked calf-deep into the river. The moon rose over the mountains and glistened on the surface of the water. The current tugged so forcefully on my legs that I wondered if I would have to give not only my pain but also my entire body to this river. As the chanting dissipated in the background and the flow of the river tried to wrest my feet from its sandy bottom, I entered a silence so deep, it was a place in itself, wrapping me in its arms. In that place of silence, I bent down into the water and carried out Swamiji's instructions.

I cupped the river's water in my hands and offered *all my pain, all my tears, and all my fear* into the water I held in my two hands. "You must forgive him,"

Swamiji had said. "Give your anger and grudges to the water, and then pour it back into the river." I stood up to my knees in Mother Ganga until the moon was directly overhead, all the while calling forth every image that had ever caused me pain, that had caused me to dissociate, that had propelled my head into a toilet, vomiting. I recalled countless images that had formed the unbearable background of my life.

Then, in the midst of these images, I saw him—my biological father, Manny—and from this *place* of imperturbable silence, I saw not a monster but a troubled man who had made mistakes. I saw the violence and the sin he wrought upon me as simply mistakes of this disturbed being. I saw a man now far away who could no longer harm me, whose life was just as haunted by these choices as mine. And I saw a man who loved me despite his inability to express it. I saw a man I could forgive.

Tears mixed with the water in my hands, and I prayed and cried and prayed and cried, all in silence. These were tears not of yesterday, but of today, tears of release rather than terror, knowing I needed to embrace what *is* rather than what *might have been*. I called his image to mind again, stared deeply into my father's eyes, and said, *"I forgive you."* Then I let the water pour from my hands back into the river. *"Take the pain,"* I prayed. *"I give it all to You."*

In the weeks and months that followed, the pain that had coursed through body and mind my entire life lost its grip. I tried recalling memories of abuse to make my body shudder again, to bring back a state of unbearableness within my own body that was far more familiar than the peace I was experiencing. I called forth every scene that had triggered terror and dissociation, to no avail. The memories were there, no less vivid than before, but I no longer identified with them. They weren't "me." I could no longer dissociate; there was no longer more than one part of myself into which I could split. There was nowhere to go but here, whole and complete.

The only split that remained was the part of me that *knew* the pain had been released and the part that could neither fathom nor accept concepts of spiritual healing, grace, or the possibility of a life without pain and pathology. The latter tried to shake the former back into victimization, while the part that "knew" remained quiet and still. Slowly, over months and then years, the knowing has become pervasive.

When I spoke to Pujya Swamiji about the miraculous transformation inside me and told him that I no longer felt like the same person who identified with this suffering, he nodded and said, "Once the switch is found and the light is turned on, it no longer matters how dark it had been or what the molecules of darkness were made of, or from where the darkness had come. What matters is that now there is light."

CHAPTER 1

"You'll Come Crawling Back"

SUMMER 1990

I was nineteen years old. The head of the eating-disorder unit at the Midway
Medical Center in Los Angeles beseeched and berated me as I signed my own
discharge papers. "You'll come crawling back," he said. "You're sick. We've seen
this hundreds of times. You need to be here. If you leave . . ."

I had completed less than a week of the six-week intensive in-patient program
after years of spending day after day stuffing myself in order to vomit again. Bulimia
is the willing (sort of), conscious (sort of), controlled (not really), purposeful
vomiting after ingesting large quantities of food. I wasn't even interested in the food.
I just needed *something* to throw up— sometimes food, sometimes gallons of water.
My psychiatrist had put me in the hospital for the second time in four months.

The administrator continued in his rote administrative voice, cautioning me about the illusion of recovery and making sure I understood that the hungry demon of bulimia sat heavily on my shoulder and would swallow me whole again, most likely soon. My only chance for survival, he made crystal clear, was to stay.

But I couldn't. Nurses peering into open bathrooms to be sure I was peeing and not throwing up, never having even the privacy of a closed door, had rendered me exhausted and constipated. I felt like someone in a prison scene out of a Dickens novel or a group-therapy scene from *One Flew Over the Cuckoo's Nest*. This was not the place for me.

"I have to leave," I'd told him the day before.

"You can't. It's a six-week program. You're sick, and you need to be here."

Finally, he acquiesced, but as I filled out the forms and checked the boxes about taking full responsibility for my own life, not holding the hospital liable, and acknowledging I was going against his professional advice, his voice changed. "I guarantee you'll be back, crawling on your hands and knees."

I walked out onto Olympic Boulevard knowing I would *never* go back there. And I knew I was in deep trouble.

I had grown up in a land of privilege, in the coveted world of Hollywood. We lived in Studio City, just up the hill from Universal Studios. I went to a private prep school with actors and actresses and the children of actors, actresses, directors, and producers. I even auditioned for commercials when I was in elementary school and had a full set of headshots taken of my innocent face, looking sometimes giggly and sometimes sultry. I spent innumerable hours exclaiming, "Moist and chewy, it's delicious" in every possible permutation of speed, tone, emphasis, and pitch as I joined a child-star friend for commercial acting classes at his house.

I wasn't supposed to be in this much trouble. This was the summer of 1990. I had just finished my first year at Stanford and had spent the last few months in and out of eating-disorder clinics. Over the next six years, I did everything I could to heal. I went to therapy—sometimes daily with a psychiatrist, sometimes weekly with an analyst. I took Prozac and Zoloft, selective serotonin reuptake inhibitors that have shown great potential for treating depression, anxiety, addictions, and eating disorders. I hit baseball bats into pillows until my arms felt like noodles, envisioning my father, who had sexually abused and then abandoned me. I recorded my dreams and tried to make sense of them. I completed my bachelor's degree and the first half of a PhD program in psychology.

I went to Overeaters Anonymous, the twelve-step program for people with addictions to eating (or to starving themselves, or to eating and then throwing up). "Hi, I'm bulimic," I would say at the start of the few meetings I attended before realizing it was not the right program for me. The required admission of my own powerlessness and surrender to a higher power gave me exactly the excuse I needed to continue to throw up. "My higher power was taking a nap and didn't come through for me," I'd say to my sponsor. "Not my fault."

I started and then quit smoking cigarettes, as it seemed the thing to do in recovery but actually nauseated me. I dated continuously, looking for a father in a range of twentysomething-year-old boys. I got married to a supersmart man who seemed to know me better than I knew myself. And still I suffered.

Some of it helped. The therapy, for sure. Knowing the reason I wanted to eat the entire world and throw it back up was an important first step. Realizing that the dissociated numbness I yearned for in Sara Lee cheesecakes and Mrs. Fields cookies was not due to being crazy or sick but a normal, natural response to unexamined trauma gave me the courage to explore and be present with the trauma so I didn't have to eat my way into a catatonic stupor. Knowing that the hatred I had toward my body was due to this very body having been the object of abuse gave me a vocabulary to address myself and the problem. I learned to say, "You can't eat his love or throw up your pain. No matter how sick you get, no matter how many hospitals you get admitted to, Manny isn't coming back." Sometimes it worked. The bulimia, and my life, became manageable, and frequently, I even felt happy.

The occasional relapse into vomiting didn't worry me, and I was usually able to bounce back without descending too deeply into the hell of self-loathing. Eating was still an effort, but I held myself on the OK side of pathology by a tightly wound coil of restriction and control.

My biological father was still a huge trigger, but fortunately, his name didn't come up that often. I'd learned to navigate my way through life without thinking about him, other than the occasional fit of sobs when my husband, Jim, left for work, as though I were three and watching my father drive away forever, rather than twenty-three and watching my partner head off to work. Movies that ended in death or separation, AT&T's commercials with the slogan "Reach out and touch someone," and summer-camp goodbyes elicited not mere teary-eyed bittersweetness but abject, inconsolable misery.

I also cried in yoga class in *Shavasana*, the final pose of a session, lying like a corpse, still and silent on my back. Gentle sobs wracked my body, and I couldn't lie still. And every time Jim rolled over in bed, shaking the mattress, I woke up startled, unable to get back to sleep.

Frequently, anorexia—and, sometimes, bulimia (my condition combined the two)—are much more about control than about food. When we feel out of control in life, we turn to something we can control—our food, our weight, our body. Whenever I loosened the viselike grip I had on my food intake, I would slip back into self-starvation, or bingeing and vomiting. Starving myself or throwing up was my response of choice to stress.

The continued struggle and low-grade suffering seemed like something I would face forever. I had heard everywhere—from in twelve-step meetings to at the hospital—that struggles of addiction, depression, and childhood trauma are with us always. We can gain some control over our lives and not engage in the addictive behaviors, but the internal mind-set and emotional patterns are always there. The hungry ghost may not gobble us alive, but it will be there forever, occasionally whispering insidiously in our ear.

I knew, even more surely than I knew the day I left the Midway Medical Center, that I would never be on my hands and knees, desperate for the help of that kind of hospital. I had my life together enough. I was getting straight A's in my PhD program and successfully navigating my way through early adulthood. Didn't everyone cry during AT&T commercials?

CHAPTER 2

"We Have to Go to India"

SPRING/SUMMER 1996

"India," Jim said. "We have to go to India."

Oh, God, I thought, standing in our kitchen in the suburb of Millbrae, west of San Francisco International Airport, conveniently located between Palo Alto, where I was getting my doctorate in pediatric neuropsychology, and San Francisco, where Jim was getting his master's in East-West psychology. I was holding a bowl of extra-firm tofu chunks in homemade teriyaki sauce ready for skewering and barbequing.

"Seriously?" Memories of our year in Ecuador flashed back, children in the burn unit of the hospital where I'd volunteered, a facility that might have been created for a *Twilight Zone* episode: babies in diapers overflowing with feces screaming while nurses sat by polishing their fingernails and watching *telenovelas* (soap operas) on a small black-and-white TV with rabbit-ear antennas. Beautiful young children burned by exploding gas canisters their moms cooked dinner on or from falling into vats of boiling water, children electrocuted while reaching playfully to touch exposed electrical lines.

Jim and I had traveled to Ecuador the year after I graduated from Stanford so he could teach English—an opportunity for him to travel, explore, and serve. He's a year older than me, and he wanted to join the Peace Corps after his graduation. Instead, he stayed back to wait for me to finish my last year.

All my previous travel had been in Europe—vacations with my parents, summers in Switzerland, a trip to France my last year of high school. Traveling in the Third World hadn't even occurred to me. Over lunch breaks in high school, my friends and I would weave fantasies of romance on Greek isles, lying on white-sand beaches while modern Adonises rubbed tanning oil on our backs. We never gave a thought to poorer parts of the world.

But I was in love with Jim and aware of the sacrifice he'd made by postponing his stint with the Peace Corps to wait for me. Plus, I had no immediate plans after graduation and didn't know what I wanted to do. A year abroad teaching and exploring sounded like an adventure.

Teaching, I discovered, came incredibly easily. I could draft lesson plans on the school bus in the morning or on Sunday evenings for the week ahead. I loved my classes and the students, but I had too much free time. We returned home each afternoon by three, and I grew tired of backgammon afternoons with the din of honking horns in Quito's traffic.

One day, while walking through our neighborhood, I discovered the local state-run children's hospital and learned they needed volunteers in the burn unit. I soon began filling my afternoons changing diapers and rocking young children to sleep. I barely spoke Spanish, so I couldn't communicate verbally, but it didn't matter. The children craved only touch. Staph infections were rampant, and each day, I arrived to learn that three or four children had died the night before. "I don't think you can take this," Jim told me one night as I sobbed over yet more deaths.

Other than my students at the school and our weekend trips to Baños, a quaint mountain town named after its hot springs, I had few fond memories from our year in Quito. Now, India?

I didn't know anything about India other than how much I loved Indian food. I had been a vegetarian since age fifteen, and Indian restaurants were always my first choice. I didn't have to grill waiters in languages I don't speak. Indians understood vegetarianism. There was no stealth chicken stock, beef bouillon cubes, or oyster sauce in the soups or stews, no eggs in the pasta or naan. But there was an Indian restaurant on our corner in Millbrae, so why go to India?

Jim was on a spiritual quest. We often went to meet gurus visiting the San Francisco Bay Area, and he had a small shrine in our apartment where he meditated every morning. To me, the only enjoyable part about the excursions to meet gurus was the food they served—sweet, milky chai in Styrofoam cups, along with crispy samosas with tangy mango chutney. The singing and prayers didn't move me. I sat through them, trying to connect with the music but really waiting for it to end so we could eat the samosas, drink the chai, and go home.

As I got ready to go to class each morning, Jim sat at his shrine, meditating to Indian chants playing on a nearby cassette. The music was nice, but I never thought of closing my eyes or singing along. The shrine Jim had created, populated with pictures of Indian masters, incense, and paraphernalia, did not entice me to join him. "This is spirituality," Jim explained. "I'm going to get enlightened."

Since reading *Zen and the Art of Motorcycle Maintenance* in college, Jim had immersed himself in the pursuit of expanding his consciousness. He spent afternoons doing past-life regressions and practicing lucid dreaming and weekends doing holotropic breathwork to access higher states of consciousness.

If there was one thing that interested me, it was Andrew Harvey's mellifluous voice speaking about Rumi or Ramakrishna. I had a crush on Andrew and wished he would just keep speaking into my heart forever. None of the rest touched me. I wanted to want to be inspired and enlightened as much as Jim did, but the actual desire for it just didn't come. Jim explained that shrines and chanting and gurus are the stuff spirituality is made of, and we came to a shared understanding that I simply wasn't spiritual.

So, India? After my brain's instinctive rebellion against suffering in another poor and distant country, I assuaged myself with the idea of going to Pune to study yoga with B. K. S. Iyengar. I was already practicing yoga; I loved studying Iyengar Yoga in San Francisco. But I knew the rules: You had to have attained a level of proficiency far greater than mine to study with Iyengar in Pune. So that was off the table.

Jim remained adamant. *We had to go to India.*

CHAPTER 3

Takeoff and a Vow

SEPTEMBER 1996

"You can always come back," my yoga teacher told me. Obvious, perhaps, but it hadn't occurred to me. And now it was only two days before our departure, and I was no more convinced about this trip than when Jim had first spoken of it. It made no sense. "No one is saying you have to stay the full three months," he reminded me. "You can change your ticket and return early." Tickets issued, bags packed, and a semester off school had rendered three months in India inevitable and intractable. Yes, of course I could come back early. I hadn't registered for the fall semester, but I could still get practicum units; I could get started on planning my research and dissertation; I could continue the volunteer work I was doing at the Family & Children Services drug-rehabilitation center in San Jose, where I rocked heroin babies to sleep while their mothers received addiction counseling.

The mere possibility of changing my ticket, though, did bring the breath back into my lungs and loosened the grip of desperation. Jim told me that if he found a guru, he'd likely want to stay longer, and alone. His unspiritual wife would be a burden. And while the idea of wandering through India with Jim was bearable, the notion of doing so alone was not.

Our flight to New Delhi, via Singapore, was scheduled to depart in two days, on the morning of September 11, 1996—or so we thought. Rereading the tickets, we realized the flight was actually leaving the night of the tenth. "Oh, my God," I told Jim, "that's tomorrow!"

Anxiety about the trip transformed into frenzied packing—electrolytes, broad-spectrum antibiotics, water purifiers, a blank journal, vaccination cards, and cotton skirts and pants that covered my ankles to respect local custom. I had no more time to think about the rightness or wrongness of the trip. There was barely time to buy locks for our suitcases.

I had been many things by that point, but never an aimless wanderer. All travel was purposeful. The best summers of my life were at an international teen camp in Chailly-sur-Lausanne, Switzerland, where, if my mother had known what went on, she'd never have sent me. Despite the directionless decadence of hanging out in cafés, bars, and pizzerias, the bonds of friendship have been lifelong, and the depth of interfaith, intercultural love in a world of wars over borders imprinted deeply on my psyche.

My trips to the mountains of California and throughout the United States during college vacations were responses to the call of the forest. I felt connected to myself and the universe when lying atop fallen needles beneath towering redwoods. These ancient trees called out to me across freeways, over the tops of malls and office buildings, through the doors of Stanford and my apartment and reeled my heart in, along with my body.

Now, here I was on a plane headed neither to friends nor to my beloved redwoods. I was going to New Delhi, a city I knew teemed with lepers, beggars, mosquitoes, and far too many people. It made no sense.

Although I was neither religious nor spiritual, I always had a deep belief that the universe has a Plan. I didn't bother myself with Who or What the Planner was, but I did not believe anything was random. So, as our plane flew over

Southeast Asia, I thought, *There must be a reason you're on this trip. You just don't know why. Just keep your heart open, and you'll come to understand. If you can't stay open, return to California. It'd be stupid to wander around India if you're too afraid to find out why you've gone.* So I vowed then and there to keep my heart open.

CHAPTER 4

We Get Adopted
en Route to Rishikesh

Connaught Place was the only place in Delhi to get a real cup of coffee. "Are you sure it's not powdered?" I asked the waiter. "Not Nescafé?" Despite implicitly trusting the vegetarian-ness of Indian food, I was still grilling waiters half a world away. "No, ma'am—filter coffee," he assured.

Our first morning in India, and I had found a place with real coffee. We sat in a restaurant overlooking the circular center of New Delhi, Connaught Place—or Connaught Circle, as it's called, nearly correctly, for it's actually two concentric circles, inner and outer. American Express, Citibank, travel agents, and touristy restaurants line the circumference. I pulled out the Lonely Planet guide and flipped through the pages.

"Let's go to Rishikesh," I said. "It seems nice. It's only a few hours from Delhi, and they have a lot of yoga programs. It's on a river and at the base of the mountains, so we can go to the mountains too.

"Also," I added, "it's full of ashrams and gurus."

Just like that. Simple, and seemingly inconsequential. "How did you come to Rishikesh?" people would later ask, expecting a fantastic story in which I dreamed of meditating in the Himalayas while the word *Rishikesh* flashed across my mind. But rather than manifest in a vision, it appeared in actual ink on the top of the page to which my fingers were drawn, in a guidebook I skimmed through over a cup of filter coffee.

Jim reached for the book and read about Rishikesh. "Sure," he said. "Sounds great. There are so many ashrams to choose from. We should probably book a hotel and scout out the situation when we get there." He continued to read, and added, "Badrinath is supposed to be a sacred temple, and it's straight up the mountain from Rishikesh. All the jeeps and buses leave from Rishikesh, so we can go to Badrinath too."

After a few days sightseeing in Delhi, we headed to Rishikesh. On a "luxury" bus that wasn't luxurious at all, I sat next to two girls who went to school in Delhi and were returning home to a city called Roorkee. They were in their mid-teens, and exhibited a blend of the gregarious diffidence I have encountered only in young Indian girls. Internally, they bubbled with exuberance, but they had been so acculturated to be demure that excitement seemed to push the edges of their modesty. I could feel the thin layer of propriety loosen as they bent across each other to practice their English on me and ask every imaginable question, ranging from "How many sisters and brothers do you have?" to "What do you think about our country, India?" to "What do you eat for breakfast in America?"

As someone with a lifelong history of motion sickness, I need to sit in the front of any vehicle, and even at the very front, waves of nausea usually overtake me. I try to avoid travel by road unless it's a straight shot, which this wasn't. I was, therefore, not in the mood to chat. It took all my attention and my will not to vomit.

But these girls were enthusiastic conversationalists. They talked continuously about their school, the hostel they lived in, the drab food served there (they couldn't wait to get home to eat Mum's cooking). And they wanted to know everything about me—past, present, and future. "What will you do in Rishikesh?" "Do you study yoga?" "Will you have children? How many children do you want? Do you want boys or girls?"

During the third or fourth hour, they endeared themselves to me when they persuaded the driver to pull over so I could pee in the dirt along the side of the highway. An avid water drinker and infrequent bus traveler, it didn't occur to me that I'd have to hold my bladder for hours. The driver ignored my requests in English, and only when the two of them implored him in Hindi did he slow down and pull over.

Their home city of Roorkee, they explained, was an hour and a half from Rishikesh. They would not, under any circumstances, allow us to continue to Rishikesh that day. "You absolutely must come home with us," they declared. As the bus driver had given in to their demands, so did Jim and I.

"Don't you have to ask your parents?" I asked. I could only imagine my own parents' faces if I had come home with two foreign strangers. "Of course not," they exclaimed. "They will be so happy to have you."

The bus stopped at Roorkee, and we alighted along with them. They guided us to a bicycle rickshaw. I had seen these in Delhi but hadn't ridden in one. A male driver sits on the bicycle seat and pedals while up to eight passengers sit in a carriage mounted on the back. It seemed cruel to make him haul so much weight while balancing a rusty bicycle, but the motorized rickshaws we'd ridden in Delhi were nowhere to be found, and so we reluctantly agreed. After bouncing across dirt paths and gravel roads for half an hour, we arrived at a long, narrow road with brightly colored houses on both sides, and at the end was their family's two-story concrete home.

It was the end of a long summer's day. The sun was dipping behind the neighborhood homes, and dusk began its prolonged arrival. There were no yards or lawns, but there did seem to be a park, or an open field with a bit of grass, at the end of the road. Before the rickshaw even stopped, the girls stood up and started yelling excitedly in Hindi to a man standing on the second-floor balcony, looking down over a stuccoed parapet. The man was in a sleeveless undershirt and appeared to have just woken up from his afternoon nap. As the girls gesticulated, he bent over the parapet to get a closer look, and a huge smile formed across his face. He shouted something into the house, then quickly disappeared inside.

The elder of the girls paid the driver, and we all grabbed our bags off the carriage floor and walked up the steps to their home. "Are you sure this is OK?" I asked one more time. I still couldn't imagine a world in which bringing two strangers home would be acceptable. The door opened, and a voluptuous middle-aged woman with a beautiful round face and wearing a yellow cotton saree stood in the doorway. The girls gave her a quick hug and began talking on top of each other. The woman smiled and said in English, "Welcome. We are glad you have come." *Wow.*

"Please come inside," she said, motioning as the girls darted into the living room to put down their bags. By this time, the man had put on a long-sleeved white cotton top, which I've since learned is called a kurta. These traditional tops for both men and women hang down anywhere from mid-thigh to mid-calf, and he wore his with thin white cotton pants.

"Sit, sit," he said, warmly motioning us to the largest couch, a brown fabric-covered sofa with a cream-colored cotton sheet draped over it. "Sit, sit," he urged again until we finally did. Over the next few minutes, at least fifteen people streamed through the front door into the living room, walked straight up to us—clearly, we were the reason they'd come—and greeted us with a dozen variations of "Welcome—you like India?"

Jim and I were dressed for bus travel. He was in jeans and a T-shirt. I was wearing thin blue cotton pants and a T-shirt. Neither of us had even showered that morning. The bus had been scheduled to leave Delhi at six o'clock, and we'd read horror stories about finding the correct bus at the terminal, so we left extra time to navigate the chaos. We'd departed our hotel early, and I hadn't even had a cup of coffee. After spending six hours on a bus, where I prayed not to throw up and Jim was squashed between passengers and farm animals, we arrived at these lovely people's house. Suddenly, I felt underdressed for the occasion. I hadn't even seen a mirror since predawn, and I was sure we must be filthy.

No one seemed to mind, and they squeezed tighter and tighter together on the other couches and chairs as more people kept arriving. Some sat easily on the floor. Suddenly, from the kitchen, the yellow-saree-clad woman appeared with a plate of squiggly, light brown circles. She placed the plate in front of us. "You eat this. It's very nice. Fresh *jalebi*. You take sugar in tea?"

"Sure," I mumbled, still not quite sure what was going on, where we were, and how this had all happened. How had these people just opened their homes to us with no questions? They had given us the nicest couch, had invited the whole neighborhood, and were serving us the crispiest, sweetest, drippiest meal I'd ever tasted. Jalebis consist of sugary batter dripped into boiling oil and deep-fried in overlapping circles, like figure eights. The first bite is crispy, and then the melted sugar pours onto your tongue.

We ate plate after plate of jalebis and drank several cups of spicy, sugary chai. It was so much better than the stuff in Styrofoam served at the guru programs Jim had taken me to back home. The neighbors asked the same questions the girls had on the bus: They wanted to know about our parents, what they did, how many other family members we had, when we planned to have children, what our jobs were. What had made us come to India?

I finally gave up trying to figure it out. It was just happening. Yes, we'd been welcomed into these random people's homes. Yes, their neighbors were spending the evening inquiring into our lives with friendliness and ease as though we'd known each other for years. Yes, dinner in this dream world consisted of fried sugar batter and spicy tea.

After a few hours of sitting with a constantly changing group of people— neighbors and friends would casually come in and out—the girls showed us to our room. It was the master bedroom. "We can't take this room," Jim and I protested to the girls' parents. "It's your room."

"Please," they said. "It is your room." Fatigue and carbohydrate stupor prevented us from fighting any further. We thanked them as profusely as we could for opening their home to us with so much love, and we collapsed on the bed to sleep.

A hard knock on the door pulled me from deep slumber. The room was dark, and it took more than a moment for me to remember where we were. Oh, yes, at the home of the Nicest People in the World, who had popped out of some children's storybook to stand at their door and welcome us. Now, they were knocking on our door in the middle of the night. Why? Maybe it had all been a mistake. Maybe they'd thought we were someone else, someone they knew who was much more worthy of an evening of jalebis and chatting.

I groggily felt my way for the door and opened it. The woman of the house, whose name I never did properly get, still looking fresh in her yellow saree, stood there with the bluish tint of fluorescent light streaming from the room behind her. "Come, it's dinner time," she said. "I hope you've rested well."

I laughed. I didn't mean to laugh—it just happened. A bodily reaction, like a cough or a burp. She looked at me, confused. "It's OK, yes? Everything is OK? You are comfortable?"

"Yes, yes, of course—everything is amazing. You are beyond generous and loving and kind. I just thought we already had dinner."

"No, no. That was snack," she said, and now she laughed too. I had laughed at how anyone could possibly be expected to eat dinner in the middle of the night after eating platefuls of jalebis earlier in the evening. She had laughed at how anyone could possibly think jalebis are dinner.

"Get ready and come soon. Dinner is ready."

Jim and I tried to stifle our giggles as we washed our faces. It was insane. We had been awakened in the middle of the night to eat more food.

As we dragged ourselves out of the room, back toward the living room, I noticed the guests had left and it was now just the four of them.

"This way," the younger of the two daughters said as she escorted us into the dining area, where a square wooden table stood just off the kitchen. We sat down to plates that had already been served for us: heaps of fragrant cauliflower and potatoes, a bowl of brown garbanzo beans in sauce (called chana), another heap of what looked like mixed vegetables, and a chapati (Indian flatbread) the size of a dinner plate. I looked at Jim, and we both bit our lips to prevent bursting into laughter. *Seriously?*

Luckily, Jim could eat and digest pretty much anything. Healthy and athletic, he had an appetite that never waned. I was not able to eat much, though, as the jalebis still took up most of the space in my stomach. "Just a little, just one spoonful," each of the family would coax in rotation. I kept laughing inside, as it seemed like a comedic dream. Finally, after Jim had graciously eaten for both of us, they let us go back to sleep.

The next morning, the father, whose name I did know at the time but have shamefully forgotten since, personally escorted us past their local bus station and all the way to Haridwar, the famous religious city, situated about halfway to Rishikesh. Haridwar being a much larger city than Rishikesh, the main bus routes ended there, so he took us there and put us onto the correct bus to our destination.

With hugs and promises to meet again, which we all knew we would not keep, we bade each other a love-filled farewell. Had it really been less than twenty-four hours since we'd met?

CHAPTER 5

Arrival at the Green Hotel

I had chosen the Green Hotel from the Lonely Planet guidebook. Rishikesh is an official holy city, designated by the government of India, so no meat or alcohol is permitted in the entire municipality. Thus, the reviews of the hotels were all nearly identical: singles, doubles, A/C, non-A/C, vegetarian restaurant. As an ardent environmentalist, when choosing among seemingly identical hotels, I chose the Green Hotel, which we later discovered was so named simply due to the color of its walls—pale, pastel green.

Rishikesh is laid out on two sides of the Ganges (correctly, Ganga) River, a bustling downtown on the western side and a quieter area on the eastern side. The southeastern quarter centers itself near Ram Jhula, a swinging footbridge named after Lord Rama, the divine hero of the Ramayana, while the northern part is centered around Lakshman Jhula, a similar bridge named after Lord Rama's brother, Lakshman. Lakshman Jhula is where most of the hotels, shops, and restaurants for tourists are. The Ram Jhula area, also known as the Swargashram (literally, Heavenly Abode) area, is lined with ashrams.

In September 1996, the Green Hotel was the only hotel in the Swargashram area of Rishikesh, sitting on a small lane that runs parallel to the Ganga, just behind the ashrams. Of course, Lonely Planet did not mention that in order to reach there, you have to schlep your bags across a nearly half-mile-long footbridge. So, when we arrived at the Ram Jhula taxi stand to discover that our hotel was across the water, the driver instructed helpfully, "You cross bridge." No mention of the large, convenient motorboat that pilgrims can use to travel easily from bank to bank of the river, no offer to find a coolie—the driver simply pointed his finger toward the swinging footbridge, more than 300 yards past where he had to drop us off.

You couldn't find a hotel that doesn't require schlepping our bags across a river? I berated myself as we found ourselves sharing a bridge, barely two feet wide and precariously suspended a hundred feet above water, with stray cows, sugarcane-laden bullock carts, fruit and vegetable vendors, motorcyclists, and two-way foot traffic. I was sure we had walked onto the set of the Indian version of *The Bridge of San Luis Rey*. Finally, hot, sweaty, and already done with India, I followed Jim through the doors of the Green Hotel.

CHAPTER 6

The Grace of Ganga

"How do you get back to the river?" I asked the clerk after we'd checked in and dropped our backpacks in the sparsely furnished room. The Ganga called me. As we had crossed Ram Jhula, our luggage strapped to our backs, the river flowed quickly and deeply below. Each year in the monsoon, the water level rises tens of feet and her springtime gentle flow becomes a rush of summer waves. By mid-September, the rains subside. A brief afternoon storm in Delhi was our only experience of the tail end of the monsoon. However, the Ganga was still brimming from mountain rains and melting glaciers.

The hotel clerk directed me down a narrow alley that ran in front of the hotel between two large ashrams until it dead-ended at a small road lined with tea stalls on the banks of the river. I did not want tea, however, or any of the jewelry or religious statues for sale in the marketplace. I wanted to put my feet in the river. After walking upstream along the riverbank a few hundred feet, I found clean marbled steps leading down to the river.

Pilgrims gathered on the lowest steps, pouring water over their heads from small brass pots or grasping tightly onto chains while they dipped themselves once, twice, thrice in the rushing river. Parents held their naked children close to their chests, scooped up water, and let it drip through their fingers over their children's bodies. Rubbing the holy water onto their own and their children's heads, backs, stomachs, and legs, they chanted "Jai Gange!" "Jai Gange!" (Glory to Mother Ganga), and the children squealed. At the far end of the long row of steps sat some meditators with malas (strings of beads) in their fingers, palms open on their knees.

As I walked down the marble steps to the river, I eyed a spot slightly downstream, far enough from the bathers to protect me from their splashing children. I stood, staring at the flowing water and at the dark green mountains on the opposite bank.

And then it happened—an experience that twenty-five years later, I still struggle to articulate. From the landscape of river, mountains, steps, and bathers came an image of the Divine. Woven into and out of the treads of my visual field, occupying every frame of perception, out of the light and colors and shapes and hues and textures of the world I had been watching came a divine form, an image of divinity that blended into and yet stayed distinct from the background.

The next thing I knew, I was seated on the steps without remembering how I went from standing to sitting. I was sobbing, breathless, yet with no experience of either the sadness or happiness that typically accompanies tears. The tears were not foreign or external, not due to some effect or impact. Rather, they were myself flowing out of myself as the waters of Ganga flowed by my feet. Waves of water outside and waves inside.

The image of the goddess Ganga formed out of every color, shape, texture, and aspect of my visual spectrum. Here She was. And here I was. Yet, it wasn't really a Her; rather, it was an All, an Everything. And I, I was part of that Everything. There was nowhere I ended and All began. There was nowhere She wasn't. I stared—eyes open into Her form over the flowing river. I had come home.

I sat on the cool marble steps, crying into the river. They were tears without thought, not the type I usually cried. These tears were not connected to any idea or memory or anything someone had said or done. They were simply tears of being in the presence of truth.

Minutes, hours, days, and lifetimes passed while I sat beside Ganga's flowing waters. My mind had become nonverbal. The only thought that arose periodically was, *Oh, my God.* It came not as an intellectual thought but as an outburst. *Oh, my God, it is amazing! Oh, my God, it is so beautiful!*

As I shifted my eyes from the river to the families on her banks, to the marble steps, the background of my visual field changed—first, flowing water, then, bouncing children and pious parents, then, the inanimate structure of the steps. My visual field had become split into foreground and background. The background changed based on where I looked and what I was looking at: a person, a pillar, a rock, a statue. But the image of the Divine stayed as the foreground of my visual field and did not change. Whatever I saw—a child, a mother, a marble pillar—I cried. Each varying background was the undulating canvas of color and energy on which the Divine was painted.

At some point, Jim came down. "Hey," he said in words I no longer understood. "Pretty beautiful, no?" My mind was still nonverbal—all senses and awareness and knowledge had dissolved like salt dolls into the watery soup of my consciousness. I was unable to tease apart the various ingredients from the rest of the soup. Words, too, blended into the soup, unable to be extricated. I looked at him and cried as I smiled.

"Wow," he said as the tears poured out of my eyes, onto my clothes, and onto the marble steps between us. He sat down quietly next to me.

CHAPTER 7

"You Must Stay"

The next days run into each other, timelessly. Rushing at the first light of day down to the river worshipped as the Mother, being pulled at night back into the sparse, green-hued hotel room with flickering blue tube lights, days of meditating on the banks of the river. I would not, however, have used the word meditating, for I had no semantic framework to put any of this in.

One afternoon, as I walked up the steps from Ganga toward our hotel, I discovered an alternate route. Rather than walk downriver to the alley, I could stroll through an ashram just in front of the marble steps. The ashram's central pathway ran parallel to the alley and was, I soon discovered, much cleaner. The alley was the typical Indian gauntlet of cows, dogs, homeless people, and all their waste, bodily and otherwise. The ashram, on the other hand, was sparkling clean and reminded me of the children's area at Disneyland. Enormous blue statues of Shiva and Krishna filled the pathways. Out of another huge Shiva statue, a fountain of water flowed from the goddess Ganga poised above Shiva's matted hair. Lush gardens with flowers of many colors lined the central pathway, broken only by a host of life-size depictions of gods, goddesses, and scenes from Hindu scriptures.

As I learned later when tasked with writing about the statues for a visitors' guide, one is the half-man, half-lion Narasimha avatar of Vishnu killing the demon king Hiranyakashipu with devoted Prahlad looking on. Another is Mother Yashoda seeing the universe in the open mouth of her young son, Bhagawan Krishna. Yet another is Saint Raidas, with his chest cut open to expose his heart, upon which lie the sacred threads. If I had been in a small boat touring the ashram, the tune of "It's a Small World" would have seemed perfectly in place.

The ashram became my pathway between the hotel and the banks of Ganga, a walk I took several times a day, rushing out of the hotel early each morning and inevitably having to return to use the restroom at least a few times before Jim came to get me after sunset.

One day, as I walked through the ashram, I heard a clear, stable voice, a man's voice, saying, "You must stay here." I looked around to see who had spoken, but the pathway was empty. I looked up, and there was no one on the balconies above. If the voice had come from the central gardens, it would have had to be a shout, not the gentle voice I'd just heard. *No one* had spoken.

If no one was around, there couldn't have been a voice, I reasoned. I must have imagined it. So I kept walking. Thirty seconds later, I heard it again—a soft, calm male voice, as though spoken by a gentleman in the seat next to me on a plane or a train. "You must stay here." Again, I looked, and the pathway and balcony were still empty.

Meditative though I had become, I was sure I hadn't lost my common sense. Clearly, if there was a voice, there had to be a speaker. If there was no speaker, there was no voice. The only people who heard voices were schizophrenics and Joan of Arc. My experiences since I had first laid eyes on Ganga had been expansive and whole, not the fragmentation of schizophrenia. I was not delusional. Yet, if I wasn't delusional and I wasn't Joan of Arc, *who had spoken?* No one was there, so no one had spoken. I could not have heard a voice.

Then I heard another voice, recognizably my own. It said, speaking in the authoritative, commanding second person to which I was accustomed, *You are about to ignore a very strong sign. You are about to pretend that you didn't hear a voice, just because it doesn't make sense. You're free to do that. But it is a violation of your vow to keep your heart open. You promised you would keep your heart open to any signs of why you came to India. You promised that if you couldn't keep your heart open, you would leave. The internal reproach continued: So, if you are going to pretend that you didn't hear a voice, you must go back to Delhi and get on a flight home to San Francisco. You cannot break your own vow.*

I was not in the mood to navigate a return trip to Delhi or to leave India yet. Along with the ecstasy, I was fighting a cold. I had, therefore, one choice. Conceding to my own ultimatum, I walked off the central pathway and onto a smaller pathway in the Parmarth Niketan ashram toward a large sign with OFFICE painted on it in English.

"I would like to stay here," I told the man behind the counter. He and three other gentlemen sat cross-legged on a thin mattress behind a low wooden desk. He did not respond; he just looked at me.

"Excuse me. I would like to please stay here," I repeated, slower and louder, careful to enunciate my words. He continued to stare at me. Was I actually speaking? Were my lips making sound, or was I imagining this as well?

"Is it possible? Can I stay here? How much does it cost?" He continued just to stare at me—not the kind of lascivious stare that makes you feel naked; he just stared as though it were too much trouble to move his eyes away. He clearly had no intention of responding.

I turned to the other two men. They immediately busied themselves shuffling papers from one side of the desk to the other. "Excuse me, please." I tried again. "Can I please stay here?" One of the paper-shuffling men rose and returned a moment later with a fourth man, who spoke to me in English. "You want to stay here?" he asked. "Yes, please," I gasped, grateful for someone who spoke at all and doubly grateful it was English.

"There is nothing for you here," he responded matter-of-factly. "All of our programs are in Hindi. Even the yoga classes are in Hindi. There is nothing in English. Also, you must get up early in the morning for the five o'clock prayer ceremony, and that is also in Hindi. You should go to the ashram down the road. They have classes in English."

"Oh, thank you so much." I walked quickly out of the ashram, excited to tell Jim that I had found a place with classes in English, and equally pleased to ignore the implication of the mysterious voice I had heard.

When we arrived at the ashram further downriver, I immediately felt repelled. This was not where I was supposed to be. They did have a full day's activities in English—yoga, meditation, philosophy—but I needed to get back to Parmarth

Niketan. The voice had become a rope pulling me back.

I hurried back to Parmarth Niketan and pleaded with the man in the office who spoke English, "I will get up at any time that you say. I will sit through whatever you say I need to sit through, whether I understand it or not. It doesn't matter. I just want to stay here. Please."

"Actually," he replied, "we do not have the authority. You are a girl, and you are a foreigner. You can only stay here with permission from our president."

"OK, great. No problem. Please let me meet the president so I can ask him."

"Actually, he is out of town."

"Oh," I replied, my heart sinking a bit. "When will he return?"

"Maybe tomorrow," the tall man replied.

"Great. I will come back tomorrow."

I had not read the section in the India guidebook that explains that people in India, and especially in the service class, will tell you whatever they think you want to hear. Truth is less important than goodwill, and the highest goal is to keep you happy: "Is my faucet fixed?" "Oh, yes, Ma'am, faucet is fixed." You're happy to hear this news, so his goal is accomplished. However, what he hasn't taken into consideration is how short-lived your happiness will be when you discover that actually, no, the faucet has not been fixed, and your bathroom is flooded.

So, when the gentleman in the office said, "Maybe tomorrow," I took it to mean, "Maybe tomorrow," not recognizing that it really meant, "I have no idea."

For the next many days, I returned to ask, "Is he here yet?"

"Not yet," was the daily reply. "Maybe tomorrow."

CHAPTER 8

Surrender to the Divine

"He's here, he's here, he's here!" Pratap rushed toward me, breaking the silence of the bustling central pathway at the ashram. Breathless, my new and only friend grabbed my hand. "Come meet him. Come meet him."

I had long since given up waiting for the phantom president to arrive. Parmarth Niketan ashram is the largest ashram in Rishikesh and one of the largest spiritual institutions in India. The man at the front desk of the Green Hotel provided me with all the details I wanted about this magical place with life-size statues and disembodied voices. He told me they have more than a thousand rooms—"And I can't even get *one*?" I wondered—plus a wide range of spiritual, charitable, and humanitarian programs. "It's the most famous ashram," he said, clearly impressed and proud to be in such close proximity.

So, I figured the people working in the office must've had more important things to do than field questions from a teary-eyed American woman twice a day.

They clearly did not want me to stay but were too polite to tell me. I assumed that to avoid hurting my feelings, they must have simply invented a phantom Higher Authority who would never arrive. They knew I'd eventually go away, and they wouldn't have to insult me by telling me I wasn't welcome. The office staff was simply employing, as I had learned by then, the socially acceptable solution of white lies to avoid upsetting someone. I decided to stop harassing them and turn the focus of my wonder elsewhere.

Inside me, movie music was playing nonstop—not the hit tunes you sing inside for decades, but the wordless music that announces, "It's about to happen." You don't know what *it* is, but instinctively, you reach out to hold the hand of the person next to you or tighten your jaw. When I heard the voice at Parmarth Niketan, I felt "it" was *there*, but with the men in the office thwarting my path, I decided "it" would probably come from the mountains. So Jim and I were headed to the mountains the following morning, on a five o'clock "luxury" bus that would, barring breakdowns, landslides, avalanches, road closures, or other seemingly inevitable hurdles, arrive in the sacred town of Badrinath by nightfall.

We had been planning to leave that day, Monday, September 23. However, after an ecstatic music concert at a local music teacher's home the night before, we sat on the banks of Ganga, the moon hanging low, holding us in her glow. Suddenly, instinctively, I suggested, *"Let's go Tuesday instead of tomorrow."* Why? I spoke the words before I even thought them.

Mountains have always been my refuge. Every spiritual experience I had prior to coming to India took place melting into the wet earth beneath huge redwood trees or hiking alone through high-altitude pine forests as my breath merged with the alpine air and I felt my existence merge with the mountains. Mountains were my vacation of choice—whether for a day trip or for several weeks. So, heading from Rishikesh to the mountains was natural for me. To postpone a departure, though, was unprecedented. Yet I'd just said it. Jim agreed easily; he would take another day of yoga and philosophy classes at the nearby center.

The ecstatic tears that streamed down my face—now nearly constant prisms through which I saw a world of rainbows—carried away the self-doubt to which I'd grown accustomed as a teenager. The power of whatever had grabbed hold of me, whatever had thrust me into this experience of bliss, was one I trusted.

Now, Monday morning, as I walked back from the steps on the Ganga through Parmarth toward the hotel for a quick bathroom break, my new friend Pratap saw me from the temple where he sat. A retired professional from Maharashtra, a large state in western India, he spent several months a year at the ashram doing seva, or selfless service. The service given to him was to sit in the temple, at the place where people passed after having darshan of the deities, a Hindu tradition that refers to seeing and being seen by the Divine, typically in the form of deities in temples. Pratap's responsibility was to hand everyone a bag of *prasad* (blessed food)—in this case, puffed rice. With thousands of visitors per day, it was no seva for the lazy.

Pratap's English was impeccable, and I had discovered him earlier in the week as I roamed through the ashram, pining to stay. I began to visit him daily. Sitting on the ground in front of his low desk, on which were piled bags and bags of the holy blessed rice, I listened to him expound on the nature of the universe.

As he handed the prasad to pilgrims, Pratap talked about God. "Prayer is like a broom which sweeps out your heart," he told me one day. I had never heard anyone speak about prayer other than in jokes that typically began with *"So, there was a priest, a rabbi, and a minister..."* Pratap was not concerned by the tears pouring from my eyes or the seeming incoherence with which I tried to explain my experience. As I stumbled for words, he smiled knowingly. "Ah, you have seen Ganga Maiya, the Mother Goddess Ganga. You are very blessed."

He had, according to Indian tradition, fulfilled his *grihastha ashram* phase of life, the householder stage: He had had a good job, had raised a family, and was now shifting into the *vanaprastha ashram* phase of moving away from the material world toward a spiritual life. Later, should he follow tradition, he would further shift from *vanaprastha* to *sanyas*, the stage of full renunciation and dedication only to spiritual practice. Pratap had embraced the concept of life as something for which the highest goal is spiritual awareness and experience, and his conversations emphasized the mundane nature of the world. "Pleasures come and go," he told me. "You can never hold onto them. Their nature is to be fleeting. The only nonfleeting joy is in divine connection."

Pratap knew I was waiting to meet the president. He also knew about the daily "Maybe tomorrow" answer I got from the office regarding the president's arrival. He didn't know I had given up waiting and was headed to the mountains. Why insult a man who had been so generous with his time and wisdom by telling him that I realized there was no president, that I knew this phantom Higher Authority had simply been invented so the office staff wouldn't have to tell me I couldn't stay?

I had stopped asking, stopped expecting, and stopped waiting for my Indian Godot. I would simply leave. I knew something important was about to happen in my life. I could feel it in my breath, and I could hear it in the wind. I just didn't know where it would come from. So, on this Monday morning, as I walked back to the hotel to go to the bathroom, no longer stopping to inquire after the president, my friend Pratap, a man well into his seventies, came sprinting out of the temple onto the main ashram pathway, shouting, "He's here! He's here!"

In those days, the ashram president, Pujya Swami Chidanand Saraswatiji, usually called Pujya Swamiji or Swamiji, met people twice a day for open darshan. *Darshan* means "seeing the divine" in Sanskrit, "being seen by the divine," or "divine sight." The word is used for beholding images of God in temples (e.g., "We are going to the temple for darshan"). It can also pertain to sitting in the presence of an enlightened master, who sees the Divine in each person and encourages us to see ourselves as divine too. Looking deeply through the eyes of an enlightened being, we have the opportunity to see the Divine. On another level, *darshan* refers to any meeting with a saint: "I'm having darshan with Pujya Swamiji tomorrow." In those days, Pujya Swamiji gave open darshan from 10:30 to 11:30 a.m. and from 4:30 to 5:30 p.m. For someone off the street, as I was, these were the only times it was possible to see him.

It was 10:45 when I walked through the ashram. As Pratap tugged me excitedly, he advised, "Be sure to do *pranam* when you meet him."

"Do what?" I asked, suddenly nervous. I had planned only to ask permission to stay, which in itself had seemed pure fantasy, as I was sure he didn't exist. Now, surprisingly, I felt agitated.

"You bow. *Pranam* means you bow very low on the ground."

"I'll do whatever you do," I told him. "Just show me, and I'll follow." I didn't know a thing about the president except that he got to decide whether I could stay. Now, I was supposed to prostrate myself before him. I guessed he was more than a high-level administrator, quite possibly a religious figure. I was suddenly curious and still a bit nervous.

We reached the reception area, which was next door to the office where I'd been asking about his arrival. Pratap gently opened a screen door and motioned for me to walk in. The room was large and bare, save for a burnt-orange carpet on which thirty or forty people were sitting. Some were poor, others well-to-do. Some were professionals; others looked like they lived on the street. They all faced the front of the room, where, on a thin, saffron-colored cushion, sat the most beautiful man I have ever seen.

Pratap signaled for me to sit next to him in the back of the room. I longed, more strongly than I could remember ever longing for anything, to be near this being at the front of the room. He wore orange-ish/pinkish robes, lighter than the orange of the carpet and softer than the shiny saffron of the cushion. Long black hair and a long black beard covered most of his head and face, out of which shone black eyes with a light that pulled me straight into them.

After a few minutes, Pratap pulled my hand. Come. I followed him as we walked up to the front of the room, gingerly stepping between widowed grandmothers in white sarees and upper-class professionals in pressed kurtas, their children sitting obediently with straight backs and crossed legs. The space between people was practically nonexistent—a tiny patch of orange here, another over there. I tiptoed from patch to patch in my bare feet, conscious already of being called up from the back of the room, out of turn, special treatment due to my beloved Pratap, who had said something in Hindi to a young man at the door as we entered.

As we walked forward, I felt the eyes of the president drawing me nearer and nearer, as though he had cast a fishing line into my heart and was now reeling me in. Rather than flapping and flailing to my death on his hook, however, I felt drawn into life.

Around the cushion was a small area of empty space into which people moved, one by one, to have an audience. Pratap knelt into that space and then lowered his forehead to the ground in front of his bent knees. He stretched his arms out in front of his head, inches away from the president's cushion. I did the same, peeking out from under my elbow to see when to raise my head.

When we sat back up, Pratap spoke in English and explained that I wanted to stay here, that I had been waiting for the president's return in order to ask. When he finished, I added that we were now planning to go to the mountains, to Badrinath, tomorrow, but maybe I could stay when we returned.

The president looked at me and said in perfect English, "This is your home. Stay whenever you'd like. I will be here for a few days, and then I have to go out again, but do not worry. I will tell them, and they will give you a room whenever you come back from Badrinath. You are always welcome."

I had lost myself in his eyes, which seemed to hold my entire being—past, present, and future. Mountains, rooms, dates, and staying were from a different plane of existence. I'm not sure how long it was before I realized I was supposed to respond.

"Oh, thank you so much," I stammered, distinctly aware of the musculature required to form words with my mouth.

Our two minutes were up, and Pratap whispered, "We have to go now." Again, we bowed and walked toward the back of the room and out the screen door.

"I am so glad you could meet Pujya Swamiji," Pratap gushed. "It was such Divine Grace that he came and you were also walking in the ashram at the same time. The Divine Plan is always perfect."

"What did you say his name was?" I asked. Up to now, he had been simply "the president"—first real, then phantom, then real again—the person whose permission my stay at the ashram depended on. I had envisioned a man wearing a coat and tie with a briefcase sitting behind a desk, accepting or rejecting guests based on some mysterious criteria. It hadn't occurred to me that "the president" was a holy being in whose presence I would feel eternal time and boundless space.

"His full name," Pratap, my friend, confidant, and now guide of the intricate pathways of the ashram and its president, explained, "is Pujya Swami Chidanand Saraswatiji, Muniji. Muniji is a nickname his guru gave him, meaning 'one who observes great silence and austerity.' Most people call him 'Pujya Swamiji.' *Pujya* means 'worthy of reverence.' If that's difficult, just say Swamiji. That is also OK."

"Wow" was all I could say. A few moments later, when my breath returned, I added, "I didn't realize he was such an incredible being. This wasn't at all what I had expected."

Pratap smiled. "Ah, yes. Pujya Swamiji. We are very blessed here to have his darshan every day when he is here. People from around the world long to meet him. He travels to every country and has many, many followers. He has built temples around the world to spread the glory of our heritage. He has been in the United Nations." Pratap's chest puffed up perceptibly as he spoke about the president's accomplishments. "People wait their whole lives to have a moment with him, and we are blessed to see him every day."

We sat outside the president's darshan room on lime-green benches. I hadn't noticed this area before, but now that the president had returned, it was a flurry of activity. Young men raced in and out, no less serious than Wall Street brokers. Every few moments, another person or group would emerge from the screen door, all of them smiling as though some great burden had been lifted. Many people would inquire in Hindi of one of the young men and, on receiving a response, enter the room. Even without understanding the language, it seemed clear to me that they were asking whether he was back. Everyone wanted to see him.

Why had no one told me I was waiting for one of India's most revered religious leaders? I berated myself for imagining a businessman and nearly missing the opportunity to meet him. I vowed, at least in India, to always be patient, for it was clear I had no idea what was coming, when, or from where.

I practiced saying, "Pujya Swamiji, *Poo-jya Swaameejee*" as streams of people entered and left the room like meandering streams joining with a great river, replenishing, then branching out again to irrigate individual fields and lands. Finally, I rose and said to Pratap, "Thank you so much for taking me to meet him. I'm so glad to have permission to stay here. We are leaving early tomorrow morning. I'll let you know as soon as we get back, and I'll come and stay here."

Pratap smiled and jiggled his head right, left, right again, in the way only Indians can. It means, "Sure, sure, no problem." Then I watched him walk down the path alongside the hall where, soon, I would sit from five to six o'clock every morning for prayers, then back to the temple complex.

I turned and walked toward the iron water pump in the center of the ashram complex, midpoint between the small road in front alongside the Ganga River and the small road in back that connects the back gates of all the ashrams lining this stretch of Swargashram village.

I turned right at the water pump to head back to our hotel, where I would tell Jim the great news of what happened. We could stay here after our trip to Badrinath. He was looking for a guru, and, fortuitously, I had found one for both of us. But the moment my body turned right, I couldn't take another step. My feet were stuck to the ground. I looked down. Had I stepped in something? Indian chewing gum that had welded my bare feet to the concrete pathway? There didn't appear to be anything on the ground. Invisible Crazy Glue, then? What was it? Something was holding my feet to the ground. They wouldn't come up, no matter how hard I contracted my leg muscles to raise them. I scrunched my toes to see if I could feel something on the ground, but it felt just the way the concrete always does—warm and smooth, certainly not like chewing gum or Crazy Glue.

Oh my God! I realized. *I've contracted some horrible disease. One of my vaccinations didn't work, and I've lost the use of my legs! I must have polio or tetanus or Ebola or some other disorder that is slowly eating away my muscles or nerves. Oh, God, please help me!*

As I flailed my arms, trying unsuccessfully to extricate my feet from the ground, a wave of calmness suddenly washed over me. And as the wave descended, it drew the energy from my eyes, which had widened in fear, and down into my abdomen. After a few breaths, I calmly realized that fatal illnesses probably don't come on like this—suddenly, with no pain, no other symptoms, no warning, no infection or fever. Still not convinced, but calmer, I tried to think of other explanations. Maybe my legs had gone to sleep. We'd sat on the floor in Pujya Swamiji's room for a while, and I wasn't used to sitting on the ground. Maybe it was a delayed reaction and my legs had fallen asleep. I put a hand on each calf, but they weren't numb or tingly. No pins and needles. They were not asleep.

I closed my eyes. This was ridiculous: Normal, educated, scientific, healthy American students do not get themselves stuck to the pavement in an Indian ashram. There must be some simple explanation and obvious solution. I visualized the motor cortex in my brain—right for my left leg, left for my right leg, communicating with my cerebellum, as acetylcholine was secreted into my synapses. The motor neurons sent the signal down their axons into my spinal cord and ultimately into the muscles of my legs: *Contract! Contract! Contract!* Nothing.

A small crowd was gathering around me. Being white was unusual, and I had found myself being stared at frequently during our days in Delhi. Now, however, I was not only white, but I was also flailing my arms in the middle of the courtyard like an airplane trying to take off.

At that moment, a group of children came racing down the central ashram pathway. Many of the ashram workers live in rooms around a courtyard in the back gardens, and most have children who, of course, run and play. They were playing an Indian version of tag and raced after each other at high speed. Instinctively, I stepped backward to prevent being knocked over.

The children passed, and I realized, *I'm free. I just moved backward. My feet aren't glued to the ground anymore!* Immensely appreciative of the ability to lift one foot after the other off the ground, I turned again toward the back gate to make my way out of the ashram.

And again, my feet were stuck—now in a slightly different place, a few inches behind where they had been "glued" before, but the feeling was identical. I could not contract a single muscle. No instruction from my brain, no amount of forcing or coaxing, could get my feet to move.

I just moved backward, I thought. *I definitely did.* For some inexplicable reason, I could walk backward only. If someone had told me I'd contract an illness whereby I was restricted to backward motion, I would have laughed at the sheer idiocy of it. Your muscles work, or they don't. Your brain works, or it doesn't. You might develop a proprioception issue whereby you can't properly navigate your surroundings, but to be able to walk backward but not forward is absurd, unheard of, and medically impossible. But it was true. I had such a disease. OK.

With my feet still seemingly glued to the floor, as I had no other option, I swung around and shifted my weight so I now faced Pujya Swamiji's area, with my back to the ashram's back gate and the hotel just past it. *I'll just walk out of this ashram backward*, I thought, not at all distressed at the idea and actually feeling proud at having successfully diagnosed my weird Indian ailment.

But no. As I leaned back and tried to pick up my feet to follow the rest of my body, they wouldn't come. Neither of them. They would not budge.

The crowd around me was growing, and I tried to ignore them. I had to figure this out. I'd tried, first facing forward and then facing backward, to walk out the ashram gates, and my legs wouldn't move. I could not walk out of the ashram. However, I'd been able to move backward when the children raced by. There was only one possible explanation. It was not the direction of my body that mattered, it was the direction I tried to move. I could move toward Swamiji's room, but I couldn't walk out of the ashram.

As my eyes filled with tears, I tested my new hypothesis. I was already facing Pujya Swamiji's room, for I had swung around while trying to walk backward out of the ashram. Could I walk forward, then, toward his room? I lifted my right leg easily and the left just as easily. As though walking on the beach in footsteps already imprinted in the sand, I walked back toward his meeting room. I entered the room and realized that only a few minutes, perhaps five or seven, had passed since I had left it the first time.

I stood in the doorway, not sure what to do, as I no longer had Pratap to choreograph my every movement. Pujya Swamiji was surrounded by a family— parents, a white-saree-clad grandmother, and two young children who sat stiller than I'd ever seen kids sit. The mother was speaking to Swamiji in Hindi, and he listened intently while every once in a while moving his eyes to make eye contact with each of the children and the grandmother.

Suddenly, gently, he lifted his gaze from the family to me standing by the door. "Yes?" he said with a smile that did not have even a trace of surprise. "I think," I began slowly, still undecided about my next move, "I think I am supposed to stay now." Swamiji continued to smile gently, nodded his head, and said, "*Welcome.*" He then turned his gaze back to the family at hand.

Once I decided to move immediately into Parmarth Niketan, my feet no longer prevented me from walking out. I returned to the hotel and gushed excitedly to Jim that I had found the guru he was looking for. I had found the most incredible being, a famous guru of the famous ashram, and now we'd been granted special permission to stay.

Jim declined.

"I need to find my own guru, not one you find for me. I'm tired of my life revolving around you and your life. I will not move into the ashram. I'm going to Badrinath. You can either come with me or stay here alone." Excitement turned to shock, then shock to stillness. I was sad but not afraid. I knew I would stay; there was no question.

For me to stay back while my husband traveled up the mountains was an unprecedented act of courage and defiance. I had had severe abandonment issues since my biological father, Manny, had left our house when I was three and then my life when I was eight. I had clung to boyfriends and moved seamlessly from one to the next, sure to never be alone. Jim had warned me, as we prepared for our trip to India, that I should be ready to travel alone should he find a guru with whom he wanted to stay, free from any marital encumbrance. Less than two weeks after touching down in Delhi, that is exactly what I did. But it was I who'd found a guru!

Jim's imminent departure neither worried nor upset me. A hand had reached out and grabbed onto my life. I was being held by an experience, a power that made the power of all relationships pale in comparison. I no longer needed my husband to protect me. I was being protected. I did not need him to heal me. I was being healed. I had assumed that this would be a journey together, and when I met Pujya Swamiji, I assumed that Jim would find in him the guru he had been longing for. Yet I was barely affected when I realized this was not to be. Something had already healed in me so deeply in those few days of sitting on the steps of Ganga that I no longer depended on Jim as the foundation of my life. If he was there, wonderful. If he wasn't, that was fine too. My roots had found deep, nourishing soil. I trusted fully for the first time in my life.

I moved into the ashram the next morning, and Jim took the dawn bus to Badrinath.

CHAPTER 9

"Just Don't Give
Them Any Money"

"Oh, my God, it is *so* beautiful here. It's amazing. I see God everywhere. It's so beautiful. And Swamiji. He is so beautiful. It is all just so beautiful," I cooed through the phone lines to my mom and dad (Frank, who began as my stepfather when I was seven, quickly became all things Dad, and finally legally adopted me when I was nineteen). Although the internet existed and we had email in California, neither Rishikesh nor most of India had it yet. I had promised my parents I'd call once a week, on Sunday evening, which would be Sunday morning for them. My mom's stress threshold regarding my health and safety is seriously low. Even today, as I cross fifty, she always wants travel itineraries and text messages as I take off and safely land.

So, once a week, I would call and assure them I was all right, the same arrangement we'd had when Jim and I had spent a year in Ecuador. Mom could make it a week anchored in her own resources of comfort, but on the seventh day, she needed to reconnect to be sure I was OK.

I had called from Delhi the first Sunday after we arrived. We'd seen the Red Fort, Delhi's most iconic monument. It was huge but, to me, not that interesting. I was much more intrigued by the crowd that gathered amphitheater-style, squatting and unabashedly watching me take photos, a not uncommon experience for foreign tourists in India. And I'd found a cup of real coffee overlooking Connaught Circle.

The second Sunday, I called from Rishikesh during my mystical intoxication with Ganga. "I see God everywhere," I babbled on. But my inebriation over the divinity of a river seemed innocuous enough to them. Mom knew I loved nature, always connected profoundly with mountains and trees, so for me to blather on about the divinity of a river didn't set off any alarm bells, especially since I was staying in a hotel with my husband.

But now I had moved into the ashram and had uninterrupted days of ecstasy. It was Sunday, and time to call again. "Oh, my God," was all I could say to describe the last week. "I met the president, the guru here, Swamiji, and he is *amazing*. He is so divine. Everything is just so beautiful. I see God everywhere. And Ganga, oh, my God. Jim? Yeah, he's great. He's gone to the mountains. Yes, I'm here alone, but I'm so not alone. I am with God."

It was too much for them. I was not just cooing harmlessly about a river while staying with my husband in a hotel. I had now moved into an ashram, my husband had gone off alone to the mountains, and I couldn't put together a coherent sentence. Something had to be done.

Looking back years later, I realize that when we have a spiritual experience, we forget that the rest of the world has not had the same experience with us. When day becomes night, it is dusk for everyone, so to refer to the oncoming darkness is understandable. When night becomes day, it happens for all too. But when darkness becomes light *inside* of us, the experience doesn't automatically include others who are in our life. The veil over my eyes had been lifted, but the vision I had was *within my consciousness*, my energetic connection to the universe, not in everyone's. Mom and Frank were clearly not experiencing what I was. "It's so beautiful," I kept exclaiming on auto-repeat. My parents said nothing to alarm me, nor did they hint that I had alarmed them. Only later did I learn that they had considered flying to India to rescue me.

"I called my friend in Pune," my mom later explained. "And I told him that my daughter had been kidnapped and brainwashed by a cult and we needed to free her from them. 'I will bring the cult deprogrammers,' I told him, 'but you need to get the Indian police, because I don't know whether they'll become violent when we try to rescue her.'"

Her Indian friend was, of course, quite concerned, both for me and for the reputation of his country, and assured my mom he would do everything to help. "However," he said, "you have to give me the name of the ashram and the swami so I can inform the police. They will need specifics."

"I don't know the swami's name," my mom said. "Only that he is the head of Parmarth Niketan ashram, which is where she is now staying in Rishikesh."

"OK," her friend said. "Give me a few hours to get back to you."

Later that day, her friend called her back. My mom's voice began to crack as she told me this part of the story. It happened during Frank's sixty-fifth birthday celebration in 2011, fifteen years after that babbling phone call from Rishikesh, and Swamiji was present in our backyard in Los Angeles with all my parents' closest friends gathered together. "He said, 'If that swami gives your daughter permission to stay at his ashram, it will be a blessing not only to her but to your entire family for generations to come.'" In typical disregard for rules she doesn't agree with, my mom leaned over and gave Swamiji a big hug. "Thank you for blessing her, and all of us," she said.

But in fall 1996, she was not yet appreciative. Her friend's reassuring phone call was enough to postpone her scheme to bring deprogrammers from LA to India and to know that I was, at least, physically safe.

"Whatever you do, don't give them any money!" she pronounced, finally, on the phone, capitulating in a battle I didn't even know had taken place.

CHAPTER 10

Seva

People ask, "How did your seva begin?" "How did you start working for Pujya Swamiji?"

The seva began on the fourth or fifth day after I arrived. My eyes were flooded with tears, the beach within my heart being shaped by waves of love rising and crashing on the shore, each wave so high I was sure it would drown my very heartbeat.

I saw Pujya Swamiji three times each day: at morning and afternoon darshan, and in the evening aarti, during which I joined the yellow-clad boys and orange-robed sadhus (Hindu monks) to stand on the steps leading to the river's edge and sing along to words I didn't understand.

Each evening as we sang, I felt a hand gently reach into my chest, grab hold of my heart, my lungs, and every physical aspect of "me," and carry me by my internal organs the way a mother cat carries her kittens by the skin of their necks to a plane of existence I'd never before encountered. It was not a physical plane. There were no distinct mountains or rivers or grassy fields. It was not a visual experience at all. It was an entirely different state of being.

When I opened my eyes, I was still physically there, on the edge of the flowing Ganga River. Yet I was carried to a different level of perspective and experience, one in which there was no yesterday, today, or tomorrow. Time wasn't linear; *simultaneous* moments overlapped in a carefully woven tapestry of existence.

Nor was space linear. When I opened my eyes, I could recognize that the legs that moved by force of my brain were standing atop some marble steps that led, one after the other, into the river. So I knew I was "here"—this was where the body stood—and yet I was not here. I was taken to a simultaneous, separate plane of existence, carried deeper and deeper by the songs Pujya Swamiji sang. Each note took me into a realm where I was both the legs that came out of my torso and the legs that came out of everyone's torso, and also I was *everyone's* torsos, arms, heads, and ears, and the steps on which we stood, *and* I was the water flowing over the marble. With a gentle shift in focus, I was all of these.

After aarti, after the wave of yellow- and orange-clad students and renunciants receded back into the ashram, I continued to sit, my eyes merging and melting into the water, now incandescent in the moonlight. It felt to me like there had never been a moment prior to this one. All of time was now. The twenty-five pre-India years of my life seemed a canvas on which a child had painted and I had once glimpsed and smiled at.

One afternoon, as Pujya Swamiji stood to leave from the afternoon darshan, he looked down at me, still seated on the ground, waiting for my legs to regain sensation so I could stand. "You can come at 6:30 a.m. tomorrow, after the prayers," he said. *Come? Come where?* He had already brought me to what seemed to be the furthest reaches.

"Where should I come?" I asked in a whisper, as though my vocal cords had gone to sleep with my legs.

"Just come here to this room," he replied. "One of the boys will bring you in to see me."

With that he turned and left, vanishing through the magic door into his quarters—his sleeping, eating, and meeting rooms. Beyond that door, it had seemed to me, was the land beyond the Phantom Tollbooth, a Kingdom of Wisdom I'd never be able to visit.

The next morning, I was up before my alarm buzzed at four o'clock. All through the prayers, which include Hindi and Sanskrit chanting and then a Hindi discourse, I was edgy with excitement. *What would it be like in the inner sanctum? What would Swamiji say? Or do?* Each previous morning, I had effortlessly entered a state of meditation. The words of the songs *and* the lectures were music to my ears. Not understanding Hindi was a blessing. When we don't speak a language, the language center seems to shut off, and sound is processed as just sound. And each word brought tears to my eyes.

If I didn't understand, why was I crying? What was touching me so deeply? We process only the most superficial aspects of communication through our language centers, I believe. The rest of communication takes place elsewhere—perhaps in the body, the nervous system, or the soul. In any case, meditation came easily each morning, as I was undistracted by the meaning of what was being said. The chorus of men and women on separate sides of the hall bursting forth into *"Hari Om"* as the clock tower struck five soothed my mind to stillness.

On this morning, my mind was not calm. My heart beat rapidly. I couldn't lose myself or merge with the sounds. I kept looking at the clock, waiting for the prayers to end. Then, a quick cup of coffee, and I'd be taken in to see Swamiji, granted entrance into his sacred quarters for the first time.

Since I had started driving at sixteen, I'd had a morning coffee habit. In high school, on my way to class, I'd ritually stop at 7-Eleven to get a thirty-two-ounce cup of coffee, filled not quite to the top to leave room for flavored nondairy creamers: French vanilla, vanilla caramel, hazelnut. I'd pour them cupful by tiny cupful until the bitter junk that passed for coffee smelled like a candy shop. The irony of getting the greatest percentage of my daily caloric intake from nondairy creamers was lost on me at the time, and each morning, I kept myself awake in history, social studies, and other eight o'clock classes by virtue of thirty-two ounces of caffeine.

As I got older and gourmet coffee became as ubiquitous as frozen yogurt, my tastes got more nuanced. By the time Starbucks opened in Palo Alto, I'd graduated to triple soy lattes. A huge cup of hot, frothing soy milk with three (sometimes four) shots of espresso was the perfect antidote to collegiate sleepless nights and drowsy afternoons.

Before arriving in India, I had never tasted Nescafé. The idea of powdered coffee was beneath me. I spoke fluent French, vacationed on the Champs-Élysées and in Chamonix, and spent summers in Chailly-sur-Lausanne. There was no place in my affected self-identity for instant coffee.

Then, I came to northern India, where, if you want to drink coffee, Nescafé it is. In fact, what passes for coffee in India is much closer to melted coffee ice cream than to any serious stimulant. Tiny spoonfuls of brown powder are mixed into sugary milk (sometimes fresh—sometimes the milk is powdered too). In a fancy setting, one might get a flaking of additional coffee powder sprinkled gingerly on top of the white foam. It was wonderful, of course, as melted Häagen-Dazs coffee ice cream would be. But it was not coffee in the *I need to wake up* sense.

Hence, I quickly developed and perfected a morning ritual: The man at the local chai shop would give me triple the serving of Nescafé for "only" quadruple the cost. Therefore, instead of paying five rupees for a cup of mildly coffee-fragranced sweet milk, I paid twenty rupees for three heaping spoonfuls of Nescafé in my steaming milk. It was bitter and unpalatable but at least offered the fix of coffee. I soon discovered that by stirring heaping spoonfuls of sugar into the concoction, I could drink it without gagging.

So, my morning ritual was set. After morning prayers, I walked to the marketplace, where, fifty yards down, the *chaiwallah* greeted me with an enthusiastic "Nam-*aa*-ste." He sat cross-legged on a raised wooden platform in front of the small café. In front of him brewed a vat of tea, into which he periodically dropped more loose tea leaves, or another ladleful of milk from an uncovered pot nearby.

He and I, even without a shared language, had worked out a routine. He would remove the huge vat of chai from the single gas burner and, in its place, put a small pot of milk. As the milk came to a boil, he poured once, twice, then three times from the small packet of Nescafé. He then picked up a large steel glass (twice the size of the tiny glasses that most people drink tea or coffee from) and poured the properly brown beverage into the cup, which he handed me with a flourish.

I smiled and handed him twenty rupees with a heartfelt Hindi thank-you, "*Dhanyavaad*," and took my coffee to sit on the steps leading to Ganga.

The cool marble steps on the banks of the holy river were mostly empty at that hour of the day. Ritual bathers were already gone, and those for whom sunshine was more important than tradition hadn't arrived yet. So, from 6 to 6:30 a.m., just after sunrise but not yet warm, it was remarkably quiet, populated by those in meditation and prayer rather than splashing bathers.

I sat on the higher steps, careful not to bring coffee into the sacred area of prayer and puja (worship). Once lips have touched food, drink, or a utensil, it's considered *juta* (unfit for another, and certainly not fit to be in a place of worship). Mindful not to offend cultural sensitivities, I sat high on the steps, watching the morning mist dissipate into the rays of the rising sun as they danced on the waters of the river.

That morning, the coffee was purely medicinal, so rather than walk to the banks of Ganga and sip it meditatively, I sat on a bench at the café behind my friend the chaiwallah so as not to waste time walking to and from the river.

I drank my coffee Indian-style to finish it quickly, pouring small amounts from the tall steel glass into a little bowl, swirling the bowl to cool it, then drinking from the bowl. With four or five cooled bowlfuls, I emptied my cup, handed it back to the chaiwallah, smiled, cooed "Dhanyavaad" earnestly, and walked quickly back to the ashram.

The clock tower in front of Parmarth showed 6:20 as I entered Pujya Swamiji's outer sitting room. The door to the large room was unlocked, so I entered, completely alone save for the orange carpet and a painting of Lord Krishna directly above the saffron cushion.

I had just sat on the floor right next to the Magic Kingdom door when, suddenly, it opened and a boy's head appeared. "Why are you here?" he asked in a way that might seem accusatory but probably reflected only the limits of his English vocabulary. I froze. Maybe it was all a mistake. I was a fool. Swamiji hadn't really said he would see me privately. I had only imagined it. I was delusional, and now I'd been found out. I couldn't speak. I looked down at my covered feet and felt my face flush with shame. "You are here to see Swamiji, I think," he said. I nodded abashedly. He smiled. "Come here," he said and held open the door. I jumped up and followed him excitedly, hesitating briefly in the doorway to savor the moment I crossed the threshold.

The lithe young man led me into a room with windows facing Swamiji's garden. The rays of the morning sun were beginning to stream through the glass. In one corner, next to the windows, was a large desk painted pink and topped with elegant translucent black glass. There were several piles of papers and files lined up and stacked neatly on the window side of the desk. Behind the desk was a large chair covered in a floral pattern that matched the couch on the opposite wall. Facing the desk were three smaller chairs, also covered with the same floral print.

"Sit here," he instructed me, motioning to a rug on the floor at the foot of the couch. I sat obediently, facing an empty couch. "Swamiji will come soon," he declared and then departed, closing the door behind him.

Moments passed, many of them. I could faintly hear voices coming from some other part of the complex but could not decipher anything. I was suddenly conscious of the ridiculousness of how I had gotten there and where I was. I was sitting alone on a soft Persian rug at the foot of an empty couch, waiting for a man in orange robes I didn't know to arrive *and then what*? In all the anticipation leading up to this special meeting, I'd never thought about what the meeting might be about.

Damn, I berated myself. You should have thought of something to talk about. He'll think you're an idiot. He's given you this incredible opportunity to meet him privately, and you don't have anything to say. My heart plummeted into my stomach. Maybe he's forgotten about me, I finally thought, with some relief.

Of course he's busy—how and why would he possibly remember that he told me to come see him? I'm sure he's doing something more important. I looked around and suddenly felt like a trespasser. *How dare I think I'm supposed to be in this sacred room, clearly reserved for those much more worthy than me?*

As I was about to stand and leave, the door flew open and Swamiji entered. "Yes," he said. It was not a question, but an answer, perhaps, to some unasked question. "Yes," he repeated as he sat on the couch. "Tell me."

The anxiety of not having anything to say vanished. I still had nothing to say, but felt no agitation about it. It felt absolutely perfect to sit there with him, at his feet, on the rug, in silence. He looked at me, and I knew he could see everything. Finally, words began to come. "Swamiji," I whispered, wondering where the rest of my voice had gone, "I feel so blessed to be here, so blessed to be having these life-changing experiences. I don't understand what is happening, but it's so beautiful. I feel so blessed. I would like to give back in some way, to do something." I looked up at him, and he was staring into my eyes wordlessly. "Is there anything I can do?" I repeated.

He continued to look into my eyes, and I felt his presence inside me. I knew that he had entered the core of my Self. He knew everything and could see everything inside me. It was not frightening or embarrassing. In fact, it was the most soothing and comforting experience I could imagine, as though my heart and mind, my darkness and anxieties were plunged into a warm bubble bath. He smiled as his eyes bore through mine.

Finally he spoke: "Anything?"

It took me a moment to remember what he was talking about. Oh, yes—I'd asked if there was anything I could do.

We sat in his office, a separate personal room, entry to which was restricted to one or two of the "boys" and an occasional person blessed, as I had been, to be granted permission to sit there. There was no question of being interrupted or someone walking in unannounced. Swamiji had known me only a few days and was fully aware that I did not know anyone else in the ashram or in any circles of his devotees or disciples. Our worlds did not overlap at all. He could tell that I had no idea what a Hindu saint was, what it meant, what the rules and restrictions might be. He was the first saffron-robed man I had ever seen, let alone spoken to. And of course he knew that I was intoxicated with bliss, floating through my days, my consciousness immersed in an ocean of incomprehensible ecstasy.

We sat, I a twenty-five-year-old temporarily incoherent American student, and he a forty-four-year-old renunciant whose life of celibacy had begun before he even understood what he was renouncing. And I had just offered him anything.

"Anything?" he questioned again, and continued to look not into but fully through my eyes. What was he seeing?

"Yes, anything," I whispered, the rest of my voice still absent. Suddenly, into this state of stillness, into this state of surrendering my darkest corners and deepest secrets to his loving gaze, into this state of ecstatic openness, I heard my mother's voice. It was stern and sharp: "Just get up and walk out." She was now here, in my brain, watching me sit on the floor at the feet of a man old enough to be my father in a far-off corner of the world, offering him anything.

"Just stand up and walk out right now," she instructed again, forcefully, as though I were a toddler refusing to leave the toy store. "Just leave. Now." I smiled at how her voice had found me even thousands of miles away, and how of course she'd be worried. Maybe there really was something to worry about. But, oddly, none of it mattered. I knew without any doubt that, yes, I would give him anything. Whatever he wanted.

I nodded again to make sure Swamiji knew that yes, I was fully his, fully eager to be taken and utilized in whatever way he wanted.

"Do you promise?" he asked. I raised my eyes again to see him staring down at me, unblinking.

My mother's shrill voice was joined now by the voice of Dr. Phil Zimbardo, expert on cults, mind control, and brainwashing. I had been one of the only students in his decades-long career at Stanford to get an A+ in his standing-room-only Psychology of Mind Control class.

Dr. Zimbardo's voice now bellowed through my brain as well: "You know better than this. You must leave the room right now. Be strong. Gather your wits about you and just leave." His steady voice contrasted sharply with my mom's, which had reached a frantic crescendo: "Leave, for God's sake. Just stand up and leave!"

I could hear and recognize both their voices, but they were unable to affect me. They seemed to be slightly loud background music, a grating audio track in an otherwise heavenly film. While aware of them, I was not touched.

"Yes, of course. I promise," I spoke, leaving my mother and Dr. Zimbardo in a far-off corner of my consciousness.

As I looked at Swamiji, having promised him anything, the seriousness of his gaze broke and he smiled. "OK," he said. "Three things."

"First, I want you to get closer and closer to God every day. Every day, a little closer. Second, serve humanity. You've been given so much—use it to serve the world. Third," he paused, and his gaze spread and opened to envelop every cell that had ever been part of who I was. Holding the me who had been, the me who was now, and the me who I was yet to become in the ocean of his eyes, he said, "Third, be happy. I do not want to ever see you sad. If you have any sadness, give it to me." He held out his cupped hands as though begging not for bread, but for my pain.

I don't know at what point the tears began to flow from my eyes. I became aware of them only when his now outstretched hands picked up the washcloth next to him and he leaned over to wipe my face with it.

"By the way," he said, "Can you type?"

CHAPTER 11

Jim's Return

Meals at the ashram were served in a large hall. We sat side by side on thinly woven *chattais* (cotton mats) and sang as young men in flowing yellow dhotis (fabric wrapped around the waist and tied through the legs like loose-fitting pants) and yellow kurtas (as our host in Roorkee had worn) served food to us from large metal buckets. Meals were usually a potato-and-vegetable dish lightly seasoned with cumin, turmeric, and salt; dal (lentils), typically yellow mung dal; and freshly rolled whole-wheat chapatis.

Meals had been a battle for me since I was a teenager—an internal war over what I *should* eat, what I *would* eat, what was *good*, what was *bad*. Food was love, fullness, and my numbing drug of choice. Starving myself to gain some semblance of control in my life was my alternate drug of choice. Yet here I was, swaying left and right over my crossed legs as I clapped to the tune of words I didn't understand, in one of six parallel lines of people singing and sharing a meal.

Meals were at 11:30 in the morning, just after Pujya Swamiji's open darshan, and 6:30 in the evening, just after the aarti. The bell rang once and then twice. If you missed it, you went hungry.

From the moment the first scoop of potatoes simmering in cumin seeds was dropped onto my metal plate and a round chapati tossed down thirty seconds later, I no longer obsessed over food. The waters of the Ganga that had washed over my feet and through my awareness had also, inexplicably yet irrefutably, washed away the notion that I could eat my biological father's love in a cheese sandwich; that somehow, if I ate enough slices of toast with butter, I could fill the hole in my heart. Mother Ganga's waters washed away the notion that by starving myself, I could control my life. I no longer headed to the bathroom after a meal to regain, by vomiting it back up again, the control I had lost in eating. The cumin-cooked potatoes were a friend, not an enemy. Was this really me eating chapatis and potatoes so happily? Where had this new "I" come from?

After dinner, about a week after my feet had been glued in place, I stood on the same central pathway, chatting with new friends in a mix of broken English and hand gestures in the after-dinner glow of absorbed nourishment, when I felt a hand on my shoulder. Jim had returned from Badrinath. He had intended to stay seven days but had returned after four or five. I smiled at him, gave him a quick hug, and introduced him to my new friends as we continued our conversation.

"I need you to come with me to the hotel," he said. I bade my new friends goodnight and accompanied Jim up the ashram pathway. As we walked out the back gate of the ashram toward the Green Hotel, I reminded him that the ashram gates closed at nine, so I needed to watch the time.

"Seriously?" he asked. "I just traveled ten hours by bus, and you're going to stay in the ashram?"

"Jim, stay with me," I offered gently. The ashram, the experience, Swamiji—none of this was intended to replace my marriage or be a threat to Jim. It was just a new dimension. I thought the experience I'd had, the awakening, the discovery, would be something he could dive into too, something that could bring us closer to each other and ourselves. I hadn't anticipated his response.

"No, I'm not going to stay in *your* ashram. I'm not going to eat in that dining hall. I'm not a horse, and I don't eat out of buckets. I am going to stay at the hotel, eat at the hotel restaurant, and if this marriage matters to you, you'll stay with me."

"I can't," I said, although in retrospect, I realize it would have been more honest to say, "I won't." I wasn't being held prisoner at the ashram. I *could* have stayed out for the night and come back in the morning. There were no nightly room checks. But I was rooted in something deeper, more stable, and more real than fear of abandonment. I was no longer worried about Jim withholding his love or me not being the woman he longed for. My roots were now held in the rich soil of the ashram; my Self was being watered and nourished there. And that was where I needed to be, not back in the Green Hotel.

"Jim, I have to go back, but please come with me. Give it another chance. You really will love it." It was Jim who was on a spiritual path, Jim who was searching for a guru and enlightenment. I was convinced that if he just gave it a chance, he would see this was the right place for both of us.

"It can't be the right place for me," he said, his jaw so tightly clenched, his teeth barely separated from each other, fighting back his own rage. "It's *your* place. You have already become queen of the ashram, with everyone standing around you with folded hands and drippy smiles on their faces. It can never be my place. I need to find someplace where you are not already the star. I'm tired of everything revolving around you."

That was it.

We sat in silence for many minutes while he ate dinner at the Green Hotel. When he spoke, he told me about the girl who sat on his lap for ten straight hours, throwing up out the window of the bus the whole way to Badrinath; he told me about the flu and fever he had had, about what he'd gone through to get a bus back. Not a word about what was happening to us.

"I have to go," I said quietly after dinner. "It's almost nine. Are you sure you don't want to come?"

"I'm sure," he replied casually, the earlier anger and sarcasm having dissipated. "I'll see you tomorrow." As I walked back toward the ashram, I thought, "Maybe he will be OK. Maybe he'll come around and realize how amazing this place is. Maybe some of what is happening to me will happen to him."

CHAPTER 12

The Marriage Cracks

Jim stayed in Rishikesh for a few days, recovering from the cold he'd caught the week before, exacerbated by the frigid temperatures of Badrinath and endless mountain bus rides. Finally, he agreed to move into the ashram, at least to save money. One evening, I brought him in to meet Swamiji in his garden.

Swamiji sat in a folding chair, and we sat on woven mats on the grass. On a small table next to him was a phone. "Oh, you have a cell phone?" Jim chuckled sarcastically while I bowed. "It's only a cordless," Swamiji responded, slowly and softly.

"You are blessed to go to Badrinath," Swamiji continued. "It is a very holy and beautiful place."

"Yes, it was beautiful, but I was sick the whole time and came back early," Jim replied, the majority of his words left unspoken.

"Tell me," Swamiji said. It's something he says frequently, offering open-ended space into which, with grace, truth can flow.

"Tell you what?" Jim asked. He was not going to flow into that empty space. He'd made up his mind before he entered the door.

The meeting lasted only another few minutes, with Swamiji inquiring as to whether Jim was comfortable, did he have a clean towel? Enough toilet paper? Was he eating well? Embarrassed by Jim's coldness, I responded for both of us, "Yes, Swamiji, it is all wonderful. Thank you so much."

"One moment," he said and rose. A few minutes later, he came back with a box of cold Belgian chocolates. "You must have sweets. Someone brought these for me." He opened the box of chocolates and placed one in each of our mouths. I could see Jim's eyes roll as Swamiji reached out his hand to place the chocolate in his mouth. At least he took it.

I bowed to Swamiji before Jim and I rose. As we walked out of his garden, I turned to give Swamiji an "I'm sorry" look. He smiled and motioned with his hand not to worry. He then extended his arm outward, as though he were hugging an invisible person. I didn't understand. He pointed to Jim and again motioned with his arm. Ah—it was a signal for me to put my arm around Jim. I did and looked back. Swamiji put his thumb and forefinger together, forming an A-OK sign, and smiled.

The next day, Jim announced he was going to Mussoorie, a quaint hill station established by the British in the mountains about three hours from Rishikesh. If I didn't join him, he said, our marriage was over. I had no interest in going to Mussoorie. I had no interest in leaving Rishikesh for any reason, even to save our marriage.

I told Surya, Swamiji's main attendant, that I needed to speak to Pujya Swamiji privately. A few hours later, Surya came to the small room where I was typing letters on a manual typewriter and said, "Pujya Swamiji will see you now."

"I know I should care deeply that my marriage might be falling apart," I said, sitting on the floor of Swamiji's sitting room. "But I don't, really. Yes, I would love Jim to be happy and to be happy here. He wants me to come to Mussoorie with him and says that if I don't, our marriage will be over. But I am so happy here that if I have to choose between staying or being married, I would rather be here."

Swamiji smiled gently. "Go to Mussoorie," he said. "Go with your husband. It is the right thing to do." In a newfound joy of doing the right thing, along with knowing Swamiji would be away for the next few weeks anyway, I agreed.

In some ways, I was excited to leave Rishikesh, eager to see whether whatever was happening to me had a half-life. Would the ecstasy dissipate as I drove away from Rishikesh? Was the joy that consumed my days and woke me in the night for no reason other than to revel in it situation dependent? My heart knew it wasn't, but Dr. Zimbardo's straight-A student was a bit eager to find out.

So, we took the three-hour bus ride up to Mussoorie, and the streams of tears flowed from my eyes the entire way there. "It's like being married to Ramakrishna," Jim joked sadly. It would have been funny if I weren't his wife.

I found a wall in our hotel room at which I could meditate every morning and evening, something I had never done before coming to Rishikesh, where it often happened spontaneously wherever I was. But now that I was in a hotel rather than at an ashram, now that there was a road in front of our hotel rather than Ganga, I wanted to make sure to stay connected. So, I sat cross-legged on a pillow with my back against the wall of our hotel room every morning and evening; I closed my eyes and re-melted into the spaciousness that was growing inside me.

One evening, Jim said he needed to go to Lucknow to visit another spiritual teacher, from whom he wanted to learn. He invited me to come. "I need to go back to Rishikesh," I told him. I knew I needed to get back to Ganga and to Pujya Swamiji. I could call them forth in my mind and heart, but I also needed to be there physically. I wouldn't have had the experiences I was having if I were meant to be roaming around India.

It would be more than a decade before Jim's heart opened fully to Pujya Swamiji and nearly twenty years before he came back to Rishikesh. Jim had a picture of what and who he wanted in a wife, in a marriage, and in his life, and it did not include living in an ashram in Rishikesh. So, early one morning, after three days in Mussoorie, he boarded a bus for Lucknow and I boarded one for Dhanaulti, a lush, secluded mountain town on the way back down to Rishikesh.

I loved Jim—I still love him—but the attachment to his physical presence, the fear of losing the secure bond of marriage, which gave me an identity (being "Jim's wife"), no longer existed. I could love him whether he was with me in the ashram or not. I could love him whether he was sleeping with other women or not. I could even, I discovered, love him when his anger took the form of scathing faxes that he sent me from cities throughout India, berating me for the choice I made and describing the affairs he was having with other women. The love I was able to access came from a seemingly bottomless and boundless source within.

I did, though, wonder whether I was going crazy. Was I really not bothered that my husband had left me to travel around India and be with other women? I poked and prodded my psyche, trying to get a reaction. "There must be some sadness, some fear, some loss." But there wasn't. There was just love for him. The only sadness I felt was sadness for what he was going through and for how I was the cause of it. If being with other women helped, so be it.

The waters of Ganga had pulled my attachments, like sheets of Velcro, off the objects to which they had been adhered. Whether it was Jim, triple soy lattes, sinking into a thick mattress, or warm water streaming over me from a strong showerhead, the waters of Ganga washed so completely over everything I had identified with, everything I thought was essential for a happy life, that simply basking in the sun as she rose over the Himalayas and danced on the waters of the Ganga was enough.

I had no thought of divorce or of my spiritual experience and my guru *not* being compatible with my marriage. I had no thought that we would not walk the path of Parmarth together and sit at Swamiji's feet together. Spiritual experience was a new, amazing *additional* layer of my life, not something to replace my marriage.

Now, with twenty-twenty hindsight, I see that this is the way it needed to happen. I was being pushed through the first levels of an initiation into *sanyas* (renunciation). The easy detachment from my marriage was crucial. If it had been painful or wrought with uncertainty or longing, I could never have made this decision.

I was not an abstainer of anything by choice. I did not value austerity. The only role simplicity and renunciation played in my life was in camping and backpacking. I could easily renounce a deodorant or a change of clothes if it lightened my pack. I never thought about the extra baggage burdening my mind.

But here was a grace that began to work through me, slowly removing all the baggage I carried around—fear, emptiness, a longing to fill the space, drama, and anything that might soothe the anxiety. Slowly, through no merit of my own, this baggage was being lifted along with the weights that bore down on my shoulders, heart, and life.

CHAPTER 13

Losing My Questions, Finding the Answer

During my first weeks at the ashram, I spoke to almost no one other than Swamiji, and that only every few days. I sat twice daily in his open darshans, times when anyone could walk in and meet him. And everyone did: Sweepers, shopkeepers, widows, high-court justices, and wealthy industrialists from all over India and around the world came and sat on the orange carpet to receive his blessings. I sat in the back of the room, my back against the wall, listening and watching.

As I could not understand his words, I noticed instead his tone, his expressions, and the rise and fall of his volume and pitch. Actually, I closed my eyes most of the time. The experience was so overwhelming that even visual input was too much. I closed my eyes and melted into the ocean of his presence, the ocean of love, listening to the ebb and flow of his pitch, the comfort, interest, and care with which he addressed each person.

Every time I opened my eyes, a different person was in front of him, a different recipient of his boundless river of love and compassion. But it was all in Hindi, and I didn't understand a thing. Once every few days, there was an opening before the sixty minutes was up, and Swamiji would then turn to me, smile, and say, "Yes?"

I was an academic, a straight-A PhD student. Surely, I would have an intelligent response to "Yes?" But I never did. After the teaching about fear and faith, after unbelievably giving my pain to the river, I found my mind empty each time the opportunity to ask a question arose. Like a cookie jar from which even the crumbs have been emptied, there was nothing to grab hold of, no vestige of my former inquisitiveness.

Asking and answering questions had always come easily to me. Being the only child of highly verbal parents, combined with an education that prepared me to go forth into the world proud to have a question, unashamed to raise my hand and ask it, entitled to show up unannounced at a professor's door to see if she had an extra minute to explain something, I was a question asker. At eight o'clock in the morning, in 200-seat lecture halls, I'd be the one in the front row raising my hand: "Excuse me—I don't understand the last point. Can you clarify it?" and my teachers were astonished someone was actually paying attention.

That was not the same woman as the one who could only stare blankly at Swamiji's "Yes?" Not to have a question was OK, but not to have *anything* to say—not even a comment, an elaboration, a request for clarification? Where had this woman come from, and where had all her brains gone?

When not in his presence, I could think of perfectly intelligent things to say, valid questions to ask. *Ah, thank God,* I told myself. *At least next time he asks, I'll have something to say, and he won't think I'm a brainless idiot.* But the next time he looked in my eyes and asked, "Yes?" my mind became clear and smooth once more, with nary a ripple of movement nor a wave form of question or comment. I was simply nonverbal. It was all I could do to produce a small smile on my lips. *He must think I'm a fool.*

After repeatedly staring blankly in response to his inquiry, I decided to make a list of spiritual, cultural, and personal questions I might ask so I'd have something to say the next time I heard "Yes?" And so I folded the list into the small purse that held my room keys and a few rupees.

That afternoon, darshan was filled with a large group who wanted just to receive his blessings on their return from the sacred temples of Badrinath and Kedarnath. Thirty or forty of them bowed and left together. Swamiji finished well before 5:30 p.m. I sat, my back against the wall, eyes closed. Then I heard the word: "Yes?" I opened my eyes to realize the room was empty except for the two of us. I jumped to my feet and hurried to the front of the room to offer my pranam, to bow at his feet. "Yes?" Swamiji repeated, with a smile. "Tell me."

I had my cloth purse on a thin string across my chest, and I excitedly unzipped it to pull out my list of questions. The paper was gone.

My keys were there. Fifty rupees were there. My ChapStick was there. There was nothing else in the purse. Like a frantic woman in an old comedy routine, I turned my purse upside down and shook it on the floor. Nothing. There were no pockets, secret compartments, or holes through which it could have fallen out. I felt my face flush, and I looked up at Swamiji, who smiled at me with a mix of compassionate love and obvious amusement.

"I had a list," I stammered. "But it's not here." He said nothing and kept smiling. "I'll be right back. I must have lost it along the way. Do I have time to quickly run to my room?" He nodded and I jumped up, ran out the door, and scanned every square foot of the path back to my room as quickly as I could.

My list was not on the road. I flung open the doors to my room. Maybe I hadn't put it in my purse after all? Although I vividly remembered folding it and putting it inside, maybe I'd imagined it. Maybe it was still on the end table, where I wrote it. Nope. Only my alarm clock, journal, and pen. I pulled the sheet and blanket off my bed and the pillowcase off my pillow. It must have fallen between my sheet and blanket, or in my pillow.

Fortunately, no one was there to ask, "And exactly how would your list have fallen into your pillowcase?" I scoured every corner and surface of my tiny bare room and, acutely aware of the ticking clock, I walked back to where he sat on the beautiful golden saffron pillow, waiting for me to return. I bowed again and sat with legs folded behind me, my eyes lowered to the ground, waiting for him to come out of meditation.

After a few minutes, he opened his eyes and looked up at me. Before I could explain that my list had disappeared, he smiled and said, "Yes." This time, however, it was a statement, not a question. He did not follow it with "Tell me."

Just "Yes."

Yes. Yes, I had made a list. Yes, the universe had snatched it from my hands and caused it to dissolve back into the elements from which the paper had been made. Yes, I thought I was going crazy, and yes, I was not. Most important, yes, here we are. Here now. In this breath. In this intersection of time and space in a time and a space that are infinite. Right here, right now, there are no questions; there is only stillness. The stillness was the answer to my questions. He had already answered them.

CHAPTER 14

Expansion

A few weeks after I arrived at the ashram, a group of Americans led by a medicine woman/Aphrodite/Kelly–from–*Charlie's Angels* came to visit. Her outfits ranged from hippie–meets–Earth Mother to Native American leather bedecked with tassels and feathers, and she brought a bevy of followers with her. These were the first native English speakers I'd met since my arrival in Rishikesh.

Since I arrived in 1996, Rishikesh has become a hub of tourism—the "yoga capital of the world." At that time, while it wasn't exactly off the map, especially since the Beatles had come to Rishikesh in the sixties, it was still far from a tourist destination. The southeastern part of Rishikesh, Swargashram, where Parmarth Niketan lies—across Ganga and south from the hotels and restaurants—tended to attract more Indian devotees than Western tourists. Here, among the ashrams, tea stalls, and small shops, you could buy rudraksh malas (strings of prayer beads made from the seed of the sacred rudraksh tree), Ayurvedic medicine, oil lamps, and statues of the many manifestations of God. Back then when I walked in the market, heads would turn, and calls of "Madam, madam, shawl, madam, mala, madam?" resounded. I could feel the eyes of every shop owner and chaiwallah on me—not lasciviously, but simply resting their eyes unabashedly on someone who was new and different.

Today, foreign tourists are ubiquitous. Signs are written not just in Hindi and English but in Hebrew, Russian, and other European languages too. And about half the people on the roads are non-Indians.

The group leader was Jacqueline, and when her group arrived, my world shifted from the internal to the external. I was drawn into socializing, which had been absent during my first weeks in the ashram. Other than occasional words with Swamiji, which now focused on work and projects, and basic discussions with the kitchen staff about an apple or a clean towel, I barely spoke. There were no cell phones, Zoom, or FaceTime. There wasn't even a landline phone at the ashram I could use. I could make calls only from the phone booth in the marketplace—inconvenient and expensive.

Jacqueline and her twenty-five American spiritual seekers were middle-aged, mostly interested in energy healing, opening their chakras (energy centers), and indigenous rituals. While there wasn't much connection between us in age, background, or interest, we were all spiritually inclined Americans who spoke American English. That was enough for me, and I spent most of my time with them. We ate together, walked together on the banks of Ganga, and laughed at people farting and picking their noses in public.

One evening, they invited me to join them for a Reiki workshop. Upon their request, Pujya Swamiji had brought in a Reiki master to teach them. I knew nothing about Reiki, but at that point I was excited about everything. My life was an adventure, and I had no idea what the next moment would bring. I was in God's hands now. Walk on the Ganga? Sure. Tea? Sure. Reiki? Of course.

When I entered the room, the Reiki master was explaining the Level 1 initiation he'd be giving that evening. I had missed the introduction, and as I entered, he was saying, "So, my assistants and I will be initiating each of you. As I mentioned, you will not feel our physical touch on your bodies, as Reiki works on the energetic body."

Chairs were assembled, and one of the members of the group reached her hand out to me and said, "You should go in the first batch, because you must have work to get back to."

I sat in the chair in front of the Reiki master. "You missed the introduction," he said. "But don't worry. Just close your eyes and allow whatever is meant to happen to happen."

After a few minutes, he spoke again: "Your chakras are so open, much more open than I expected to see in anyone. We are only giving Level 1 initiation, but your chakras are so open, I think you're ready for Level 2 initiation too. If you'd like, I can give it to you now."

My vocabulary was formed by SAT (Scholastic Aptitude Test) and GRE (Graduate Record Exam) preparation books, AP (Advanced Placement) English classes, and the Word-a-Day game my parents had initiated when I was in junior high. "This is fun," they would announce each evening after dinner when it was time to play. I didn't find it fun. None of my friends had to play Word-a-Day at home with their parents. It was not only not fun, it was a violation of my precious free time. But they were insistent: "Sit down. This is fun." In any case, none of my vocabulary preparation included words like *chakra* or *Reiki* or even the word *initiation* the way the Reiki master was using it. I had no idea what he was talking about, but sure, why not?

"OK," I said. The Level 1 seemed to have taken only a few minutes. He hadn't even touched me; I had just had to close my eyes. How much more could Level 2 be? I smiled to myself in amazement at this incredible and unimaginable adventure on which God was taking me.

At some point later, a voice seemed to travel from somewhere into my ears. "OK," I could hear it say, barely audible. "You can get up now." The voice was a physical sensation, traveling from somewhere outside me, into my ears, through my ears, and into my arms, which reached to my sides to grasp the sides of my chair. It traveled through my ears into my legs, and I leaned forward to rise. I had no idea how much time had passed since I had sat down or what had happened.

"How do you feel?" the Reiki master asked. The words traveled through my ears, and I could feel them in my body but could not conjure a response. I think I smiled at him before I walked out of the room and went to find Swamiji.

It was evening time in early autumn, and Swamiji was in his garden. The air was fragrant with jasmine, and I could feel the beginning of the cool fall breeze as I walked into the garden, the dewy grass wet between my toes. Swamiji sat, as always, in a corner of the garden, this time on a thin mat of woven jute rather than a chair. The small group gathered in front of him also sat on a thin woven mat, and they hung on every word he spoke. I bowed as I approached and sat cross-legged behind the group.

I closed my eyes and immediately felt a surge of heat and energy rise, it seemed, from the cool grass beneath me straight up into my body, as though I had sat on a geyser at Yellowstone National Park—except that it wasn't water. It was a geyser of heat and energy. It felt like bodysurfing on the California coast, except the wave moved through my body rather than taking me to shore. After the wave hit what seemed to be the inside of my skull, it receded down and out below my navel and back into the cool grass.

I opened my eyes, and Swamiji's eyes caught mine. He was in the midst of a passionate discourse in Hindi that played like divine music across the background of my consciousness, the musical score to my internal drama. His eyes fixed on mine for a moment.

A few minutes later, the group bowed and rose. I too bowed and rose, and I followed them toward the door. Suddenly, I heard Swamiji say, "Come here." He had already started walking into the building of his residence and inner meeting rooms. He did not speak again or turn back toward me, but I knew I was supposed to follow. He turned a key in one of the smaller doors at the end of a hallway. Opening the door, he switched on the light in a room I hadn't been in before, a small library-cum-storeroom with no windows, lined with shelves and cabinets. Books in both Hindi and English, gifts still in their boxes—many wrapped in colorful, shiny paper—small pads on which he had made notes and plans for decades, and other miscellaneous items filled the shelves. On the floor was a beautiful Persian rug.

"Lie down," he said. I did, thinking my Indian adventure was about to take a new, exciting turn. However, Swamiji just turned off the light and left. I heard the key turn in the lock from the outside. Alone in the storeroom, lying on my magic carpet, I felt my consciousness being pulled forcefully inward, as though a vacuum cleaner inside me was sucking "myself" inward. I didn't feel called to fight it. I was free to let go of the glue that held myself together, the glue I had held so tenaciously to over the decades of my life.

I let go into the waves of energy that rose and crashed through my body. As the waves came in, my whole being expanded. Bones, skins, muscles, all borders and boundaries became a vestige of my former body. I was boundless, and it seemed the most natural thing in the world. There was no running commentary explaining my energetic expansion. The waves swept away everything, and the commentator in my head had drowned in the ocean.

According to the scriptural story of the goddess who took the form of the river Ganga, when the rambunctious, intractable Ganga first came down from heaven, She swept away the sages and priests performing their pujas on the riverbanks. The surge of Her uncontainable waters washed everything away. Ganga was now flowing into and through me, razing and annihilating everything made of matter, everywhere I ended and the universe began.

I was the universe. As I inhaled, my chest rose and rose above the shelves of books. I filled the room, and I was still inhaling. These shelves and walls, too, crumbled into the waves of my breath.

My awareness rode the waves, existing not in the gray-and-white matter of the brain inside my skull, but in every molecule of the world inside me and outside me. There was no distinction. It all was me. The air around me, the room, everything pulsated with my breath, and grew and expanded. The walls and shelves obeyed, and they, too, made room for my ever-expanding being. It all was me.

After an indeterminate amount of time, a sound in the door reached through my ears, through my brain, and found me floating somewhere beyond it. The noise took hold of a part of my consciousness and carried it back into my body, into my skull, into my brain. By the time Pujya Swamiji had opened the door and turned on the light, I had processed the sound: *ah, a key in the lock.*

Standing in the doorway, hair, beard, and robes merging into one extraordinary formless being, Pujya Swamiji looked down at me. I could not make the borders of his body or clothes stay in one place. They kept dancing, merging into and out of the space between him and the doorframe. But his eyes were sharp, clear, and in focus.

"How are you feeling?" he asked. I exhaled, and my consciousness escaped on my breath into the dark brown of his eyes, into a world I'd never visited. A fragment of awareness left back in my brain registered that he had again turned off the light, closed the door, and once again turned the key in the lock from the outside. His form had left, but I was still in the world inside his eyes.

At some point, after another indeterminate amount of time, I felt my awareness draw itself back into my physical body. The room and walls and shelves no longer moved in rhythm with my breath. I was aware, for the first time, of the softness of the rug beneath my bare heels and on the back of my hands, which, I noticed, lay to my sides. My eyes were closed, but when I opened them the room was so black, I wasn't exactly sure when they were open and when they were closed. I blinked a few times and finally realized the room was dark; I had not lost my sight.

I was again aware of the rise and fall of my own chest and belly as I breathed, and my own body was once again able to contain the breath. My skin tingled, and I floated in my ocean of joy.

A short time later, I again heard the key in the lock. This time, the sound did not have to reach through my brain to find me. I had heard it the first time, and I understood it would be Swamiji coming back. But it wasn't him. It was the cook, the lovely cook, who, as he turned on the light, looked at me as though it were perfectly natural for me to be lying, awake, on a rug on the floor in the storeroom with the lights turned off. "You must eat," he said. "Swamiji say you must eat."

He bent down and took my hand in his. I had no awareness of muscle or muscle tone. I giggled to myself as I realized that I could not figure out how to make my limbs move. I knew they should move, but how to make that happen was a nonconcerning mystery. Eventually, the cook was able to peel me off the ground, and as he helped me stand, my coordination returned.

Hand in hand, I followed him into the kitchen, where he sat me down on a woven mat and placed a tiny wooden table in front of me. He disappeared and then reappeared with a bowl of hot kichari—lentils and rice cooked together, the Indian version of chicken soup. Whatever ails you, kichari is the answer, according to traditional Indian medicine.

I discovered that night that kichari is also the perfect post–spiritual initiation "Welcome back to the physical plane" meal.

CHAPTER 15

"You Are Not a Pen"

The morning sun rising over the Himalayas streamed through the window onto Swamiji's face. We were sitting in his office across the desk from each other. Each time he raised his eyes from the papers and looked at me, the light was breathtaking. His eyes, always a dance of light, now reflected the sun's rays as mirrors. My heart stopped each time his eyes met mine.

"Write to Dr. Rao in Columbia," he said, referring to the chief editor of the *Encyclopedia of Hinduism*. "Get a new, latest chart of how many articles are still left to be assigned and how many are left to be received out of those that have been assigned already. Tell him I want to know the status."

My pad was about half used. I'd been in Rishikesh nearly two months, and every few days, I was called into Pujya Swamiji's room to receive more work. He had found an eager and competent typist, and I'd found something to do, a way to serve, to give back to this man and this place. My seva consisted mostly of letters to write. It was simple correspondence. Swamiji would open a file full of letters he'd received and his own handwritten notes in Hindi. Flipping through the papers one by one, he instructed me what to say.

Sixty days ago, I had been taking final exams in Advanced Psychodynamic Psychology: The Biological Bases of Behavior and Neurological Assessment. I researched and wrote papers on psychopathology and psychodiagnosis. That, too, had already begun to bore me. "How many more hoops do I have to jump through before I can actually start helping someone?" I groaned at my neurology adviser, my parents, my friends, and anyone else who would listen.

Now, I spent hours a day typing on a pale blue manual typewriter—the kind I'd never actually seen except in movies, with huge keys that bounced up and down. Finger yoga, with no Delete button. Mistakes had to be painted with Liquid Paper and typed over once the liquid dried.

The work was mostly typing short letters to devotees across the world, blessings on weddings, birthdays, anniversaries, all with the essential question "When are you coming home to Rishikesh?" and the invitation "The holy waters of Mother Ganga and the sacred Himalayas are calling you." Pujya Swamiji's arms and heart were open to all. The call was universal: *Come home to Rishikesh. Recharge your batteries in this sacred land.*

Most of the rest of the correspondence was follow-up on projects, mostly the *Encyclopedia of Hinduism*, which was being overseen by K. L. Seshagiri Rao, the editor, and his team at the University of South Carolina in Columbia, with satellite offices in Bangalore, Madras (now Chennai), Delhi, Nagpur, Benares (now Varanasi), and London.

The irony of trading research into serotonin reuptake disruption for birthday blessings was lost on me. Neurologic and psychodynamic papers and studies felt meaningless, while ghostwriting blessings was exhilarating. I was too intoxicated to notice the paradox.

On this autumn morning, I finally bought a pair of socks. Chill had begun to creep into the blue skies, and the marbled floor of my room at 4 a.m. reminded me of a favorite poem by Judith Viorst titled "Thoughts on Getting Out of a Nice Warm Bed in an Ice-Cold House to Go to the Bathroom at Three O'Clock in the Morning": "Maybe life was better / When I used to be a wetter."

So I purchased a pair of synthetic brown socks that had a space for my big toe and a larger one for the remaining toes, to facilitate wearing them with flip-flops.

When I returned from shopping, Surya, Swamiji's main attendant, came to my room, walked in without knocking (as always), and announced, *"Pujya Swamiji is calling you."*

So, here we sat across from each other at his dark, glass-covered desk while I watched the light streaming through the window into his eyes. He read each paper quickly, then either placed it back in the file (work for another day) or removed it and began to dictate instructions.

I scribbled on my makeshift pad—made by stapling together papers with writing on only one side. Without a recycling infrastructure, the only environmentally friendly way to live in India is to reduce and reuse. Nothing is wasted. Every paper that arrives in the ashram—from envelopes to wedding invitations and everything in between—is reused. My pad had been created, like so many others, by cutting used paper in half, then stapling the sheets into a pad.

I scribbled his dictation—follow up with Dr. Rao, birthday blessings, replies to letters requesting Swamiji's presence at functions he would not be able to attend—knowing they were all props in the drama of why I was here. I made brief notes of people's names, and crucial points. The language and the rest I would compose on my own.

Really, what I wanted to do was just stare at the light streaming from Swamiji's eyes in the glass tabletop. He did not notice me doing this, as it looked as if I was gazing at the table, on which rested my pad and his file. I took just enough notes to ensure that I could complete the tasks and would be permitted to keep sitting there.

The light reflected and refracted off the glass table into my own eyes, causing them to tear. Were the streams of water running down my face physical reactions to the light in my eyes, or was I crying? Where did the outer end and the inner begin? It didn't matter. Nothing mattered except sitting there as the sun rose gently over the Himalayas, pouring more incandescent rays onto his face and into my body, which was quickly dissolving into the chair on which I sat.

Suddenly, Swamiji looked up from the file, held his pen in the air, and said to me, "You are not this pen." I laughed. Was he really saying this, or was I imagining it? Pulled out of my dreamy journey on the rays of light, I realized he was saying something quite deliberate. "You are not this pen," he repeated. Although I could see he was serious, I laughed again. Of course I was not the pen. Had I melted my brain cells staring into the bright light? Was I unable to grasp the meaning of his statement? There were certainly many things about the world I did not know, but that I was not a pen wasn't one of them. Why was he saying this?

"Yes, Swamiji," I said, trying to restrain my giggles at the absurdity of his statement. "I am not that pen." He didn't laugh, and his eyes no longer reflected the sun's rays but generated a light of their own that seared straight into my chest and made my heart stop.

"You laugh," he said, "because you know you are not this pen. But you still think you are that body. You think you are all the experiences it is having, all of its beauty, intelligence, emotions, pleasures, and pains. You still think that is you." My breath disappeared. I couldn't speak. "Someday," he continued, "you will laugh in the same way when I say you are not that body."

His eyes broke their hold on mine and returned to the file. "Now, *agay baro*." (Let's keep moving). "Next," he said as he picked up a Hallmark card covered in hearts and flowers with the rounded, bubbly handwriting of a young girl. "Now write, 'My dear divine Kuku. I have received your beautiful card.'"

I am not this body. OK, that makes sense. I've had experiences of being "out of my body," not being the skin and bones of my physical frame, of melting and merging into the world around me. I had whirled and twirled on LSD at Grateful Dead concerts, and merged into the tall grasses, sandy beaches, and warm afternoon sun of the Mendocino coast as Jim, some friends, and I spent a Saturday eating psychedelic mushrooms. Over these months in Rishikesh, unassisted by chemicals or plants, I had experienced nearly continuous expansions of consciousness beyond not only my body but also the walls, doors, and rooms in which I sat or lay. I understand I am not the body. But not *the experiences*? Not what had happened and was continuing to happen? Not my emotions and the identity that generates them?

In the three or four meetings of the twelve-step group for eating disorders that I'd attended, the first thing we said was, "Hi, my name is such and such. I am bulimic." Or "I am anorexic." This was the nonnegotiable opening line. In group therapy, we began by sharing, "I am an abuse survivor." What I felt, thought, struggled with, reacted to, longed for, I had been told, was due to these aspects of my history and identity. The depression and anxiety, the recovery from depression and anxiety, the recovery from the bulimia, the ability to forgive—surely, all of this was who I am. They were and are all inherent parts of "me." How could I not be what I felt, knew, and experienced? If I'm not those things, then who *am* I?

Each night, as the aarti lamps are placed in a neat line along the bottom step above the flowing waters of Ganga, at the conclusion of the ceremony, as the blazing ghee-soaked wicks burn themselves out and thick plumes of camphor rise into the wind, we chant this mantra from the Upanishads: *Purnam adah, purnam idam purnat purnam udachyate; purnasya purnam adaya purnam evavasisyate.* I had memorized these words before I knew what any of them meant.

In time, I learned that this fundamental teaching of Indian philosophy says that the Creator, the Source, the Origin is full, complete, and infinite. This which has come out of That, which has been created from That, removed from That, is also whole, complete, and infinite in itself. This mantra is the spiritual equivalent of the mathematical properties of infinity. Infinity minus ten is infinity. Infinity divided by ten is infinity. Infinity divided by 7.7 billion is infinity.

I found it difficult to concentrate on the papers Swamiji was handing me across the desk. The teaching he had just given was swirling through my mind and didn't leave much room for instructions about correspondence. Fortunately, a few minutes later, one of the boys came in to tell him that the people he was to see at 12:30 p.m. were waiting in his garden. "OK, that's enough for now," he said and walked out the door.

I went to lunch and pondered the infinite nature of round chapatis.

CHAPTER 16

Young and Celibate

I was in love with Swamiji. At first I thought it was awe. Then I thought it was ecstasy. Slowly, I realized that I not only revered him but also loved him. The fact that he was twenty years older than I seemed irrelevant and actually added to the excitement and allure. To be in love with a man my own age would be commonplace. To be in love with a forty-five-year-old holy man was quite special.

It was a being-in-love-ness that I had never experienced before, and it aroused desire not in the usual places. This desire sprang from a geyser deep within me that had been buried and capped my whole life. Every time I looked at him, the cap blew off and a rushing, surging explosion of yearning crashed through me.

But the yearning was different. Typically, yearning stems from lack, wanting to obtain something we don't yet have. This yearning shared space with attainment. It coexisted with fulfillment. It was a yearning born not of emptiness, but of fullness.

As the shower of offerings from the universe poured into my tiny cup, rather than let it runneth over, I tried to expand the cup. I wanted more, and so if I could just keep expanding and expanding, I would be able to absorb increasingly more ecstasy. In fact, I wanted the cup of myself to shatter so that, with no limit, I could absorb the bliss. The closer I got to Swamiji, the larger my cup seemed to grow.

As my eyes fell on him, whether he was singing as he led the aarti, working at his table, or meeting people in the garden, this surge of desire exploded into, it seemed, an already full—actually, overflowing—river of gratitude. "I cannot believe it," I kept saying, to myself, aloud. "I cannot believe it." From my eyes streamed tears of fullness, and my chest heaved as I gasped, trying to breathe enough to stay present in each moment.

And in the midst of the fullness and gratitude and expansion was also the bursting geyser of desire. I loved him and was in love with him. I yearned to be even closer, to experience even more oneness, more expansion. I yearned for absolute union on every level.

Swamiji was not the least bit interested. Each time I walked in front of him, he looked through the self with which I identified, through my body, through my organs and limbs with which I yearned to connect, into the intangible source of me. He didn't even have to say it. I could feel it. As a woman knows when a man undresses her with his eyes, I knew that with him, my entire physical frame was an optical irrelevancy, a dust-covered window through which he saw the "me" I was just learning to meet.

In the beginning, I thought it would just take more time for him to become interested in me that way. He had been celibate his entire life. He knew nothing else. But as the days became weeks and months, there was no shift in his energy. Despite the now numerous times we'd been alone in his room, he had not reached out even once to touch me. Despite making myself as energetically available as I could, he responded only by turning my energy inward, by sending me back into myself.

After more than two months, I noticed a slight pull within myself. When the river of ecstasy was flowing within me, some part seemed to stay behind, locked out of the ecstasy by a dam of self-doubt. A seed of anxiety, planted when I wasn't aware, began to sprout now and push its way through my joy. Did he really not want me? What was wrong with me? The concept of conscious, conscientious celibacy, abstinence by choice, was foreign to me and thus meaningless. Why would anyone choose that? What's wrong with sex?

Months later, I read books by Swami Sivananda on the importance of conserving and protecting the *ojas*, our sacred bodily energy, and began to understand the philosophy behind the tradition of celibacy. But at this point, my interpretation was that there must be something wrong with me. I was young and beautiful. I was devoted and surrendered. I was available. How could he *not* want me?

But he didn't. His disinterest was not personal, of course. The concept of any life other than as a celibate swami had never occurred to him, just as the life of a celibate nun had never occurred to me. He had made a deeply conscious decision at a young age that this was the life he would lead, this was the life he was born for, and this was his dharma.

Later, when I was back visiting San Francisco, my yoga teacher Manouso explained to me how the specific yogic practices given to young monks actually change the very biology and chemistry of their bodies. Swamiji, as incredible as it seemed to me at the time, just did not experience any desire. It was not a battle of the wills to conquer desire. He simply, due to the intense decades of sadhana (daily spiritual practice), meditation, and yoga, had restructured the systems of his body/mind to be free of desire at all. There was no fertile field within him for that seed of desire to be planted. The question of it sprouting was moot.

But at the time, I didn't understand. All I knew was that he didn't want me romantically or sexually. He *did* want me spiritually. He did want access to the deepest presence of spirit within me. He did want my heart to expand so I could love God more and more each day.

So much of how I'd always identified was physical. Being attractive, having a nice body, being noticed, appreciated, and desired were the ways I knew I existed. Every time I looked in a mirror and liked what I saw, I knew I was worthy to occupy space on the planet. I belonged. I was loveable. To be desired was the height of worthiness.

Now, here was someone saying, "You're wonderful. You are divine," someone who poured love from his eyes through mine into parched and withered corners of myself. But he didn't desire me. How could I know I was wonderful if he didn't want me? How could I believe I was special when he was content to pat me on the head?

He clearly had allowed me in closer than normal. While lines of devotees waited outside for his darshan, I was brought in directly. If he didn't want me romantically or physically, then what could I offer him? What was it he wanted from me? Why me?

I struggled with this question without finding an answer. In the beginning, I couldn't ask, for fear that merely speaking the words would make him realize what a horrible mistake he'd made and send me back to America. It was better to be quiet, I thought.

When I asked him finally, several years later, he said, "I took it as God's plan. I knew God had sent you for a special purpose. The way you arrived, the way you were, the purity of your heart, and the way love for God flowed through you, I just knew you had been sent for a reason. I don't question God's plan. I just follow it. So I kept you."

That was enough for Swamiji. But for me, the question seeped into my mind like the contrast dyes they inject before an MRI or CT scan. It soaked into all parts of my conscious awareness—whichever part of my brain was "on," the questions were highlighted: "Why me?" "What does he want?"

In twenty-five years, I have found no intellectual answer. There is no one *thing* that I can point to in hindsight and say, "Ah—that's what he wanted. Ah, that's what he saw." The answer is one of *knowing* rather than figuring out. Figuring out is an intellectual process, brain stuff. *Knowing* is a state, an ability to rest in truth and expansion. In this place, I know now what he knew immediately—he wanted me to be there because it seemed to be God's plan. He had no other motive than that.

Nor, in twenty-five years, has he ever wanted anything from me other than to just "be there" and allow grace and service to flow through me. The work that has flowed from me being there—programs and projects, public speaking, leading and teaching—is all a by-product of me just being there. It's what I "do" now, from a place of just being. What Swamiji saw in me was not actually in me. He simply saw the "Plan."

CHAPTER 17

Obedience and Disobedience

No one ever told me that obedience was expected in the guru-disciple relationship. Respect, of course. Reverence, of course. Devotion, of course. But obedience? And unconditionally, even in the absence of reason? It was early December 1996, and Swamiji asked when I'd be going back to America. He asked it casually and straightforwardly, perhaps offering to help me make arrangements to get to Delhi. He's sometimes like a doting mother. "Have you had your meal?" was how he began most of our conversations those first months.

If I ever said, "No" or "Not yet," he would end our conversation abruptly, ring the bell by his side, and instruct the young man who came running to immediately feed me. "Go. Go and eat. Then come back." So the question about travel plans seemed innocent and kind.

When I'd arrived at the ashram three months earlier, the registration form had asked, "Expected date of departure." "December 15," I had written. My flight to

San Francisco had been scheduled for the evening of the fifteenth, and graduate school classes were to resume the first week of January. But I had filled out that form before everything in my life changed, before I knew that this was where I was meant to be, before I knew this was home.

Go back? I thought. Had this whole experience been a Narnian adventure? Was I now required to walk back through the wardrobe, leaving behind a world of love, beauty, vibrancy, and truth? I wouldn't! I had eaten no forbidden apples. I had disobeyed no divine instruction. Why was I being kicked out of the Garden of Eden?

Go back? I could think no other thought. With each repetition of the question, I sank from the heights of joy to shock, anger, rebellion, and terror. Was he kicking me out? I hadn't done anything wrong!

"I don't want to leave," I whispered. My voice had left with my joy. Not only the rug but also the floor and the very foundation had been pulled out from beneath me, and it carried my breath along too. "I want to stay," I gasped, and I wondered whether the floor I was sitting on was sturdy enough to support me as I crumbled.

Swamiji appeared surprised by my reaction and looked at me across the low wooden table. Had he not realized this was forever? Could he really think I would leave? I thought we'd agreed that it was God's Plan for me to be there, and to me, that meant forever. I don't know which was harder to accept—returning to California or that Swamiji didn't realize I was meant to stay.

He tried the cultural argument: "You will not be comfortable here forever. You will miss so many things. Ashram life is not easy. You are used to comfort. You have loved this for a few months, but forever is different."

I could not believe it. Couldn't he see deeply into my soul and know I had already been given more than I'd ever imagined possible?

Like a mother explaining to her child at the dinner table, lovingly but pointedly, "Yes, honey, you can have ice cream for dessert, but only after you finish your spinach," Swamiji said, "But you have to go back. You have to finish your psychology PhD degree." My what? A piece of paper that indicates I've successfully learned to identify pathologies and put people in boxes? A degree that required me to believe only what could be supported by research already completed, that offered a rope of innovation that was only as long as the list of supporting documents? A degree to heal traumatized children that seemed mostly to bolster my own ego?

My voice shook as I explained, "Swamiji, I don't want to finish my degree. It's unnecessary. I entered this PhD program to help children. But here I am, with only my research and dissertation left, and I have not helped one child. The only thing being helped is my own ego. I get A's on exams, and my ego likes it. A teacher pats me on the back for a smart comment in class, and I like it. I get the highest IQ scores, and I like it. But it's just ego. It's not benefiting children or the world.

"Tens of thousands of people get PhDs every year, and the world is not a better place," I continued. "There is no connection between a PhD and alleviating misery, despair, and trauma in the world. You live every minute of your life making the world a better place. Through some crazy, amazing gift of grace, God has given me an opportunity to be part of something that actually makes the world a better place. How can I leave this to go back for a piece of paper?" I was pleading.

He ignored my arguments and simply said. "You must go back and finish your degree. Then, if you still want to come back, you can come back." He smiled at me, as though this were a good and practical thing to do. I should be happy. He was giving good, practical advice.

Although I was still sitting on the ground, my legs seemed to give way beneath me. I couldn't breathe. Should I beg? Cry? I'm the daughter of a great lawyer. I had won every debate in school. I would not be victim to such a ridiculous fate without an argument. "Swamiji," I said, keeping my voice as stable and firm and yet polite as I could.

"Yes?"

"May I ask you something?"

"Of course."

"I want to understand. Please correct me anywhere I say something that is not true."

He smiled.

"You say God is omniscient, right? He knows everything." Swamiji nodded. Of course God knows everything.

"And you say He is omnipotent, right? He is all-powerful and can do anything, correct?" Again, Swamiji nodded. These were such basic questions. Where was I going with this?

"You say He is good, right? He is all-loving and all-compassionate, He wants only the best for all of us?"

"Hmm," Swamiji replied with a smile at his disciple the advocate.

"So," I, able protégé of *Law & Order*'s Jack McCoy, concluded, "if God is omniscient, it means that He knew I was going to have this experience when I came here. He *knew* I still had two years left in my PhD program to finish my research and dissertation. If He is omnipotent, He *could have* made me not have the experience I did. He also *could have* made me come here after I'd finished my degree. If He is good, then He certainly doesn't want to send me back, after having had the experiences I've had, simply to suffer in a meaningless program for the next two years.

"Therefore—" I could not look at Swamiji—I was on too much of an intellectual high. If I'd made eye contact, it would have broken the spell of how well my mind was working. "Therefore, either God is not omniscient and didn't know I'd have this experience, or He is not omnipotent and couldn't have done anything about it, or He is not good and therefore wants me to suffer, or—" I paused for effect, "Or, it means I am meant to stay here."

Silence.

I took a breath. There it was—the truth as I understood it. Irrefutable, in my opinion. I half-expected a gavel to appear and bang itself on the small wooden table in front of Swamiji. "Objection sustained," the court would say; I could stay. But no magical gavel appeared and no universal judge spoke. There was silence.

"OK," Swamiji finally said. "Let's do one thing." He did not respond at all to what I had said. He did not try to argue or explain or justify his instructions. My intellectual advocacy exercise existed in one plane, and his knowledge of what needed to happen was on a different plane.

"Go back and finish just the next semester, the one you are already registered for. The one your parents have already paid for. Get your straight A's, and then, if you still feel it's right, go through the proper channel to leave, and then you can come back. It won't look nice to just call and cancel your return now."

"It won't look nice" is one of those Indian expressions that used to exasperate me. "To whom?" I would ask. Who's looking? But as time went on and I learned Hindi, I understood the phrase from which it's literally translated: "*Tik nahiy lakta hai.*" Really, it means, "It's not right" or "It doesn't appear to be correct."

One semester sounded like a fair compromise, although far from ideal. "Why?" I whined, as I hadn't since childhood. "Why do I have to go back? Why do

I have to finish the semester?" I was as sure of the illegitimacy of his instruction as kids are when their parents explain about waiting till after dinner for dessert. "But *why*? Why can't I have my ice cream first?" When something is so perfect, how can there possibly be a good reason to delay?

Swamiji looked at me, leaned back in his chair, and, resigned that I was not going to just obey and crawl away, began to explain: "You see only what you want to see. You see only what is happening to you. You see only what feels good and right to you. I see more. If you do not go back now, people will say you were brainwashed, that you joined a cult, that you ran away. That is not useful. If you are going to stay here, you must stay as a model of someone who has renounced something she had, not something she didn't have. To renounce that which you're failing at is not renunciation. To give up something you are losing anyway is not noble.

"If you come back here, you will be a model of someone who chose the spiritual path over the material path," he added. "To be a model, you have to do it right. Otherwise, people will just think you went crazy or got brainwashed. You will be of no use." The part of my brain able to be rational understood his meaning—that my life as a renunciant, and even as a teacher, a leader, or inspiring figure, would not bear fruit if people could write me off in those ways.

Now, nearly twenty-five years since we had this conversation, I am no less impressed by his vast understanding of worlds he's never inhabited. Swamiji never—in this lifetime—lived in a college dorm. He never went to summer camp. He never attended a slumber party. He never experienced the challenges of married family life or the subtleties of social circles in modern societies. Yet, his understanding of emotional triggers, expectations, psychological games, and nuances in the dance of relationships is profound. The causes of and solutions to insurmountable and irreconcilable differences in marriages, parenting dilemmas, and extended-family dramas are clear to him, as though acquired from some universal book of knowledge.

He knew, without ever meeting my parents, exactly how they would respond. He knew, without having ever lived in America, how my academic and social community would respond. I, who had known my parents for a quarter of a century, who had grown up in my community, who had spent nearly seven years in the world of Palo Alto's academia, imagined that everyone would understand. I'd never really thought about it; it was just obvious. I would call home and tell them I was staying in India. I had found God and found my guru. Of course they would understand.

I would call my school and tell them I wasn't coming back, that they should refund my parents' tuition money. Whether they understood or not was unimportant to me. I was done. And society? My world of grande soy lattes with three shots of espresso, salad bars and nondairy frozen yogurt, burritos at the beach and naked Sundays in the spas of San Francisco, memorizing facts to recite back at professors, stressing over exams and then celebrating each A, that world existed in some forgotten dimension. Who cared what they thought?

When I was around three years old, I had a whole community of plastic Little People made by Fisher-Price, and I played with them constantly. They had their own houses and schools and parks. One day, I flushed them all down the toilet to see if they could swim. That they never returned from their swimming adventure did not disturb me. I can still see my mother's face as she came into the bathroom at some ungodly hour of the morning to find me standing over the toilet as I kept flushing and reflushing. "I want to see if the Little People can swim," I explained.

Then, with the last flush, they were gone. If they could swim, they were swimming in some other dimension. If they couldn't, they had gone to the land of people who can't swim.

I did not mourn for my Little People, for they weren't "gone." They were swimming or not swimming in a magical land on the other side of the toilet bowl, their own Wonderland. They were no longer with me, but that was fine. They were living in Toilet Land, and I was living on Hargis Street in Los Angeles.

On that December morning in 1996 in Rishikesh, twenty-two years after I'd flushed the Little People down the toilet, my feelings toward everyone I knew from *my other life* were similar. Everyone I knew was living in *That Land*, and I was living in *This Land*. They were fine; I was fine. Why was Swamiji so concerned about what they thought? As the sun burst through the early-morning fog, unveiling the fluorescent purple bougainvillea hanging from every rooftop into Swamiji's garden, as I watched the rays of sun rise over the Himalayas, everyone seemed fine.

In retrospect, I realize that if I were not living my own spiritual experience, if I could not feel the tears of ecstatic union with every blade of grass, every tree, every drop of Ganga pouring out of my own eyes, if I didn't feel the nearly constant surge of expansion and connection with each breath, I would have said I'd become a sociopath. Let them live in *That Land*! My family? My friends? Those who had been the very foundation of my life for twenty-five years? The nearly instant detachment I felt from that first moment on the banks of the Ganga was something I would understand only many years later. At the time, though, I knew it was rooted in love.

Swamiji understood it all. He lived in every Land simultaneously, and just as he knew, simply by looking in my eyes from fifteen feet away, when I needed to be locked into a room, he knew what my parents and community needed without having met them. So, as per the original plan, I boarded a flight back to California on the fifteenth of December.

Pollution in India is much worse in wintertime than summer. In summer, rain cleans the skies. In winter, it's dry and cold. People living and working on the streets burn whatever they can find to stay warm. Piles of flammable trash are ubiquitous in Delhi, so nearly every corner will find homeless people and day laborers huddled over burning mounds of trash, warming their hands in toxic fumes.

November and December are also the months when the husks of autumn's crops are burned. With no functional system of composting and no waste management infrastructure, the farmers of Haryana and Uttar Pradesh spend the latter part of November and December burning husks and other unusable parts of rice, corn, millet, and sorghum from their autumn harvest. Visibility in Delhi in daytime is worse than most cities at night. The sun is eclipsed not by the moon but by a thick impenetrable layer of smoke.

As my flight took off from Delhi for San Francisco, as I watched the city, faintly visible beneath the veil of smog, get smaller and smaller, I cried—not with ecstasy or truth this time, but with bottomless sadness. The Indian woman in the seat next to me tried to make conversation. "Married?" she asked. "Yes—to Ganga," I told her.

CHAPTER 18

I've Committed a Felony

Jim extended his ticket and stayed in India to continue his adventures and to explore a new relationship with a woman he'd met traveling. He asked me to be out of our apartment in Millbrae before he returned in early January.

He was furious and hurt. This was not how it was supposed to happen. My heart ached when I thought of him. If only, somehow, I could make it better for him. If only, somehow, there could be space for Ganga and Rishikesh and Parmarth Niketan and for Jim. I yearned for him to understand that this new, unexpected experience was not *instead* of him; rather, there was enough room— more than enough room—for ecstatic spiritual experiences and a marriage.

But that was not the life he wanted, and it had already become my life. I could not squeeze back into the life I'd lived previously any more than I could squeeze into the size 6x skirts I had worn as a child. Being the target of his anger did not upset me viscerally. There was no place in my psyche to feel triggered. But it saddened me, and I prayed he would heal quickly. I was ready to do whatever was necessary to expedite that, and I agreed to move out.

I wanted to be in the United States only until my last exam of the semester, the deal I'd made with Swamiji, so I moved into a furnished apartment near San Francisco Bay on a month-to-month basis. During the moving process, I called Swamiji one evening to kvetch, "It's such a headache to deal with the moving guys and the boxes and the van. I'm so worn out."

"How far is your new apartment from your old one?" Swamiji asked.

"About a mile," I replied.

"That's not such a very big problem," he explained. "It's very close."

"Yes, but Swamiji," I explained back, "it's not the distance but the boxes and the packing and the moving guys and everything. It's been two full days now of this headache."

"Ah," he said. "So the problem is the *stuff*. It's your stuff that gives you the headache. If you didn't have the stuff, you would just put on your shoes and walk from one apartment to the next. It wouldn't even take you twenty minutes." I laughed.

"Either get rid of your stuff," he instructed, "or realize how blessed you are to have it and stop complaining."

Yes, the very stuff I had lived so easily without for the past three months. The stuff I left at home every time I went backpacking. The stuff that was never with me during the most important or joyous moments of my life. Every time I felt deep contentment, it happened sans stuff. Lying at the foot of redwood trees or in pine needles, reaching the summit of a mountain and staring off into the infinite vista, being in love, nearly every moment of my three months in India—at none of those times did I have my stuff. Not one of those moments included large suitcases or boxes or moving vans or shelves and closets full of belongings. Yet there was a fullness, a felt sense of expansion and abundance that I never experienced sitting in my living room surrounded by possessions.

So, why was I so attached to stuff? Stuff requires energy to pack, move, and unpack. It has to be sorted and cared for. If these possessions weren't generating joy, why lug them from place to place? The next day, I asked the moving guys to place all the boxes in my new living room and hallway not stacked, but next to each other, so I could access each one. Opening the boxes one by one, I searched for items I really needed or wanted or couldn't bear to part with for any reason. The rest I left in boxes, all of which I took to Goodwill the following day.

I chanted prayers of gratitude as I placed boxful after boxful of what had been "mine" into large bins in the Goodwill center parking lot. "*Sarve bhavantu sukhinah, sarve santu niramaya.*" May all beings be happy. May all be healthy. May my former possessions bring joy, warmth, and health to one who lacks. "*Swaha,*" I chanted loudly with each thump of clothes into their bins. "I offer it to You. *Swaha.*"

In Rishikesh, each evening, we have a sacred *havan* or *yagna*, the purifying fire ritual. As we place seeds and offerings into the fire, we chant, "*Swaha.*" *I offer to You my ego, my attachments, my challenges, my obstacles, all that I think, say, and do, all that I am, all that I achieve and acquire, I offer it to You, O God.* "*Swaha.*" Without actually lighting the bins on fire, I had my own personal yagna in the parking lot of the Goodwill store. Next time I had to move, I would just walk for twenty minutes in the sunshine, carrying little more than my photo albums and, of course, my cappuccino maker.

My new apartment was less than a mile from the bay. I pretended the bay was Ganga. Thick fog blanketed my windows each morning. As it burned off by midday, giving way to the bright sun and blue sky, I reexperienced the veil that was pulled off my own eyes, revealing the image of the Divine, as I stood on the banks of the Ganga, having come only to dip my toes in the water.

That moment, just three months earlier, had become the axis around which my life now revolved. Pre-Ganga and post-Ganga became the eras of my life's journey. Post-Ganga felt real. It was three-dimensional. I could see, hear, taste, touch, and smell it. I could feel it not only with the nerves on my skin and the receptors in my spinal cord and brain but also in my breath, in every expansion and contraction of my lungs. I could feel it in my pulse and in the constant beat of my heart. Each pulse was a knock from the inside on the walls of my awareness. *Thump, thump, open up, open up, thump, thump, I'm coming through, thump, open, open, open* . . . . As I breathed, the walls of my awareness gave way to the beating of my heart.

Pre-Ganga felt two-dimensional. It existed, and I could *remember* its flavor and feeling, but I couldn't feel it in my body. It didn't push at the walls of my consciousness. It didn't flow in and out on my breath.

Pre-Ganga seemed like a long, elaborate dream, with a full cast of characters and changing sets, its own villain and heroes. Now I had awakened from that dreamworld, and it was fading into obscurity.

It was New Year's Eve, and I'd been living in my new apartment for almost a week. In a few hours, 1996 would become 1997. I had three parties to go to. One was organized by high school friends who lived in San Francisco, another by friends from graduate school, and a third by undergraduate friends from Stanford. The first was in the City; the other two were in Palo Alto.

I planned to attend all three, each briefly. I wouldn't be drinking alcohol. The idea of ingesting any substance that would, even slightly, alter the magnificence of what my mind had become was by now anathema to me. So I planned to go to Palo Alto first, then drive to San Francisco to spend the midnight hour with my high school friends.

The first thing I wanted to do on returning to California was to replicate the temple Pujya Swamiji had built into his wall. Of course, I couldn't build into the wall of a rental apartment, but I could hang a shrine that would mimic Swamiji's as best I could. When I meditated, I wanted to feel that I was sitting at his temple, with Ganga flowing just outside the door. I envisioned a large picture of Gayatri Ma in the middle on her multipetaled pink lotus flower, her hands holding a conch shell, a chakra, and so much more, and two pictures of Krishna, one as a child, the other with flute in hand. Then I'd put a small, silver oil lamp in the center.

So, my first day back in California, I went to The Home Depot and showed the salesman a photo of Swamiji's shrine. I wanted it to be low enough so I'd be at eye height with Gayatri Ma when I sat cross-legged on the floor. My hero at The Home Depot cut the wood, glued the pieces together, and attached hooks so I could hang it without violating my lease. It imitated Swamiji's Rishikesh temple nearly perfectly. The only difference was that mine hung half a mile off Highway 101 in San Mateo, and not in the lap of the Shivalik Hills of the Himalayas. I placed a picture of Swamiji in the center, next to the oil lamp.

Before leaving for Palo Alto on New Year's Eve, I showered and sat down at my new shrine. I filled the lamp with sesame oil and placed a long, narrow piece of cotton I'd rolled between my fingers, and lit the end of the oil-soaked wick. Then, I sat down to meditate. The lamplight flickered on the images, and it seemed Gayatri Ma's eyes blinked slowly as I looked at Her.

My next recollection is opening my eyes to the familiar gray backdrop of Bay Area winter mornings, squeezing through the sides and bottom of my bedroom blinds. Morning? I was still sitting at my temple, but now my back was against the wall and my legs stretched out toward my bed. Gayatri Ma, Krishna, and

Swamiji watched me from the side. What? Where had the night gone? My bed hadn't been slept in, and I was still in my bathrobe from the shower. I'd sat there all night long.

That morning, I found messages on my answering machine from friends in three places, wondering whether I was coming. Apparently not. I had been in my own temple, having a private New Year's party, dancing without moving to music that had no beat. I looked down and found three pieces of paper. I had written letters to God, each with a title written across the top. The first title read, "Thank You, God, For:" The second one read, "My Vows for 1997." And the third read, "Please Bless Me With."

Three lists: what I was thankful for, what I pledged, and the blessings I requested. I began to remember sitting before my temple, the oil lamp still flickering while I loved God through the pen in my hand. *Thank you, God. Thank You. Thank You for all these incredible blessings You've bestowed on me in this last year. Thank You. Thank You, God, for India, for carrying me, against my will, to the world of wakefulness. Thank You for the experience on Ganga, for showing Yourself to me, thank You for gluing my feet to the ground. Thank You, God, for Pratap. Of course, thank You for Swamiji, the glue who brought and held all other pieces of my experience together. Thank You for Jim, for his yearning for a guru, without which I would never have considered going to India. Thank You for my parents, who even though they don't understand, love and support me so completely.* The list grew and grew.

> *Now, as I've been so blessed, as You've bestowed on me, clearly through no merit of my own, such grace, now, here is what I will do for You; here is what I promise. I vow, God, not to forget You, not to forget what You've given me, what You've shown me. I vow to keep my eyes and my heart open without fear, to be a vessel for Your will to flow. I vow to continue loving Jim, even if not as a wife, from this ever-expanding source of love within me, and to treat him only with kindness and tenderness. I vow, God, to use my life, as Swamiji asked of me, in service of You, in whatever ways You think best.*

Last, I know, God, I've been blessed beyond what I could ever have imagined. I know I don't deserve this, but, O God, should You see fit to keep blessing me, and for those blessings to expand, here is what I would like in the coming year. It was my spiritual Christmas list: Please bring peace to Jim. Help him heal and understand. Please bring me back to India as soon as possible. Let me again be free on the banks of Your waters, let me not be bound by an identity that no longer fits, one everyone here tries to stuff me into. Let me, again, live each day bathing in the rays of the sun as they rise over the Himalayas, bouncing off the bougainvillea in Swamiji's garden, coming through his windows onto his face and then into my eyes and heart. Let me, again, walk, as the sun sets into the waters of the Mother, pulling tears from my eyes as I watch the rays dance on Your waters. Please help me be a clearer, a purer vessel.

The lists were long, each covering a full sheet of paper. The thank-you list ran halfway down the back of the page as well.

What to do with them? In India, I became convinced of the power of ritual. Not for ritual's sake, not just hand gestures or words or phrases or actions, but the power of deeply present, deeply connected sacred rite and sacred ceremony—from my "giving" my pain to Ganga to the impact of each evening's aarti apparent on the faces of all who attended to the ecstasy of walking thirteen miles barefoot around a mountain that Lord Krishna had held up with His pinkie. Everything in India was a ritual, and it made every day ripe with possibility.

Swamiji always said that wherever we invoke Ganga, Ganga will be there. He taught me the prayer Indians say each morning while bathing:

Gange cha Yamune chaiva

Godavari Sarasvati

Narmade Sindhu Kaaveri

Jalesmin Sannidhim Kuru

Om shanti

*(O sacred rivers of the Ganga, the Yamuna, Godavari,
Saraswati, Narmada, Sindhu, and Kaveri, I invoke you
all in this water in which I bathe. Bless me with your
presence in this water.)*

Hindus may be bathing from a Mumbai municipal water tank or from a hand pump in a village in Kerala, but the heartfelt invocation of the sacred waters renders ordinary molecules of H_2O holy. "Pray to Ganga when you stand in San Francisco Bay," Swamiji told me. "She will be there."

Suddenly, I realized I needed to offer the letters to Ganga, to whom everything is offered: our pain, our sorrow, our ignorance, our sins, anything we want Her to "take care of." Every few weeks in Rishikesh, I received scathing faxes from Jim, belittling and berating me for still being in the ashram. "What should I do?" I asked Swamiji. "Offer it to Ganga," he always said. "And pray for Jim." So, I developed a ritual of burning the letters in a clay pot and then pouring the ash into Ganga. (Now, two and a half decades later, I would never dare. Now, we don't even offer flowers to Ganga after the aarti, an otherwise nonnegotiable, biodegradable "must" in traditional worship ceremonies. Keeping Ganga clean has become a single-pointed mission for Swamiji and so many other holy men and women.)

In 1996 in Rishikesh, the water still ran clear and clean. Natural, biodegradable items like flowers were offered nightly. Watching the words on the page curl inward with the fire and then disappear into ash, then offering that ash to Ganga, brought me to a stillness unperturbed by the wrath with which the words had been written. I watched the ashes float on the surface of Ganga, and then I rinsed the clay pot clean to ensure that every speck of Jim's letters were truly given to Ganga. I then would envision Ganga flowing into his heart, dousing the fire of his anger with Her waves, and taking him in Her arms. Whatever came into our lives—an unbearable emotion, anxiety over a loved one's future, anger at a past hurt, disappointing news—Pujya Swamiji always reminded us to "Give it to Ganga."

So, before the morning fog over San Francisco Bay lifted, I rose from the floor, gathered up my letters, and prepared for a ritual burning. I took a stick of incense and a matchbox from my homemade temple. In the absence of a clay pot, I grabbed a *kutori*, a small metal bowl used at the ashram for meals, and prepared to head out. When I realized I was still in my bathrobe,

I dressed quickly and, with letters, incense, bowl, and matches in hand, went out to my car.

As I passed the manicured gardens of the apartment complex, my eyes scoured the dirt for a flower that had recently liberated itself from the vine, thus volunteering to be my morning offering to Ganga. I finally found a yellow flower of unknown species that would do just perfectly. I bent down and gently lifted it out of the flower bed.

The drive to the water's edge took three or four minutes; the streets were empty. I drove slowly through the thick, low-lying fog, and when I arrived at the bay, I scrambled over boulders to the water's edge, flower and incense gently in hand, careful not to squish the thin yellow petals that had so generously offered themselves.

I set the puja items down on a flat rock and stood with my eyes closed, hands folded at my chest in prayer. "O Ganga," I said softly, "O Ganga, running through my veins, through my breath, over these rocks, and through the bay. O Ganga, thank you. Thank you for my life. Please accept these offerings." I chanted the few mantras I knew:

Tvam-Eva Maataa Ca Pitaa Tvam-Eva

Tvam-Eva Bandhush-Ca Sakhaa Tvam-Eva

Tvam-Eva Viidyaa Dravinnam Tvam-Eva

Tvam-Eva Sarvam Mama Deva

(O God, You are my Mother and You are my Father
You are my Relative and You are my Friend
You are my Knowledge and You are my Wealth
You are my All, My God of Gods)

Om Sarve Bhavantu Sukhinah

Sarve Santu Nir-Aamayaah

Sarve Bhadraanni Pashyantu

Maa Kashcid-Duhkha-Bhaag-Bhavet

Om Shanti

(May all beings be happy
May all beings be healthy
May all attain peace and experience auspiciousness
May no one suffer
May there be Peace)

I closed my eyes and focused on my breath. Allowing the sound of bay water splashing against the rocks to fill my auditory awareness, I felt myself back in Rishikesh, standing on the edge of Ganga, the waves breaking on the marble steps of Parmarth's.

I opened my eyes and sat down on the rocks, putting the letters in my lap. Then I placed the metal katori on the rock and lit a match. The wind blew it out immediately. I struck another and another, each of them fizzling out in the wet, windy fog. Finally, using the katori as a windbreak, I coaxed the match into providing a strong flame onto which I could place the corner of the first letter. The paper grabbed the fire from the match and burned quickly, curling and shriveling on itself and dropping ash into the katori. By the time I had burned every letter, the small metal bowl was nearly filled with ash. The flames pulled tears from my eyes as I watched my lists of gratitude, vows, and entreaties dissolve back into the elements from which they'd come.

I stared at the bowl. There it all was. My whole heart. For Ganga. I lit the stick of incense and waved it toward the bay as though it were an aarti lamp, forming the shape of Om, then a clockwise circle, the shape of Om, and another clockwise circle. The fragrant incense ash dropped into the cold water. After about ten minutes, when the stick had burned down, I cupped the yellow flower in both my hands, squatted to scoop up some water, and prepared to offer the flower, now immersed in two handfuls of water, to Ganga.

Pujya Swamiji had shown me the letters his mother had written him when he was very young, after he left home and was doing his sadhana, his intense spiritual practice in the woods. In one of the first letters to her son, called by God into the mountain forests and the jungles of the human mind, she wrote, "As I prepared for my puja this morning, I wondered which flower to offer to God. I wandered in the garden looking for the most beautiful, most perfect flower I could find. Then I realized that the most beautiful and perfect flower was not to be found in the garden. It was the flower of my womb. You are the flower I offer to God, the flower of my womb."

I remembered her words as I held the yellow vine flower in hand. I didn't have a flower of my womb to offer God, so I offered the flower of my heart. *May this flower, O God, be filled with all that I am, everything I have, every last piece of me. I offer it to you, O God, O Mother Ganga.* I squatted Indian-style and gently released the flower and the water back into the bay.

Finally, I picked up the small katori, from which ashes were beginning to fly. I cupped my palm over it, submerged the bowl in the water, and watched as the water carried each speck of ash out to sea. When it all had been washed out, I stood and continued watching it flow on its way to the Pacific Ocean.

My eyes closed themselves, and I sat back down on the rock and began to meditate. The wind that blew against my face felt like the wind rushing off the surface of the Ganga, blowing down from the Himalayas. The drops of dew and mist on my skin seemed to be those of the night sky over Rishikesh. As the sun slowly burned through the morning fog, unveiling the New Year on the California coast, I felt I was sitting on the marble steps at Parmarth.

As my consciousness slowly returned to the rough surface of the rock beneath my sweatpants and I heard the sounds of early-morning traffic on Highway 101 in the distance, I remembered that I was in Foster City, California, not Rishikesh or India. I rose into the sun, now almost fully visible through the fog, joined my palms together, and said, "Thank you."

Climbing back over the boulders to return to my car, I noticed a sign on a notice board stuck into the dirt, just at the edge of the rocks: "Fine for littering the Bay $1000 and prosecution." I laughed into the mist at the absurdity of my life.

"I committed a felony," I told Swamiji as soon as I got home. "If everyone hadn't been asleep, I could have been arrested."

"Oh, no!" he exclaimed. "What did you do?"

"I made an offering to Ganga," and I told him the whole story, adding, "With full love and devotion on New Year's morning, in a state of joy, peace, bliss, and gratitude, I committed a felony without even realizing it! I'm no longer fit to live in this world. You must let me come back to India."

"We'll talk soon," he said. "In the meantime, remember: Follow the rules and enjoy your stay."

CHAPTER 19

Two Choices

It was mid-February of 1997, and only a few weeks were left of the fall-winter semester. Swamiji had still not visited, even though he'd promised he would in January. I lived in my personal edition of *The Agony and the Ecstasy*. The ecstasy was more constant and replete with tears streaming down my face—in class, at the grocery store, in my car listening to the cassette Swamiji and I had made before I left India. As one of the homework projects he gave before I left, he asked me to prepare a book of the ashram's morning prayers in English—six or seven Vedic prayers, mantras, and songs that we sang each morning from 5 to 5:30, followed by his Hindi lecture until 6. The ashram had Hindi prayer books, but none had an English translation or even a transliteration.

On the morning before I was forcibly peeled off the wall of the reception office and packed into the back seat of a car to Delhi to fly back to America, Swamiji and I had sat on the floor of his meeting room and he had played the harmonium and sung each prayer line by line. He had followed every prayer with a translation and profound commentary on each line. I had recorded it all on a boom box, a gift from an anonymous devotee that had lain in storage till then and would have been the envy of Venice Beach crowds a decade earlier. I played the cassette I recorded that day over and over in my car the three months I was in California, and by the time I got back to the ashram in April , even though I still couldn't speak a word of Hindi, I had memorized all the songs.

The waves of ecstasy ebbed into stillness, a stillness *in the world but not of it*. For the first time in my life, everything was just right. No drama, no excitement, no passion in those moments, just a stillness in which my mind and I were actually friends. That was one end of the seesaw: ecstasy ebbing into stillness and stillness flowing into ecstasy.

Sitting heavily on the other end of the seesaw was my bulimia. Although I hadn't thrown up once, or even had a thought about what I was eating, during the three months I'd been in Rishikesh, the bulimia returned about a month after I was back in California. However, it had a new quality to it. Rather than me using it as a tool to stay afloat in the ocean of my inner world, a tool to numb feelings I believed would have swallowed me whole, a tool to "stuff" them, and then a tool to forcibly extricate my feelings from within me as though they could hitch a ride on the back of a Mrs. Fields cookie, now, instead, the bulimia was being used by some hitherto unknown part of my ego to make me *not* live my life. The bulimia no longer soothed me. It was no longer the bridge from anxiety and overwhelmed to endorphin-induced calm. Now, it was being used by my ego quite deliberately to convince me that I was still sick, that I was not spiritual, and that I had not actually had a spiritual awakening. Look, here I was vomiting. I could not possibly be spiritual.

Now, rather than feeling relieved afterward, I felt as though the previous owner of my home had shown up in a delusional fugue, thinking this was still her house. Each time I threw up, my ego pushed the Play button on a recorded script in my mind's ear: "You cannot go back to India. See? You are sick. You need to be in therapy. You must stay here. What happened in India was just an illusion. You are not that spiritual person you think you are. You are sick. You are crazy. You need help."

I started to believe the voice. Who did I think I was, anyway? You don't just heal from trauma by grace. Pathologies are not washed away by rivers. The whole thing must've been an illusion.

Then the seesaw would tilt and the ecstasy would wash over me, thawing out the parts that had frozen into fear. As the ecstasy rose within, it carried the rivers of my thoughts into its ocean of stillness. The vomiting ceased. I could sit again in the presence of my own breath. I was again one with the universe, beaming at every checkout clerk, every professor, every neighbor, bellowing Hindi prayers at the top of my lungs as I drove down Highway 101.

"So, what do you think?" I asked Kim, my therapist, best friend, mentor, and love of my life. "Should I go back, or not? Am I really supposed to be in India? Or should I stay here like everyone is telling me to?"

Kim looked at me and softly said, "When I look at you, I see a woman in India. Although you are sitting here in front of me today, what I see is a woman in India. You are already, on a soul level, back in India. It seems to me you really have only two choices: You can either torment yourself for the next six weeks, pretending to make a decision that has already been made, or you can spend the next six weeks packing up your stuff and preparing to move to India."

Many spiritual lineages teach that thoughts are things. They are not just empty, random, electrical firings of our neurons; rather, they are actual things, carrying metaphysical weight and energy, reaching out from the gray-and-white matter of our brains into the world, creating our reality.

Words are also things. Kim's gentle pronouncement turned our conversation of two into a party of three. Now, instead of just Kim and me, there was also Truth. Her words had, like naughty kids in a Dr. Seuss book, leaped off her tongue, rushed to the corner of the room where Truth had been hiding, pulled back its covers, and unveiled it as a tangible presence in the room. There was almost an audible "Aha!"

"Oh," I said, staring at Truth, for I didn't realize it had been hidden in the corner the whole time. "Yes, of course you are right." We both laughed, softly and gently at first in due reverence for the moment, and then in full gleeful abandonment, for with Truth now occupying most of the space in the room, there was really not much else to talk about. We laughed the unabashed laughter of seeing and being seen.

The presence of that truth—simple, unanalyzed, tangible—precluded any further presence of untruth. As darkness cannot coexist with light, so untruth cannot coexist with truth. I could wallow in the rehearsed drama of my own personal script of illness, of pathology, of brokenness, of victimhood, only as long as Truth stayed covered and cowering in the corner. The moment it claimed its presence, the untruth dissipated as naturally and automatically as darkness dissipates when a match is struck or a candle is lit.

The next day, I looked in the Yellow Pages for "long-term storage" and made an appointment to speak with the dean of my graduate school to discuss a one-year official leave of absence. I rented a storage facility for one year, took a one-year leave of absence, and arranged to have my mail forwarded to my parents' address for a year.

India was right for me. That was obvious. However, at twenty-five, I had never been one to say things like "forever" or "for the rest of my life." I could not see the rest of my life. I had no view of the future or myself in it. I could only see now, and now I knew India was home.

As I stepped from the familiar drama of a conflicted decision-making process into the truth of knowing I was going back to India, my confusion and agony ceased, dismantling the stage on which my ego performed and leaving it stranded like a confused actor still in full makeup and costume long after the show is over, the lights have come on, and the audience has left.

The bulimia ceased, for the pain that had caused it and propelled it truly was "taken" that evening in the waters of the Ganga, almost six months prior, in my early days at the ashram. The recent episodes were, I realized, simply my ego, the out-of-work actor, continuing to scream its lines from the street corners of my psyche. The script was so familiar, perhaps I would forget that the show ended long ago.

CHAPTER 20

Ecstasy in Statistics Class

FEBRUARY–MARCH 1997

"So, if there is a jar of five hundred marbles and two hundred are red, what is the probability of choosing a red marble if you pick four marbles out of the jar?" "What is the probability of choosing two red marbles?" "What is the probability of choosing no red marbles?"

I sat in the front row at a two-person table, the type that line graduate school classrooms. Undergraduate classes took place in large lecture halls, auditoriums with rows and rows of chairs sloping upward, each with an individual desk folding from the right armrest.

By age twenty-five, four quarters into the PhD degree, I was jaded. I took between nineteen and twenty-one units a quarter, instead of the normal fifteen, so that I could finish the program as quickly as possible. "Is this taxonomy, or psychology?" I once burst out in my psychodynamic psychology class. "Are we learning to help people or just to stick them in the appropriate boxes?"

My volunteer program at a county center for drug-addicted women, where I worked with their drug-impacted babies while the mothers received addiction counseling, was the highlight of my week. Holding babies whose incessant sobs had nothing to do with present-day despair and everything to do with the heroin coursing through their veins during in utero development made me finally feel that my life was worthwhile. I closed my eyes and visualized their neural circuits, their tiny limbic systems with serotonin, dopamine, epinephrine, and norepinephrine flooding their synapses at all the wrong times. As I held them, I visualized being able to heal them. I fantasized that from my hands poured forth healing energy that could reset their neural circuitry.

I was aware, though, that I could do little for them other than a few hours of weekly tenderness until I finished my degree. I needed to accumulate degrees and titles if I wanted to effect true change.

In India, I had found the ability to effect immediate change. Schools could be built where schools did not exist. Starving people could be fed. Orphans could be taken in off the streets and given a chance at life. And I could do this even without finishing my PhD. It was an opportunity to stop jumping through the hoops of academia and put my life to use immediately. And that was aside from the spiritual experience.

Being back in graduate school classes in January through March 1997 was more difficult than I had imagined. To sit through statistics class when one has no other option is hard enough. To sit through statistics class while the waters of Ganga could be rushing over one's feet, while one could be waving an oil lamp and singing Her glories, while one could be engaged each minute of each day in helping children whose eyes sparkled with a light belying their destitution, was unbearable. "I just need to make it through the semester," I kept telling myself.

"If the first three marbles I remove are all black, and I replace them each back into the jar, what are the chances the fourth marble I pull out will also be black?" The math is easy. The concentration is difficult. I open my assignment book to make a note, reminding myself to pick up my sweater from the dry cleaners on my way home in the evening.

After noting the reminder, I turn to the back of the book, where, on the glossy inside back cover, I have taped two photos. One is a picture of Swamiji I took the week before I left. It is a December morning in his garden, and the rays of the sun are just starting to beat down on the burgundy bougainvillea. He stands among them smiling.

The other picture is of Lord Krishna, but not the usual full-bodied, flute-in-hand image. This is an unusual picture, one I haven't seen since—a picture just of Krishna's face, and mostly only His eyes on a black background. There is no outline to the face, only His huge shining eyes, a subtle nose and mouth.

In November 1996, on my first visit to the sacred land of Govardhan/Vrindavan, as we walked the thirteen-mile *parikrama* (circumambulation) around Govardhan Hill, someone pressed the photo into my hands. I had walked, among thousands of others, led by Swamiji and other revered saints of India, barefoot around a mountain that Lord Krishna had held up with His pinkie finger to protect the people from the fury of Lord Indra, the king of the gods.

Walking—or, rather, gliding—over the pebbled ground, I was entranced. I was also the only foreigner. Every few minutes, someone would compassionately ask me if my feet were OK. The question seemed absurd. Feet? Really? Did I even have feet? I felt like I was being carried along, in a land so foreign and yet so familiar, by One I had never met but knew intimately.

As we passed through a tiny market, a shopkeeper rushed forth from his shop, probably to catch a glimpse of the procession, and inexplicably grabbed my hands, pressing this picture between them. It was hundreds of yards later before I had enough space on either side of my elbows to open my hands and see what they contained. Staring into the eyes of Krishna transported me through the picture into a realm where my body had no physical borders, a realm in which I breathed into the universe and of the universe, a realm in which love was the field on which all else existed.

Now, sitting in class, I look at these two pictures—Swamiji framed by blossoming bougainvillea, and Krishna with eyes like magical flowers that open their petals just wide enough to engulf me and then close again on me, carrying me deep into the source of the nectar and fragrance itself.

I notice my notes are wet before I realize I'm crying. My left hand rests on my pad of paper, on which my blue-ink calculations of red and black marbles are now smudged illegibly. I am not sobbing. No noise is coming from my mouth, and no chokes are wracking my throat or lungs. Tears are simply pouring from my eyes and dropping from my chin onto my notepad. I am not sad.

I did not even remember I was here in class calculating probability of red versus black marbles.

The images of Swamiji and Lord Krishna were vehicles into which, each time I saw them, I was carried to a place where nothing but love existed. The tears streaming down my cheeks and onto my notes were just a tributary of that river of love.

My teachers and classmates, of course, saw tears, not rivers. They saw open-mouthed catatonia, not meditative ecstasy. They thought I had gone crazy. Only my continued straight A's and relative coherence in conversation prevented them from suggesting that I become a recipient rather than a provider of psychological help.

On an afternoon at the end of February, after the Truth had become the third party in my conversation with Kim and hadn't gone back into hiding since, I went to meet with the dean. "I would like to take a one-year leave of absence," I said.

"I'm not surprised," he replied in that casual way that hints at the not-so-casual. "We expected something of the sort, seeing the change in you since you've returned from India. But I must tell you, I do not advise it. I cannot, in good conscience, recommend this path. Charity work is admirable, and finding one's inner truth is compelling, but you are a star student in this program. To take an extended leave now will surely raise questions to future employers. It will be suspicious and therefore disconcerting to those who would hire you later on. This will be a black mark on your record. Star students, capable and focused students, do not take these sorts of extended leaves for spiritual pursuit in the midst of their doctoral work."

I focused on my breath. Two inches below my belly button, at the *swadisthan* chakra, the seat of my energetic being. *His truth is not your truth*, I told myself. *There is no reason to be upset.* I had not expected understanding or support, so why was its absence upsetting?

"I must tell you in no ambivalent terms," my dean continued, "I think you are making a serious mistake."

I continued to sit on the chair facing him. I brought my attention back to my breath, over and over. It was crucial to me to be present with this. If my Truth was really Truth, it would have a power of its own. I would not permit myself to dissociate through these difficult meetings. If I was walking into the fire, it would be hot.

When my breath was slow and deep, I looked up at him. "Thank you. I know you are saying what you feel to be the truth. It is not the truth for me, though. Being in India is the truth for me, and I must return. I deeply appreciate your concern for me and your time in sharing your advice."

We rose and shook hands. I looked into his eyes and smiled, trying to give him a glimpse of what I was experiencing inside myself, trying to connect with him on a level that the words would not permit. He made cursory eye contact and then showed me the door, opening it while I walked through.

I left his office and headed into the tree-lined streets of Palo Alto. Soon I would be going home.

CHAPTER 21

Pujya Swamiji
Coming to America

JANUARY–MARCH 1997

"Don't worry," Swamiji said when he pushed me out of the ashram in December. "I am coming to America next month." He had founded the world's first Hindu-Jain temple in 1984 in Monroeville, a woodsy, hilly suburb of Pittsburgh, and had spent many months each year in the United States since then, establishing and inspiring that and other temples.

In August 1987, at the end of a special event at the Hindu Jain Temple, many devotees, including a few scholars on Hinduism, had met with Pujya Swamiji to discuss the state of Hinduism in America. Indians born and raised in India, steeped in Hindu culture, simply live these rites and rituals daily without necessarily knowing the specific meanings or significance, and it's difficult for them to explain them to the inquiring minds of their Western-raised children. Although the Hindu tradition is one of the oldest, largest, and most influential religions on Earth, with over 7,000 years of history and prehistory and 1.2 billion adherents worldwide, there was no comprehensive encyclopedia of Hinduism. So, Pujya Swamiji had proposed, "we should bring out an encyclopedia of Hinduism to provide your children and your children's children, and all the children of the world, an authentic, informative, insightful, and inspiring source of reference for Hinduism."

The others had looked at him incredulously. It would be a herculean undertaking. "Do you really think it can be done?" someone had asked. Pujya Swamiji had closed his eyes and opened them a short while later. "Yes," he had said. "It can be done, and we will do it." When I asked him how he had known to say yes, he explained, "I needed to see if I received the green signal from God. The moment, with closed eyes, I got the signal, I knew the project could be done and would be brought to successful completion." So, beginning in 1987, Swamiji oversaw publication of the world's first comprehensive encyclopedia of Hinduism.

That winter, Swamiji had founded the India Heritage Research Foundation (IHRF), a nonprofit organization dedicated to bringing out the multivolume work. The IHRF's activities have since expanded and now include innumerable projects, including free schools, orphanages/gurukuls, vocational-training programs, women's-development and rural-development projects, disaster relief, ecological-preservation programs, and much more.

So, in December 1996, as I was preparing to leave Rishikesh for California with as much enthusiasm as one prepares for a colonoscopy, work on the encyclopedia was in full swing at a network of dozens of offices around the globe, headquartered at the University of South Carolina in Columbia. Board meetings, advisory meetings, editorial meetings, and awareness-raising events took place regularly, and Pujya Swamiji's presence and guidance were crucial.

"I'll be in the US in January," he told me.

"Will you come to California? Please," I begged.

"Sure," Swamiji said.

In *Miracle of Love*, Ram Dass, the renowned Harvard professor turned brilliant spiritual leader, shared a story of his experience with his guru, Baba Neem Karoli Maharaj:

Maharajji would usually agree to any request from a devotee. People frequently invited him to come and bless their homes and to partake of the food prepared by the family. He would inevitably agree to all these requests, yet, more often than not, he wouldn't go.

When questioned by one of his devotees about his habit of making and breaking promises, Maharajji replied, "I'm just a big liar!"

If only someone had thrust that book into my hands in the beginning, it would have saved me a lot of heartache. I was being initiated into not only a world of spiritual awakening but also one in which "Yes" can mean "No." The gears of my brain had to readjust themselves; neural networks had to be rewired. In the world I had entered, "Sure" and "Definitely" do not mean "Sure" or "Definitely"; they mean, roughly, "Maybe, but quite likely not."

As "Tomorrow," in response to questions regarding Pujya Swamiji's return to the ashram, actually meant "I don't know," and was said to keep me happy in the moment, so too, I've learned over the years—but not quickly enough to prevent disappointment in early 1997—Swamiji's "Sure" means "In this moment, looking into your eyes, which are filled with love and devotion, that sounds absolutely like the right thing to plan to do." However, in the next moment, or a week or month later, it probably isn't the right thing to do, as the flow of the river of life in which Swamiji is anchored has taken a different course.

I didn't know that at the time. All I knew was that he had said, "Sure." Therefore, he would come. I daydreamed constantly about where I would take him. I'd show him the sunset at Half Moon Bay. I'd take him to walk among the redwoods in Muir Woods. I'd cook *sattvik* Indian meals from my Indian Ayurvedic cookbook. I even had the property manager of my apartment fix the sofa bed in my living room so I could sleep on it while my room served as a perfect, restful abode for Swamiji.

At a moment of devotion-induced delusion or loss of common sense, I imagined bringing him to my PhD program classes at the Pacific Graduate School of Psychology. "Today, boys and girls, for show-and-tell, I brought my guru, an enlightened master." The absurdity was lost on me at the time, and I imagined how great it would feel to have him see my school, where I studied, where I ate lunch.

In elementary school, we used to have Grandparents Day, where those of us fortunate enough to have a living grandparent nearby could bring them to school. Grandparents are interested in where their elementary school grandkids eat lunch. Indian gurus, it turns out, are not interested in where their graduate school devotees eat lunch.

Swamiji listened to me with tenderness and compassion when I would call him regularly, sometimes from the payphone in the courtyard at school, early in the morning for me in California, his evening in India, to inquire whether dates had been finalized for his visit. He never once said, or even insinuated, "Are you crazy?"

But the dates kept getting postponed.

Jim had returned from India, and we had a sweet—or, more correctly, bittersweet—evening together. We met at our favorite vegan restaurant, and over plates decorated artistically with swirls of raspberry syrup and bread dipped in tofu garlic sauce, we discussed the end of our marriage. He had kept me abreast of his Indian adventures through detailed faxes, so there was no need to repeat stories of the women he'd been with or the length and breadth of his travels. I wanted to share the immensity of the joy I was experiencing, but I knew that to Jim, it could feel like a knife piercing his heart. So we stayed mostly quiet and spoke of logistics—my stepfather, Frank, a divorce lawyer, would do the paperwork. I would leave Jim with mostly everything to help him get back on his feet and to free me from the chains of logistics conflict.

As I planned Swamiji's imminent visit, I envisioned him again meeting Jim and laying a hand on Jim's heart that would heal the wound and fill him with love.

However, Swamiji didn't come. An urgent meeting for the encyclopedia at the Chennai office forced a postponement from late January to early February. Then a winter cold caused a postponement from early February to mid-February. Something or other kept coming up and causing the dates to be pushed back, week by week. Finally, he landed in Pittsburgh the second week in March, but regrettably, he explained, he would not be able to come to California. So, on Friday, March 14, 1997, my twenty-sixth birthday, after completing my last final exam, I took a red-eye from San Francisco to Pittsburgh.

I spent a week with him in Monroeville, ten miles outside of Pittsburgh. An Indian couple had taken over administration of the encyclopedia project and moved from Edmonton, Alberta, into the house next door to the Hindu Jain Temple. A generous devotee of Swamiji had purchased it a few years earlier so the encyclopedia project would have an office, and so Swamiji could stay there and meet with people when he came to support the temple and work on the encyclopedia. Until then, he'd stayed at the temple, but now that the work of the foundation had expanded and it had its own head office, it made sense for him to stay there.

Living under the same roof with Swamiji was ecstasy. There were no boys I had to go through to get an appointment into his inner quarters. The office was on the ground floor of the house, and he spent all his waking, nonmeditating hours there, poring over files, charts, and graphs as well as plans for the upcoming summer awareness-raising tour, with the Canadian director. Swamiji had asked a local devotee to bring an extra desk and chair for me, so I had my own corner of the office. My parents had just given me a laptop computer for my birthday, and as I set it on the desk, a mere ten feet from the couch where Swamiji sat with files spread out on a low coffee table, my breath slowed and deepened the way it does when I begin meditation. I felt my lips spread as a huge smile opened across my face. I was in heaven, and it was a home office in the suburbs of Pittsburgh.

Office hours ran from about 7 a.m. to 10 p.m. Pujya Swamiji came downstairs each morning after his prayers and meditation and began reviewing papers, making notes on dozens of small pads that he called diaries. He had a different diary for each aspect of the project, a diary for each city he was going to, a diary for each person he worked with. The Devanagari script looked to me like artistic hieroglyphics, carrying secrets and wisdom within it beyond even the perfection of his lettering.

His organization, albeit relegated to tiny slips of paper bound in spiral notebooks and spread across a table, rivaled anything I had seen in any corporate office. Months later, when I gave him, on his birthday, a beautiful clothbound planner with sections for calendars, contacts, and to-do lists by day, week, and month, he smiled, thanked me, and regifted it to someone working for him in Rishikesh. "Yes," he said, "many people have given me those," extinguishing in six words the bubbling excitement of my ingenuity, "but I prefer my own system."

Each day, streams of people would float through, ranging from devotees who came for his darshan and blessings or to spend a few precious moments in his presence to board members—the treasurer balancing the accounts of payments made to scholars, the secretary and joint secretary reviewing meeting minutes and outstanding action items—and members and executives of the Hindu Jain

Temple for Swamiji's guidance on issues arising within the temple or his advice on upcoming programs, projects, and expansion plans.

I sat at my desk in bliss, understanding only random English words that have become ubiquitous in Hindi and Gujarati as they were interspersed between torrents of those languages: (Hindi) ". . . blueprints . . ." (Hindi) ". . . architect . . ." (Hindi) ". . . foundation stone . . ." (Hindi), or (Gujarati) ". . . failing marks . . ." (Gujarati) ". . . hopeless . . ." (Gujarati) ". . . giving up . . ." (Gujarati) ". . . please, blessings," as parents sought blessings for their struggling children.

My work was much the same as it had been in India. Swamiji brought a manila folder with him from Rishikesh and handed me the contents, one by one, with instructions ranging from "Please tell them I cannot attend the event but I send my blessings" to "Tell them to call the scholar and ask when his articles will be submitted—tell them time is very short" or "Ask the doctors who are coming to Rishikesh next month if they would like to run a free medical camp at our clinic. It would be good to offer services to the local people." With each instruction, my heart swelled in my chest. This was the best place, the best moment. I was the luckiest person on Earth!

As I watched myself, I laughed. I, who couldn't muster enthusiasm for research papers on the role of serotonin reuptake in depression because I thought they seemed so far from the core of true importance and understanding, was ecstatic to send wedding blessings to people I didn't know and ask for updates from people I'd never met on projects I didn't understand taking place in cities I'd never heard of, all from a home office in Monroeville, Pennsylvania.

Life, from rising early to eating chapatis to being a clerical stenographer, had become infused with excitement. The experience of my self in Swamiji's presence was qualitatively different from my experience of self anywhere else. In his presence, everything was perfect, including my perfect role in this perfect world. It didn't matter what the role was or how mundane the task—simply being able to swim in this ocean of perfection made it all worthwhile.

CHAPTER 22

Enter Hanuman: Everything Is Possible with Devotion

One evening, Swamiji showed me the building that had served as the Hindu Jain Temple while the new, huge mandir on the hill was being built. The old temple had been converted to a community center. He showed me the room that had served for prayers, worship, devotion, and chanting, now a meeting hall; the kitchen, in which he had bathed before they built him a proper bathroom with a shower; the library; and the small room where he'd stayed for so many years, sleeping on the floor, overseeing the establishment of this first Hindu-Jain temple in the world, and ultimately founding not only a gorgeous red-brick, three-domed mandir up the hill but also transforming a nearly 1,000-square-mile area of people from different parts of India and different religious backgrounds into a strong, cohesive community, connected to each other and to their house of worship, a community broad enough to encompass the myriad streams from which they'd come.

"It's amazing to see all this," I told him. "I never would have imagined being outside of Pittsburgh and feeling that I'm in a spiritual paradise. I just didn't think of Pittsburgh that way. It's crazy, isn't it?"

He smiled and said, "It's crazy when you are crazy. It's crazy because you think it is crazy. You think that if you are in some fancy place with luxury, on a beach with all the comforts, you will be happy. My child, that is not what life is for. You are happy here because you have found what most people never find; you have found peace instead of pieces. You have connected to your Self, not just to objects on your shelf. Most people think only of filling their shelves. You are connecting to the true Self."

Because Swamiji picked up English by speaking with Indian Americans, for many of whom it's a second language, it is not always grammatically perfect, but it is an eloquent, inspired array of unforgettable rhymes and alliterations. People meet him decades later and say, "I remember when you asked if I wanted to live in peace or in pieces, whether I wanted to be better or bitter. It changed my life." On that crisp March evening, as we walked across the now paved grounds of the temple, at that time a muddy hilltop, he continued, "You are a divine soul, and you will teach and touch so many others in your life. You will really make a huge difference in the world."

It was beginning to remind me of my mother saying, as I stood pitifully before mirrors as a mid-adolescent bemoaning the state of various bodily parts, that I was the most beautiful girl in the world. I knew, even as a preteen, that of course I wasn't the most beautiful girl in the world, and that my mother, being my mother, saw beauty in me and comforted my insecurities as best she could. Now, Swamiji was saying something that felt similar, and yet I knew it was far beyond any simple intention to mollify my insecurities.

"Swamiji, I agree, of course, that I have been incredibly blessed in the last six months, that I've been given something I still can't describe, but luckily you understand. I feel beyond grateful for this precious gift and for the blessings you shower on me even though I'm definitely not worthy. But here, I think you're going overboard. I am not someone who can make that kind of a difference in the world. I know I'm intelligent. I know I can teach a class on neuropsychology and get A's on exams, but that's different from touching people deeply or making that kind of real difference. That is not a skill or ability I have—but," I added, lest he feel I was rudely disagreeing, "I deeply appreciate your kind words."

"You will see," he said, and we walked the rest of the temple grounds in silence.

The next morning, next to his files on the coffee table was a yellow-trimmed, colorful paperback book with an image on the cover of three people walking in single file through a forest, and the word *Ramayana* written in bold red letters at the top. Later, I would learn that the figures were Lord Rama, Sita Ma, and Lakshman.

I had just come upstairs to his office from my bedroom, and I asked, "What's this?" as I sat back on my heels after bowing to him.

"It is the Ramayana, a very sacred book telling the story of Bhagawan Rama, God in human form. This is a simple and good English translation. You should read it."

I began reading it that afternoon and stayed up most of the night to finish. It was like an exciting novel—romance, power struggles, betrayal, jealousy, forest adventures, war, and good guys and bad guys, with the former emerging triumphant. The spiritual teachings were woven simply into the threads of the plot. Lord Rama's words and actions were riveting in the pattern of the hero's journey of exile, battles, and ultimate victory.

One of the main characters is Hanuman, son of the god of wind. Hanuman is a monkey and part of the army of animals that serve in Lord Rama's army to rescue his wife, Sita, from the demon king Ravana, who snatched her and whisked her off to his kingdom of Lanka (now Sri Lanka). Hanuman is no ordinary monkey, however. Along with his divine attributes, his single-minded devotion to God in the form of Lord Rama leads to him achieving great miracles. He is the embodiment of devotion.

During the course of the Ramayana, Hanuman performs feats enumerated in the "Hanuman Chalisa," forty verses dedicated to him, as well as in a chapter of the Ramayana called the Sundarkand, the "beautiful chapter." Hanuman flies across the ocean from India to Lanka with the Himalayan Mountains in hand to bring the elixir of life—*Sanjeevani*—to restore Lord Rama's brother Lakshman to life. He traps the waning sun under his arm to keep it from setting before he arrives to the battleground. He makes himself enormous, then infinitesimally small.

When asked how he did all these feats, Hanuman explains, "I close my eyes and recite Lord Rama's name, and the rest just happens."

The next morning, I was waiting for Swamiji in his office, too excited to sleep after I'd finished the Ramayana. As he stepped downstairs, I threw myself at his feet, then sat back on my heels and looked up at him with hands folded in prayer, the tears streaming down my face. "If a monkey can do all that," I said, "just by being devoted to God, then maybe you're right. Maybe I can do something meaningful with my life too. Maybe I can make a difference in the world. I just have to be devoted."

"See," he said, smiling. "I told you."

CHAPTER 23

Parents

When people hear my story of coming to India, they invariably ask, "How did your parents respond?" What would you expect my American Jewish parents in Los Angeles, whose Stanford grad had just announced she was abandoning a PhD program to live in an ashram in India because she sees God in the river and in the eyes of barefoot children, to say? My mom's first response was, "No." *No* is an utterance, an automatic reaction, not a word. After that, she tried to persuade me not to stay (as nearly everyone did).

I wrote my parents a letter explaining everything. I had learned over the eighteen years I had lived under my mother's roof that writing letters was the best way. It gave her time and space for the initial "No" to come out privately, for the panic to rise and then fall, so that by the time we spoke, she would have regained her composure, and perhaps even her perspective.

"I don't know where this path will take me," I said. "However, I do know where my path will go if I don't return to India. It will be a life like the one you live, the one everyone I know lives, a life I know is right for you—it makes you happy, and I'm deeply glad that you're happy in this life. I respect your choices completely. And I know that when I am fifty-two"—my mom's age at the time—"I don't want the life that you have today. I say this with full respect and love. Your life is perfect for you. But it's not perfect for me. If I stay on the same train, I will end up at the same destination. Therefore, I must get on a different train. The only person I've ever met who is where I'd love to end up is Swamiji. I won't get all the way there this lifetime, but that is the train I have to get on. I would love to go with your blessings. I will, though, go, even without your blessings. So, please don't think that withholding your blessing will prevent me from going."

She was of course sad, and worried. Yet beneath her role as an overanxious Jewish mother, I felt a deep acknowledgment. "You've become so serene," she said to me one day. "Just being with you makes me feel peaceful."

"The truth is a magnet," Swamiji had assured me. "Don't try to force it on people. Just live it. Be the truth, and you will be a magnet." As I was living that truth, the pull of the magnet was strong.

My mother had wanted to go into the Peace Corps when she was just out of graduate school. But her father convinced her that if she took two years off in some remote part of the world, there would be no good men left to marry by the time she'd get back. So she stayed. We often joked—not really a joke—that it would have been so much better if she had gone to the Peace Corps and spared us all the pain of her first husband, my father Manny, and had simply come back later, married Frank, and had me with him. But alas, she wasn't defiant enough to disobey her dad.

So she understood my yearning and she struggled with herself not to do to me what her father had done to her—force me to sacrifice the soul's longing on the altar of societal norms. I could catch glimpses of her blessings between the drama of her hysterics.

Frank did not take part in these conversations. He was present, but my mom did all the talking. At the end of a several-minute litany of the many reasons I shouldn't go to India, she'd say, "And Frank agrees me with, right?" She had known since Frank had come into my life, just in time for my seventh birthday, that the best way to get me to do anything was to say, "Frank wants this."

In a private moment, I asked him, "I know Mom is hysterical, but what do you really think?" His opinion mattered so much to me. He looked at me, and in a moment the incredibleness of which I would truly appreciate only many years later, he said to me, his twenty-five-year-old daughter who was leaving everything behind to live in India, "Honey, in twenty-five years, you have never made a decision that I think was the wrong decision. I do not understand this one, but just because I don't understand it, who am I to suddenly assume you've started making wrong decisions?" Then, casually, he added, "You're batting a thousand so far. I have to assume the trend will continue."

CHAPTER 24

Return to Mother India

APRIL 1997

I sat on the bench outside the departures terminal at San Francisco International Airport, smoking my last cigarette. I had tried my first cigarette while sitting on a park bench with friends during junior high, and didn't smoke again till I entered Woodside Women's Hospital my freshman year at Stanford. Suzanne smoked, as did almost all the other women there and in nearly every treatment center, group, and program I had gone through. It was a decent distraction from food, and the nicotine-induced rush was almost as nice as the endorphin rush from vomiting. Not quite, but almost. I had smoked off and on throughout the first half of my twenties.

In a few hours, I would be on a Singapore Airlines flight to India. This time, however, I wouldn't have Jim's lap to lay my head in or be able to laugh with him about the frequency with which Singapore Airlines serves food. "Really? Time to eat again?" Always ready for a good, spicy vegetarian meal, Jim had partaken each time the flight attendants—beautiful, olive-skinned women in brightly colored suits with matching hats—had offered.

This time, I was flying alone.

My remaining possessions were locked up in a storage facility for a year. I had a one-year leave of absence from graduate school. On a deep level, I knew that this "yearlong" sojourn in India was a charade. I was not coming back. This was not just the last cigarette I'd smoke in a year. It was the last one, ever. This was not the beginning of a yearlong adventure. It was the beginning of the rest of my life.

I had spent many minutes standing on my head earlier that evening, a technique Manouso had taught us, a way of using yoga postures to prevent airplane-induced aches and pains and mitigate jet lag. I had done backbends and twisted and balanced on my palms and forearms to help my immune system kick in for the long journey.

I took a last drag on the cigarette, filling my cold lungs gratefully with hot smoke, and held it in for as long as I could, willing the cells of my body to remember this warmth without ever clamoring for it again. "Thank you," I said out loud. "Thank you for bringing me home."

I stood up into the windy night. Mark Twain is said to have remarked, "The coldest winter I ever spent was a summer in San Francisco." I had been in shorts earlier in the day in Palo Alto and Redwood City. It was now so cold, with the bay fog rolling in, that I could see my own breath long after the last wisps of tobacco smoke had dissipated.

Scot, my closest friend, whose companionship, presence, love, and warm bed had comforted me through innumerable nights at Stanford, dropped me off at the airport. He and I had detoured through Denver one summer on our cross-country drive from his home in Meridian, Mississippi, to Palo Alto, in search of Manny, my biological father. In the phone book, I was able to locate the building where Manny worked. The information board in the lobby directed us to his suite. Scot and I rode the elevator together in silence, and he held my trembling hand.

It was only when we got off the elevator that I finally thought, "What exactly will I say to him?" Scot had no answer. "What will I do?" Between us, we had no idea.

Scot reminded me that he was only there on this wild goose chase to support me, that this detour to find and stalk the man who had walked out of my life was not his idea. He had agreed to come along out of love for me. We left the building and Denver without ever catching a glimpse of Manny.

Scot was my anchor throughout my years at Stanford and after, through my marriage to Jim and its dissolution. My ardent crush on him was neither diminished nor deterred by his homosexuality. As he dropped me off at the airport, I had no idea when I would see him again. Would it be a year? Many years? A lifetime? Would India swallow me up and hold me so deep in her womb that it would be lifetimes before I would be "birthed" again into this world? I had absolutely no idea that it would be only a few months till I returned in August with Swamiji as part of a Dharma Yatra, a national tour for peace and unity.

Walking into the bright lights of SFO, I felt like a newborn walking consciously and freely from the womb of my mother into a brand-new world—my entrance into which was marked by fluorescent lights, conveyor belts, and escalators. I landed in Delhi at the beginning of India's summer.

Swamiji was also in Delhi. He had meetings in Govardhan and Vrindavan for the next few days. We had walked the parikrama of Govardhan Hill the previous autumn, thirteen barefoot miles, stepping in cow dung and God knows what else along the paths through the villages, marketplaces, and holy fields in which Lord Krishna had danced and played with the gopis—the milkmaid devotees. On that journey, while I had been melting into ecstasy, Swamiji had been planning.

The lack of places to sit down, the lack of facilities for drinking water or toilets, even the heaps of trash strewn about the pathway through which bare feet tread had all seemed part of the divine play to me. To him, it was something that needed to be fixed for other devotees. "So many people come to this sacred land to walk around this holy mountain. Many are elderly or not physically fit. Thirteen miles is too far to go without sitting down," he announced, seamlessly weaving practicality into ritual. "There must be benches, there must be clean water for *yatris* [pilgrims] to drink. There must be toilets."

Nearly two decades before he would cofound the Global Interfaith WASH Alliance and lead a revolution toward cleanliness and sanitation, he was already building toilets and taps for drinking water. My lack of Hindi kept me from knowing the subject of talks Swamiji had had during our three days in Vraj the previous fall. I hadn't realized that while I had been swooning in devotional bliss, his bliss had manifested through improving the facilities for devotees.

Now he was traveling back to Govardhan for meetings with local government officials, other concerned spiritual leaders, and businesspeople to sponsor the work. "Would you like to come?" he asked, as though it were a question.

Less than twelve hours after landing in Delhi, I was in the front seat of a Contessa zooming from Delhi to Mathura. The vast majority of cars on the road were Ambassadors—practical, stable, chunky vehicles. The other option was the Contessa, a lower, flatter Indian version of a four-door sedan.

Before seat belts became compulsory for passengers in India in 2002, very few cars had them. In those that did, they often didn't work. "Surya, this seat belt still doesn't work," I suggested as gently and politely as I could as he drove seventy-five miles an hour down a road where rickshaws, bicyclists, and water buffaloes continually entered and crisscrossed from every side in every direction.

"Have faith in God," Swamiji's twenty-year-old driver and right-hand man would tell me. "God will protect you." Even in those early days, when the haze of spiritual intoxication blanketed most of my experiences, even while my heart was melting in my chest, even in the fullness of breath that (despite the smog) returned to me the moment I returned to India, I never stopped being scared in Surya's car.

When the seat belt law came into effect, policemen stood on street corners, peering into cars to ensure that drivers and passengers were wearing them. At the same time, luggage-strap sellers popped up on street corners—often the same corners as the policemen—selling thick black luggage straps. "Why in the world are these guys selling luggage straps on the street?" I asked.

"They look like seat belts," Surya told me. "See," he showed me the one he had purchased the day before. "You attach it here on the side of the car next to the window and place it across your body. That way, when police look in the car, it looks that you are wearing your seat belt."

Wow, I thought. Indians have figured out a way to circumvent laws whose sole intention is to save their lives. There are always shortcuts here. The fact that a seat belt would, and a luggage strap wouldn't, save your life was a fact either lost on or ignored by Delhi drivers. Why spend the money to get a seat belt installed when, for a few rupees, you could purchase a luggage strap to imitate one?

As the years went by and my role as Swamiji's assistant or secretary or close devotee or simply "the one who wouldn't go away" got more solidified, I mustered the courage to reply to Surya's admonitions to just have faith in God.

"I do," I would tell him, "and God has told me you need to slow down." At other times, I'd say, "God insists that you get your seat belts fixed." American sassiness slowly wove its way into my life in India.

On this day in April 1997, though, the threads of my courage were still loose strands. So, when I reminded Surya about the broken seat belt, he got away with saying, "Have faith in God."

"Can I come in the back with you, please?" I hesitatingly asked Swamiji, who always sits in the back. I didn't want to ask, but I also didn't want to die, the thought of which slammed into my consciousness every time Surya passed a car into oncoming traffic barreling down the two-lane highway at high speed. As the truck or car or bus coming toward us flashed its brights and honked its horn, Surya would slide back into our lane just in time. Each encounter I survived felt like it shaved years off my life, so I just had to ask if I could come in the back with Swamiji. Sitting in the back, of course, doesn't ensure one will survive a high-speed crash, but facing oncoming traffic while riding shotgun without a seat belt is much more terrifying than facing it from the back seat.

Typically, and traditionally, there is a thick line, a wide distance that male religious renunciants keep from female devotees. In some lineages, male renunciants won't even deign to be in a woman's presence, let alone speak to her. In most lineages, though, it's an intricate and delicate balance between the letter and spirit of the law. Celibacy, of course, must be maintained, and therefore most touch and even close physical proximity is shunned.

However, for those leaders, masters of their own minds and senses who have reached the enlightened state, the female body is nothing more than a differently shaped vehicle for the same genderless—or gender-full—soul. So, over the years, I've seen young girls and even women burst into tears before Swamiji, who extends his hands to pat them on the back or shoulder or head. I have seen the same openness—the awareness that although the body may be different, the soul is one—exemplified by a few other renowned saints. Their vows of celibacy are not threatened or compromised in either letter or spirit by comforting the bereaved or accepting a young girl's spontaneous, jubilant leap into their arms when meeting after a long time. Still, over the years, I'd ask, "Why must these rules be followed?" when the answer to "Why can't I come?" or "Why can't I do that?" was simply, "Because you are a girl." The letter of the law was followed most of the time.

So the question "Can I come in the back with you?" was not a simple one. If there were three passengers, instead of two, in addition to the driver, someone *had* to be in the back, especially if the third person was Swamiji's stenographer or a young student, and I could be brought into the back without much of a problem. The watchful world would understand that I was a higher-ranking social creature, despite my unfortunate femaleness, than the steno or student, and hence they would understand why I was in the prestigious back seat with the saint.

But on this trip, it was just the two of us. To bring me into the back, with an empty front seat, sent a distasteful message: "Even with other options available, I have chosen to have her next to me." But I was scared, and he had heard the conversation with Surya.

"Sure," he said. "Surya, stop the car and let her come in the back."

"I can slow down, Maharajji, if you say," Surya replied with a touch of surprise. He was supposed to be the favorite, and so Swamiji was supposed to take his side and tell me he was a perfectly safe driver and I should stop nagging about seat belts. But he didn't. He let me come in the back, where I was able to stick my long fingers deep into the recesses of the cushion to pull out the seat belt buckle and snap it into place.

I watched the sun rise over the fields as the outskirts of Delhi melted into the villages of Uttar Pradesh. Every twenty or thirty feet, the fields were peppered with stacks of cow patties many feet high. Round, thick, brown patties, having dried in the open sun, were now carefully placed one upon another into tall pyramids that looked to the untrained eye like tipis for dogs or very short people.

As we headed south out of Delhi and into southwestern Uttar Pradesh, I watched villagers go about their morning rituals. Men and children of both genders soaped themselves up by the side of hand pumps. They then squatted—soapy bodies and hair of white foam—beneath the spout, pumping the rusty iron handle with one hand and rinsing the soap off their bodies and out of their hair with the other. Sometimes they'd give the lever a few hard, quick pumps and then use both hands to scrub their scalp or belly under the running water.

Women bent low at the waist over fires in their front yards. We weren't close enough to see what they were cooking, but I imagined steaming pots of fragrant chai. Bullock carts laden with sugarcane shared the highway and obscured our view ahead.

I thought about driving down highways in the United States where trucks or RV campers beyond a certain width had bright orange signs that read, "Caution: Wide Load." I laughed to myself, imagining the job of sign makers in India if those same laws applied: "Caution: Stalks of sugarcane rolling into the road." "Caution: Unsecured tons of hay falling on your car." "Caution: Vehicle stops for no reason." "Caution: Vehicle drives against traffic."

Children squatted along the side of the road, underwear below their knees, defecating. Their parents must've done so earlier, while it was still dark.

How did I get here? I wondered nearly aloud. My friends and classmates were starting the spring quarter, calculating the probability of picking black marbles from jars, diagnosing patients from clusters of symptoms, learning about neural pathways, the associated neurotransmitters, and how they correlate with neuropsych dysfunctions. And I was in the back seat of a Contessa, less than a foot from a man revered as an incarnation of God Himself, while children pooped and bathed in the dirt along the sides of the road.

I looked over at Swamiji. He had large architectural drawings spread across his lap and was making notes in a tiny spiral pad. "Benches should be over here, not here," he whispered to himself. The sun was beginning to stream through the tinted windows of the Contessa onto his hands as they delicately traced the drawings. He must've felt me watching, for he turned his head. Now the light illuminated him from behind, silhouetting his face but not his eyes. They shone as bright as the sun itself. "Yes?"

Yes what? What to say? I could only smile, my eyes filled with tears. "I can't believe I am here," I said. "I was so worried that I might not get back."

"It's all God's grace," he said and went back to the drawings.

Swamiji spent the next two days in Govardhan in long meetings, poring over enormous architectural drawings, maps of the thirteen-mile pathway around the five-mile-long sacred mountain of Govardhan Hill. Where would the benches be placed? Where would toilets be built? Where would trees be planted? The scriptural stories of Lord Krishna's life describe woods and lush forests where cowherds and milkmaids roamed with their cows. But over the last many decades and even centuries, India—along with the rest of the world—has been tragically deforested. Tree planting has always been a focus for Swamiji. Written into the aims and objectives of his foundations, "plantation of trees" has always occupied a central place.

I walked quickly to catch up with him as he led a team of local authorities in and out of the pathways of Govardhan, beside the sacred *kunds* (catchment pools) bearing the names of Radha, Krishna's beloved, and Shyam, one of the names of Krishna Himself. I couldn't understand a word anyone said, but the excitement was palpable.

It was my first glimpse of Swamiji in action. At the ashram, I had witnessed impassioned meetings about programs. In Pittsburgh, I had seen him run the board of trustees meeting in a mix of Hindi, Gujarati, and English, a nearly full-day event of charts and graphs and numerical reports of progress on the *Encyclopedia of Hinduism*.

But this was different. We had left Delhi at 5 a.m. and driven three hours, and, after a quick breakfast, he had gone into the first meeting, which he presided over in a way that reminded me of both an orchestra conductor and a circus ringleader. His attention did not stray for even a moment, and his arms and hands spoke as much as his lips. The district magistrate, the commissioner, other local officials, and all those gathered were swept up in his energy field like orchestra instruments playing themselves or lions jumping through flaming hoops.

I sat, sometimes on the floor, sometimes on a metal folding chair, sometimes on a soft couch, depending on where and with whom each meeting was held. And in every place, I wondered, *Who am I?* and *What have I walked into?* These were places I'd never before heard of, places that didn't exist on any map I'd ever seen, places that'd had no relevance in my life till now. And at this moment, swimming in a cocktail of delirium—one part jet lag and nine parts bewilderment—I was part of detailed discussions about where toilets should be built on a dirt path designed for barefoot lovers of Krishna.

Yet it all, other than the jet lag, felt so oddly right. Of course I was here, in this world, planning for benches and drinking water. Of course I'd be scurrying along dirt paths with trees that had "Radhe Radhe" painted on them to remind visitors to chant the name of Lord Krishna's sweetest beloved so that, by grace, Krishna would appear. Of course I'd be taking notes on decisions being made in languages I didn't understand. Every few minutes, Swamiji would turn his head to me and say, "Write that down." The blank look on my face did not deter him. Fortunately, the teenage son of one of the businessmen spoke English and would tell me, "Eleven trees to be planted on the land owned by the shopkeeper who is sitting over there. He will look after the trees."

And every few hours, I would wake from my open-eyed reverie and wonder, "Where am I?" Placing it on a map was irrelevant. Like Lucy from C. S. Lewis's Narnia adventures, I had walked through my own wardrobe and, sans lion and witch, I was home.

CHAPTER 25

"The Stupidest
Smart Person"

"You are the stupidest smart person I know." Pujya Swamiji's words cut straight through the spiritual intoxication I'd been under for months. I had been back in India for about three months, engaged in an ever-expanding definition of full-time service.

What I did varied from day to day. I responded to letters Swamiji received, I sent follow-up letters to people who were overseeing various projects—mostly the *Encyclopedia of Hinduism.* What was the status of article collection, or of illustration matching? I also followed up on the schools we had adopted in a slum outside of Delhi and the curriculum of the free school on the ashram premises.

I began to edit a book on the Bhagavad Gita and an encyclopedia on the teachings of Mirra Alfassa, known to her followers as the Mother, and the founder of the Sri Aurobindo Ashram, both written by brilliant Indian thinkers but checkered with spelling and grammatical mistakes. The authors had each approached Pujya Swamiji for the IHRF to publish their works, and he had handed me the manuscripts, saying, "If you think they are good, we can publish them."

The depth of the content took my breath away. As I read them page by page, I'd stop and let my tears flow or I'd let myself drift into meditation. Good? They were the deepest books I'd ever read. But nearly every page had a plethora of spelling, grammatical, and stylistic errors. "Just fix them," Swamiji said, as though each book was a one-page memo and not a thousand pages of dense text, "and then we'll publish them."

I worked with printers and designers on brochures and pamphlets about our projects—the schools, the free medical clinic, the environmental, ecological, and animal-protection programs. "They should be informing and inspiring," Swamiji insisted, "not for fundraising. Whatever God wants us to have, He will send us." So, no perforated pages to mail in checks, just pictures and details of the work. Should people be inspired to donate, they would. Should they simply be inspired to say a prayer for the children or the hospital patients or the cows wandering along the road, that was fine, too.

A desk was set up for me in the storeroom where I'd had my post-Reiki ecstatic initiation into the expansiveness of my Self the previous autumn. A computer from the Delhi *Encyclopedia of Hinduism* office was sent to Rishikesh so I could have an actual PC rather than the blue manual typewriter.

I even had my own key. Each morning, one of the young men, the first on the scene, would unlock the outer door while he did the morning sweeping. I could then use my key to enter the storeroom/office from the public darshan room. I, who had to be coaxed and coerced, pushed and prodded, to sit down and work, was suddenly at my desk before 7 a.m. After morning prayers ended at 6, I got my coffee from the market and came to the office.

I was also the ashram photographer. I had been an avid photographer since high school, so this role was natural for me. I always had my camera with me, and I became a photojournalist, jumping onto and off of stages, gently—and sometimes not so gently—pushing people's shoulders out of the shot, feeling entitled to stand or sit anywhere. "Photographer," I would say, pointing to my camera as I jostled through crowds to get to whatever I had to shoot. Swamiji's smile when he saw me, poised behind my lens, assured me that I had every right to be there.

I managed the photo processing and album production too, spending dozens of hours on the floor of my new office, arranging Kodak prints into albums for each event—one for us to keep at the ashram, and separate albums for each of the government officials and dignitaries who had participated.

The lack of global relevance of my work never occurred to me, nor would it have bothered me if it had. I wasn't there to be globally relevant. I was there because it was home. I held Swamiji's comment about me teaching and touching millions in a corner of my mind that I rarely visited. It didn't matter. If I did end up doing something like that, well, great. If I spent the rest of my life typing his letters, coordinating schools for slum children, and taking and arranging photographs, that was more than enough. The sheer rightness of where I was made everything else right too. Each morning, I woke up and knew I was home.

People asked (and still ask), "Wasn't the transition difficult? Do you miss Western life and its comforts?" I'd respond, "Imagine that you have size 8 feet, and your whole life, people have told you that you have size 5 feet. They were not being deceptive; they really believed your feet were size 5. So you've always worn size 5 shoes. They were uncomfortable, and you developed blisters and corns, but you thought shoes were supposed to feel like that. And whenever you mentioned it to someone, they assured you that, yes, shoes always feel tight. Then, one day, someone slips your foot into a size 8 shoe. 'Ahhh,' you say. 'So, that's what shoes can feel like.' Yet people continue to ask, 'How did you adapt to wearing a size 8 shoe? Do you miss the way your size 5 shoes felt?' Of course not."

Coming back to India felt like slipping my size 8 foot into a size 8 shoe. I awoke each morning before the prayers and—just as little children run into their parents' bed, cuddle under the covers, and lie in Mom's arms before starting their day—I rushed down to Ganga. The habit has stayed with me. "Good morning, Ma," I breathe into the wind as it whips off the Himalayas and onto Her ceaselessly flowing waters. I bow to Her and drink a handful of Her divine nectar. I stand, Her waters rushing over my bare feet, an IV of life and sacredness into my all-too-human morning sluggishness. I join my palms in prayer as the sun, rising over the Himalayas, begins to reflect off Her boundless waters:

Thank you, Ma.
Thank you for waking me again today,
For letting my eyes open
In the land of your infinite grace,
Thank you for making my legs able
To carry me to Your banks, and then to my office.
Thank you for bringing me forth to this life of service,
This life of light, this life of love,
This life of God.
Let my work today be in service of You.
May You be the hand that guides mine.
And most importantly,
Please, please, let me be worthy of living on your banks.

I had no idea when I would see Swamiji. Sometimes I saw him several times in a day. Maybe there was a meeting at which he wanted me to take minutes or notes. Maybe there was an event at which I got to be the photographer. Maybe he had some important work he needed done. And sometimes I didn't see him for days, except for the morning prayers and the evening aarti. I no longer sat in the daily open darshans. There was too much to do. "Whenever you want to see me, just send a message though one of these boys," he told me, "and I will call you when I am free." It was rare, though, that I'd have a question urgent enough to warrant an unplanned meeting. It was OK, though. I could always hear him speaking to people in the open darshan, as his cushion was on the other side of my office wall.

One morning, as I was sitting on the steps leading to Ganga in the early pre-prayers hour, around 4 or 4:30, suddenly, he walked down the steps in front of me toward the river. I was surprised to see him alone. Every other time I'd seen him moving around the ashram, he had been surrounded by many people—devotees or his *sevaks*—and there was always a buzz around him. Here, however, he seemed to float down the steps to the water.

At first, I didn't even realize it was Swamiji, because he was all alone, his head gently lowered so that nothing should come into his vision other than Mother Ganga. He lay down prone on the marble of the ghat, legs straight behind him, arms straight in front of him, nearly parallel to Ganga Herself, but ever so slightly turned toward Her—there wasn't room on the steps for him to lie down facing Her. He lowered his head onto the marble between his outstretched arms and lay there for a while.

Although he was a few inches from the water, in the predawn light it seemed to be washing over him, as a mother might pull the blankets over her child when he crawls into her bed in the early morn. Then, as he rose, the edge of the water seemed to recede. His hair and clothes were dry—so the water had not physically risen to cover him—and yet, for those moments, I'm certain I saw Mother Ganga's blanket cover him.

After rising, he stepped into the river and walked, calmly and gracefully, as though the strength of the current had no impact on him. He walked several feet out into the water, and the water remained at calf height. Gazing up at the moon as it began its descent over Ram Jhula and behind the Himalayas to give way to the sun waiting to rise, he closed his eyes and folded his hands at his chest in prayer.

At that moment, there was no moon, no Ganga, no Swamiji, and no ghat. There was only child and Mother. He had come home in the early hours of the morning to spend a few precious moments with his Mother before beginning the day. The two had merged so completely and seamlessly that it was hard to imagine that a few moments before, they had been water and man. As his dhoti floated behind him, lifted by the strength of Her current, I would have sworn he had no legs—that he was not standing, but floating, immersed in and merged into the goddess Ganga.

Suddenly, I felt voyeuristic. As though watching a divine movie, I was witnessing the precious moment of Pujya Swamiji's union with his Mother. Slowly and reluctantly, I turned toward the shadows and left, and his eyes were still closed.

These were the perfect, pristine moments of my first months back. Then, suddenly, someone said something negative about me and it got back to me. In all the months since I'd first arrived at the ashram, I had had few interactions with people. My conversations were relegated to simple instructions and requests: "You eat lunch now." "A new towel, please?"

Swamiji was the only one I really talked to, and days could go by between our conversations. The only friends I had were the children of the ashram, the sons and daughters of those who worked there—the sweepers, cooks, cleaners, and gardeners. The children would hold my fingers as we walked down to the aarti each night, and snuggle into my arms and lap. We couldn't communicate in words, but it didn't matter. We laughed, tickled, hugged, and loved.

I had little to do with the other devotees and disciples. A passing "Namaste" as we walked in the halls or the dining area was the extent of most interactions. Printers, designers, and photo developers were the ones I had the most conversation with.

So, to discover that a longtime, stalwart devotee had been criticizing me hurt deeply. She criticized not my words or actions, but my very presence. Why was I here? she wanted to know. Who was I, and what did I want with Swamiji? I didn't know anything about India or Indian culture and therefore couldn't possibly be of any real help. "If Swamiji needed a secretary or a photographer, one should be hired for him and the American should be sent away."

I went to Swamiji—I finally had an urgent reason to see him—and said, "I have to go. It's all a mistake. This is not a good idea." I told him what had been discussed among the devotees over tea that day.

"I am so sorry," I cried. These were not tears of truth or bliss, but of despair. My inherent uselessness had been unveiled. My inner un-rightness had been discovered, and I needed to leave before I caused any more problems for him or the ashram.

"You are the stupidest smart person I've ever met," he said calmly, staring at my teary eyes as I struggled to catch my breath. With the shock of a Band-Aid being ripped off, his words tore straight into the moment, through the drama, the story, and the plot, with all its characters and script.

Despite having been back in India for months, living a life of spiritual ecstasy on the banks of the sacred Ganga River, despite indescribable experiences of divine Oneness, that state of merging and melting into the Universe, into the Light that is possible only through Grace, despite tears of bliss flowing down my face every day, despite being touched by a power and presence I had never imagined possible, I had, on that day in the spring of 1997, reacted to a situation exactly as I always had—as a victimized, egocentric, grasping child.

When Pujya Swamiji used the words *stupid* and *smart* in the same phrase, it was to startle me awake. He was referring to a true and deep intelligence, the presence of jnana (real wisdom) in my life. Although I was "smart" in IQ and also in the experiential understanding of Truth of self and Self, I was still "stupid" in my inability to bring that deep wisdom and experience into my patterned reactivity. I may have had wisdom, but I was unable to apply it consistently to my actions and reactions.

I had burst into tears like a wounded eight-year-old. The fear, grasping, and yearning of "yesterday" felt like it was true and present "today." My sense of not being "enough" had been triggered, and I was no longer a twenty-six-year-old swimming in ecstasy, but a scared and wounded child. My buttons had been pushed, and I didn't have the tools or integration yet to know the difference between now and what my nervous system (which has no concept of time) felt was also now, but wasn't.

In the 1980s, American Buddhist psychologist John Welwood coined the term "spiritual bypass": When a person has true, deep spiritual experiences of Oneness, wholeness, completeness, and Divine presence, states of samadhi, bliss, or union in your meditation or prayers or in the presence of your guru, it's easy to think that your inner work is complete.

When we live in the world and have to relate to other people, who have their own issues, challenges, fears, egos, and desires, at some point we realize that having had the deep, ecstatic experience of the Divine does not necessarily give us the tools to overcome the insecurities and neuroses we've had since childhood. Experiences of Grace do not exempt us from having to look at our own anger, jealousies, egos, and fears.

We all know people who do dozens of rounds of *japa* (meditative repetition of a mantra or a divine name) on their mala every day or spend hours in meditation but are provoked by the slightest insult or upset. We see people who perform extensive pujas yet are not able to get along with the people around them or who are trapped in addiction or suffering from insecurity and depression.

Meditation, prayers, japa, puja, and kirtan are wonderful ways to help us connect to the Divine and experience wholeness and perfection within the Self, but they do not erase the imprints of childhood trauma. They give us a perspective that can pave the way to healing these traumas, a deep, palpable experience that we are more than our childhoods, our addictions, our depression, and our fallible, victimized bodies. They connect us to a Self that was never abused, victimized, betrayed, abandoned, or deprived.

They give us a touch of the sun's warmth. But we have to do the work of integrating these gifts of Grace into the body/mind we have. It doesn't happen automatically. We might get a reprieve for a while as we dwell in these new states of bliss, but as Buddhist teacher Jack Kornfield reminds us, "After the ecstasy, the laundry."

Psychological work without spiritual experience can become a quagmire of darkness. It's easy to sink into the quicksand of our own histories, our wounded identities, fears, and desires, and relive them over and over again. On the other hand, a deep and honest, dharmic, fearless inquiry into our motivations, reactions, compulsions, and anxieties can be a most helpful companion on the spiritual path. We can witness our anger, ego, and grasping and the repetition of decades-old scripts with the deep presence of love and divine light, and discover our humanity to be more companionable with our spiritual insight than we'd imagined possible.

CHAPTER 26

Ganga Is Ganga

SUMMER 1997

We were on Dharma Yatra, a sacred pilgrimage. In the 1990s and into the first years of the new millennium, Pujya Swamiji led Dharma Yatras throughout North America, Great Britain and continental Europe, Africa, Indonesia, Australia, New Zealand, and Fiji, ministering to the Indian diaspora throughout the world.

When Indians move abroad, a concern that arises, especially amid the economic prosperity of the West, is how to pass on the dharma to their children. This dharma is not dogma, religion, commandments, or canon. It is fluid enough to adjust to changing times and places, yet eternal and enduring in its roots, which are nourished by and in return nourish the river of life.

These Dharma Yatra were pilgrimages to ignite a recommitment to dharma primarily but not exclusively in people of Indian origin who were living abroad—to rekindle in their minds and hearts the fire of love for their own heritage. "Be American where your professional life is concerned," Pujya Swamiji would urge on the US pilgrimages, "but be Indian where your personal and domestic life are concerned." He also said, "Don't worry about giving your children cars; worry about giving them *sanskaras*"- ethics, values, and culture.

Swamiji typically would spend one night per city leading these high-intensity spiritual events. Ardent and energetic lectures on the importance of maintaining a connection to Indian culture, devotional songs led by well-known Indian musicians, and free vegetarian feasts were the typical components for crowds numbering from several hundred to tens of thousands, depending on the city. His yatras had another component as well—to raise awareness about the work of compiling the eleven-volume *Encyclopedia of Hinduism*.

From the Sanskrit root *dhri* ("to support, hold, or bear"), *dharma* means "that which protects us and holds us together." Living in accord with dharma protects, preserves, and upholds individuals, communities, and societies. It includes but isn't limited to the concept of "right path," and it also includes aspects of traditional Indian culture and heritage—close family ties, service for the less fortunate, having a personal relationship with God, and adhering to norms established over thousands of years.

When I returned to India in early April 1997, it never occurred to me I'd be back in the United States a few months later as part of a caravan of religious leaders instilling the teachings of Hindu spirituality in second- and third-generation Indians in America.

"Swamiji, I know you say God is everywhere," I asked him when we were in Los Angeles for a day, en route between San Diego and Bakersfield. "So, why do I feel God so much more strongly in Rishikesh than I do here in Los Angeles?" We stood in my parents' living room as a car pulled up to drive him away.

Swamiji was staying with devotees he'd known for many years, but he had agreed to come to bless my parents' home. Why was he so generous of time, energy, and spirit to me? How, less than a year after I met him, had I persuaded him to spend half an hour at my parents' house? People beg him for years to make a ten-minute stop at their house just to step inside the front door and bless their home. This is a question I continue to ponder more than two decades later. I was persistent—and fragile in faith. My idea of faith included the expectation that yes, of course the object of my faith would behave how I wanted him to.

Swamiji was acutely aware of the anxiety my parents were experiencing. It had been less than a year since my life had been transformed. Everything seemed new and exciting and fresh. For them, it had been a year of wondering what the hell had happened to their daughter. A year earlier, she had apparently been happily married and on the verge of completing her PhD, and would surely give them grandchildren in the near future. Now she was celibate, living in India, chanting in Sanskrit, dressed in five yards of fabric, and traveling around the United States spreading the culture of Hinduism. Thankfully, without me having to beg, he had agreed to come to the house.

My anxiety about preparations in the house prior to his arrival was rivaled only by what I had experienced the night before science fair projects were due when I was younger. What if something had been left undone? What had I forgotten? What if it wasn't good enough, wasn't right? I spent the afternoon doing my best impression of an Indian lady. I bought roses at the florist and tied them together to make a garland of sorts to hang over the room he would occupy for half an hour. I made my mom buy brand-new sheets and towels, which I dyed orange in her washing machine. "But he's not going to sleep or bathe here," she pointed out, as if I'd forgotten the obvious.

"It doesn't matter," I insisted. "The sheets on the bed must be new. There must be a towel, whether he's going to bathe or not."

He didn't even go into the bedroom or the bathroom. He came for about twenty minutes and sat with my parents in the living room, where he drank the cup of tea I prepared without laughing at my pitiful attempt at making Indian tea, or spitting it out. When it was time to go, I remembered the elaborate bedroom preparations and implored, "Please come and see the room."

Compulsive attention to detail in bed-making and room arranging did not come naturally to me. I'm not a homemaker by nature. My high school didn't have home ec classes, and I didn't go to finishing school or cotillion. The only beds I ever made were ones we short-sheeted in summer camp, a prank to retaliate against counselors who had scolded us.

But I had channeled an Indian Martha Stewart on steroids all afternoon, and she would not go away until Swamiji saw the room. He walked in, while I made sure he noticed the roses taped to the door frame, then he looked around, smiled, put his hands gently over his heart, and closed his eyes for a moment in prayer. Then he walked out. The brand-new, perfectly dyed sheets and towels did not get touched. I assume they got blessed, though.

As we stood in the living room before Swamiji left, I asked him the question percolating in my mind since we'd arrived the day before. My parents had gone outside to the driveway to greet the people picking him up. "Why do I feel God so much more strongly in Rishikesh than I do here in Los Angeles?" I asked in a rare and precious moment alone.

He smiled and said, "God is everywhere. You know that. God is just as much here as in Rishikesh. But," he smiled even more, and the twinkle in his eyes seemed brighter than the halogen ceiling light, "but, Ganga is Ganga."

Yes and yes. Yes, God can be felt and experienced and connected to anywhere in the world. And, yes, there is a uniqueness, a qualitative difference to life in Rishikesh, where Ganga flows from the Himalayas. I could have had a spiritual awakening anywhere, yet it had happened in Rishikesh, the place where saints, sages, and rishis have flocked for thousands of years.

The Upanishads remind us, *"Isha vasyam idam sarvam, yat kincha jagatyaam jagat."* (The whole universe is pervaded by the Divine. There is no one, nowhere, and nothing that is not pervaded by the Divine.) And yet, there are whirlpools of Divine energy that grab us, don't let go, carry us out to sea, and transform us. That happened to me in Rishikesh. As my head (figuratively) bobbed up miles from shore, I realized, "I'm alive. I'm not even gasping for air, for the ocean has become my lungs. My eyes are open and clear; I can see. Perhaps I died in the current, but I continue to feel more alive than ever." Yes and yes. God is everywhere. And Ganga is Ganga.

CHAPTER 27

Dharma Yatra— A Pilgrimage of Peace

SUMMER 1997

Before stopping in Los Angeles, Swamiji and I were in San Diego. On our way to the temple where the Dharma Yatra program was about to be held, Swamiji said, "And you'll be giving a short talk on Indian culture." What? The only formal public address I'd ever given was my Bat Mitzvah speech. At Stanford, when I organized the first Earth Day event held on the campus, I gave a spontaneous impassioned exhortation to those passing by on their bikes to "Get off your bikes. Step on Mother Earth. We live on this planet—touch it!" imploring them to learn about the great environmental groups I'd brought together for this celebration—visit the stalls, read their pamphlets, understand what is happening to our Earth. But that hardly counted as a speech.

Now, with less than ten minutes till we'd arrive at the temple, I had to think about what to say and how to say it. "Swamiji, are you sure? Maybe not tonight. Maybe after a few days of seeing how these events go."

"No, no," he said casually. "You can start tonight. It will be good for people to hear it from you."

I don't remember what I said that evening, but by the time my name was called to speak, I was so drenched with perspiration that as I rose from my cross-legged position to walk onto the stage, my silk saree stuck to the back of my knees. I could feel my face turn red, then purple, as hundreds of San Diegans of Indian ancestry watched me bend over and extricate the fabric from the backs of my legs. That night, I learned why Indian women wear cotton petticoats beneath their sarees.

It turned out that I love public speaking. I learned that if I could just bear the anticipatory anxiety, the twenty or thirty minutes of sweaty palms before actually walking to the microphone, I had found a passion. "Will I get to speak here, too?" I began asking as the days went by. "Yes, of course," Swamiji always replied.

First, I loved the subject matter. I had spent almost a year being transformed by the culture of India. Yes, it was a placeless, nameless, culture-less experience of awakening when I first beheld the Divine that had changed my life. Yes, I had been given a gift deeper and bigger than any country—a gift of the palpable experience of God in my life, one I had experienced in and through almost every person I met in those first weeks. And yet, aside from the spiritual ecstasy, aside from the formless, boundaryless oneness of spirit and consciousness I felt myself merging and melting into, aside from that—everything else I'd been given and had learned was from the culture.

From the barefoot children with glistening eyes, I learned that things do not buy happiness, that being privileged might not be the same as being fulfilled. I learned that contentment can be hearing devotional music streaming through loudspeakers all day long. I learned that getting A's on exams and memorizing facts and figures do not make you smart, that the accumulation of information can block the flow of real wisdom.

From nearly a year of service, I learned how fulfilling it is to give to others. The work I would have deemed boring when done for myself became joyous when done as seva. I learned that connecting with God both within myself and outside of myself—in all the ways I'd experienced over the last year—was the stuff of which my happiness was made.

All these lessons are fundamental elements of Indian culture, what they call Bharatiya Sanskriti (culture of India). It was there in the eyes of the children, in the eyes of the sweepers, in the eyes of the old women chanting their mantras on rudraksh beads as they sat by the water's edge. It was the secret to a happiness that pervades Village India despite lack of material wealth or progress. To share these experiences with Indians living in America turned out to be great fun.

During the year Jim and I had been in Ecuador, I had discovered how much I love teaching. Standing before the class, sharing something that excited me, had been a great joy. I had known they would love the material because of how much I loved it. In the same way, I loved India. I loved all that India had given me. To stand before an audience and share what excited me was even more fun than teaching. I didn't have to worry about a lesson plan, keep notes of what I'd said so I could ask about it on an exam, or write legibly on a blackboard. I just had to speak from the heart.

Something precious happens when I speak publicly. It's deeply meditative for me, and I experience the presence of grace. I don't feel like the speaker; I feel more like a listener. That which is spoken seems to flow into me as well. It seems not to come *from* my mouth but, rather, to flow into my mouth from a well that I'm drinking from, too.

After San Diego and LA, we spent an evening in Bakersfield. I had lived in Southern California for twenty-five years, and it had never occurred to me to visit Bakersfield. As it turns out, Indians live there—many of them. There's even a large, ornate Hindu mandir. There, I gave my third public speech on the richness of Indian culture.

A year earlier, immersed in American culture, I had viewed foreign cultures as places for holidays, culinary treats, fresh mountain air, and linguistic affectations—adventures that included chocolate croissants with espresso, or hot melted-chocolate fondue served with fresh strawberries on the end of wooden sticks high in the Alps while goats and sheep nibbled at bushes nearby. Foreign cultures were things to adorn myself with, whether jewelry from the streets of Lausanne or sweaters knit in the mountain villages of Ecuador. I had been an avid traveler, but I had never really delved into the depths of other cultures.

Here I was, a curly-haired Californian, expert in the locations of every Whole Foods Market between Studio City and the Bay Area, yet so entrenched in Indian culture that I was giving talks on the importance of Indian Americans holding onto their heritage. "The most essential gift you can give your children," I urged, "is the gift of your culture, heritage, and roots. Nothing money can buy comes even close to the value of connecting to your ancient yet timeless tradition."

The dichotomy between Indians in India and Indians in America was poignant. The Indians in the United States, and particularly the younger generation, were trying to be American—too ready, I felt, to forsake their own heritage. I was saddened to see this, for it was Indian culture—the mesmerizing intoxication of the aarti and every nuance of ashram life that I felt had handed me the gift of deep peace. I wanted to help the Indian youth in America see the crucial thread between their roots and their own happiness.

So, I found myself draped in a green saree, standing before a crowd of 500 Indians in a Hindu mandir, urging them—with references to the Hindu epics of the Ramayana and the Mahabharata—to stay connected to their culture, to embody devotion to Hanuman in their own lives. And in Bakersfield, of all places.

I woke up the next morning with a smile on my face. *I'm in Bakersfield,* I said to myself as I laughed, realizing I was still sharing a body with an LA girl. By mid-morning, we were on the way to Alamo, east of San Francisco.

I drove up Interstate 5, windows closed, air conditioning gently blowing on low, cup holder containing a bottle of water, and devotional music playing from a single cassette Pujya Swamiji had with him. Swamiji and Kishore Vyasji, a renowned exponent of the epics, later to become Swami Govind Giriji, were asleep in the back. I lowered the volume to avoid waking them.

Interstate 5 runs north to south, dividing California in two as it runs through the Central Valley, a vast irrigated agricultural region that provides more than half the produce grown in the United States. The scenery stays pretty much the same for hundreds of miles—stick-straight rows blossoming with oranges, strawberries, and almonds in every direction.

As the fields blurred in my peripheral vision, I blinked to keep myself in the present moment. How many times had I made this drive from LA to Stanford and back? The trip always required a wide-open driver's-side window, out of which I'd blow cigarette smoke, plus cup holders full of icy Diet Coke, and a bag of candy to keep me going. James Taylor, Sting, or Cat Jimns would blare from the tape deck. I'd sing full throttle. The idea of a drive without constant stimulation was inconceivable. How would I stay awake? What would I do with myself while I drove if I wasn't extricating Jujyfruits from my teeth and keeping up with James Taylor at the same time?

Now, less than a year since I'd left the world of hyperstimulation, I drove stimulated by life itself and by the bewilderment at how my life had magically been changed. Was it really the same I-5? Was it the same "I"? It seemed familiar yet different, like déjà vu from a previous life.

I had graduated from Stanford exactly four years earlier, in June 1993. In those four years, I had gotten married and divorced. I had gone to India with a backpack and returned in a saree. I had successfully completed much of a PhD program from which I was now on a one-year leave. I had gone from needing sugary, artificially sweetened candy to being anchored in presence itself. The same highway, the same landmarks—but the driver of my car, and my life, had changed.

We spent July and August traveling through the United States and Canada, staying a day or a maximum of two days at each location. Each evening was a different venue—typically, a Hindu temple or community center filled to the gills with elegantly dressed Indians excited to have saints in their midst. Each program began with singing and ended with food. Sometimes a full dinner was served. Sometimes it was just crispy samosas and chai. Sometimes it was temple prasad, the blessed food given by the priests—trail mix or ghee-laden mush called halva. We never stayed for the food, as we took our meals at the homes of devotees with whom we stayed.

In Raleigh-Durham, Columbia, Knoxville, Nashville, Tampa, Louisville, and Lexington—cities I'd never dreamed of visiting—I was welcomed into the homes of Indians who had migrated to America. Each evening, after I gave my ten- or fifteen-minute talk, Swamiji and Kishore Vyasji would speak. Swamiji always began by chanting mantras, and they echoed through the hallways amid a pin-drop silence. Then he gave a lecture in a mix of English and various Indian languages.

I sat, melting into his words and his presence, as he encouraged everyone to live in peace, not pieces, to be better and not bitter. His method of teaching is so simple—connect with God, serve humanity, worship the Creator, serve the Creation, be grateful, be happy, and focus more on sanskaras than cars, more on your Self than your shelf.

Kishore Vyasji gave his talks in Hindi, and so I didn't understand, although I loved being in his presence. When we were alone or in small groups, he spoke to me in English, so I knew he could, but clearly, the Indians were happiest to hear their native tongues being spoken by these saints. "Always remember three things," Swamiji instructed. "Your mother, your motherland, and your mother tongue. A cow does not forget how to moo. A bird does not forget how to chirp. You should not forget your mother tongue."

I loved being part of a traveling religious troupe, seeing all the Hindu temples, and being places where people talked only about God and spirituality. I could now recognize which statues were Krishna, which were Rama, which were Shiva, and also which were Hanuman and Ganesh (the elephant-headed son of Shiva and the goddess Parvati). I prostrated before each in full devotion. Me, bowing to a statue—I couldn't believe it! But I did it because I was overwhelmed with gratitude and devotion.

Each marble or stone image I saw smiled at me. Each pair of eyes bore into my own. Krishna stood, flute in hand, poised elegantly on one foot, coaxing me to play. His eyes wouldn't let go till my heart was on the ground at His feet. "I love you," I whispered, as though our affair were a secret. My eyes spilled tears on the carpeted floors of temples across America.

Next to Krishna always stood Radha, the graceful epitome of devotion. In Vrindavan, in what is now Uttar Pradesh, where Krishna played in the stories of His youth, the greeting is "Radhe! Radhe!" It is said that Krishna loves His devotee Radha so much that he comes wherever she is, so people pray to Radha to appear so that Krishna will come. On a deeper level, it's not so much about her appearance as it is about our own ability to manifest, experience, know, and become her. So, in longing for the presence of Krishna, we must first *attain* or become Radha.

Radha, I would pray silently in each of these temples that had sprouted up in a country that no longer felt like my own, *"race me and bless me with devotion like yours. Let me be drowned in the beauty of love for God, as you are. Enter me, Radha. Become me. Let me become you."* Prostrating on the carpeted floors, I would raise my head and look at her eyes peering down. My chest grew as I took a breath—a bit of her was flowing into me.

My Beloved Hanuman. He is a brahmachari (literally, one moving forward on the path of Brahman, or one who knows Brahman—the ultimate supreme reality, though more colloquially used to mean "celibacy"); it is said that women are not supposed to touch even Hanuman's statue, but I couldn't help myself. Whenever I saw a statue of Hanuman—on one knee, hands in prayer at the feet of Lord Rama and Sita Ma, or standing brave and tall, his hands pulling his own chest open so all could behold the image of Rama and Sita within his heart—I had to touch him. I would sneak furtive glances behind me, lest the priest or another devotee was watching, and then, if the coast was clear, I'd reach out and touch his feet.

"O Hanuman," I'd pray, "please give me some of this devotion. Let the power of grace flow through me as well. Let me be as devoted as you. Let me be just a vehicle for the service of God. Come into me, Hanuman. Become me and let me become you." As I looked up from the ground, his face always seemed to be smiling down on me, even when it was just his profile as he knelt at the feet of his Lord. I could feel him saying, "Yes, yes, yes," a pulsing embrace. "Yes, I will come into you." And my chest would swell again as I breathed.

It was the feeling I'd had at the foot of redwood trees as my face rested in the rich, wet soil beneath them. It was the feeling I'd had lying on my back at the base of these trees, watching the refraction of the sun's rays through the interwoven lattice branches hundreds of feet up. "Yes, yes, come into me. Fill me with your light and grace, yes."

CHAPTER 28

Yosemite—Giving My Marriage to the Mountains

SUMMER 1997

I met Jim one afternoon that summer in Yosemite, an extraordinarily beautiful national park about four hours east of San Francisco. I hadn't seen him since our dinner together in February. We had come to Yosemite for our honeymoon four years earlier, a weeklong backpacking trip from which we had to return after the first night because a bear had eaten all our food and made off with our stove and gas cylinders. "A bear ate our honeymoon," we told our friends, without recognizing that it might have been a sign!

Our Dharma Yatra included an extra day in the Bay Area, during which Swamiji and Kishore Vyasji would be meeting with devotees, so I drove to Yosemite, where Jim and I spent an afternoon lying on a picnic blanket beside the creek. There was little to say. He cried, and I held him. I tried to access some sadness within me, wondering again where my tears were. The only sadness I felt was in his heart. I wished I could make it better.

We held hands and watched families playing in the water. As the sun began to drop behind the peaks, Jim put on his backpack. He would be trekking up into the mountains. I would drive back to Alamo, where I had to give a speech at the Hindu temple the next morning.

We drove together, my car following his to the parking lot at the trailhead. After a long hug—we didn't know when we would see each other again—he turned and began to hike up the trail, a trail we had trekked together several times during our years together. I watched him until his navy-blue backpack disappeared beyond a curve in the setting sun. Leaving my car in the lot, I crossed the road to the mountain's edge. The drop over the side was steep. Several hundred feet below, a river rumbled invisibly through the trees. There was a narrow dirt path on the edge of the road, alongside the rock wall that prevented cars or people from toppling over the side. I stood on the path, my hands on the wall, peering into the canyon as the last rays of sun sprinkled drops of dappled light on the leaves of the trees.

"O God," I prayed into the mountains and valley. "Please take care of him. Please wrap him in your arms and hold him. Touch him as deeply as you've touched me, or even more deeply. O God, please bring him joy and peace. Please take care of him." I looked up at the mountain rising above my head. Jim had disappeared into the setting sun. Then I looked again into the valley far below. "Please, God, please take care of him."

From the rumbling of the river, I felt a response. They weren't words, but an acceptance, an acknowledgment of my prayer. My voice had been heard, and the universe would take care of him. I felt the assurance spoken by the river and the trees. "Thank you," I said, and I exhaled deeply for the first time that day. "Thank you so much."

The first tears I shed at the ending of our marriage dropped onto that rock wall. "Thank you," I repeated into the deep green canyon. I pulled my wedding ring off my finger and held it tightly in my hands. "Thank you, God." And again, "Please, don't forget to take care of him. He is yours, as am I."

I held the ring until I could feel the mountains say "OK," until the mountain air expanded the space in my chest and dissolved the borders of my skin. I held the ring until I felt the entire Yosemite Valley, every sequoia, rock, and river, hold me, hold us. Without opening my eyes, I threw the ring into the canyon. "He is yours," I reminded God. "Please remember your promise."

I drove the four hours back to the Bay Area in silence, the sound of the river accompanying me as I drove. I arrived after 10 p.m., but the house was still abuzz with people. Pujya Swamiji had just retired to his room. "Sit, sit," the woman of the house instructed, "you're just in time for dinner."

I went to see Swamiji before he slept. He was sitting on a low cushion on the floor of his room, reading a book in Hindi with a picture of Lord Krishna on the cover. "Yes?" he said when I rose from bowing. I just smiled and exhaled deeply. He understood.

"Good," he said. "And how is Jim?"

"I think he will be OK," I answered slowly. I couldn't explain the assurance I'd received from the mountains, but fortunately, Swamiji didn't need the explanation.

"I will pray for him," he whispered into the night. "Leave it in God's hands now."

When I entered the temple the following morning and lay my head on the carpet in front of the images of God, I found a new spaciousness within me. There was more room in me now, it seemed, to be filled with Grace. I hadn't realized how much space a wedding ring occupies.

By the time we returned to India at the end of summer, I had begun to step into a new layer of experience—devotee, ecstatic servant of God, and public speaker. There weren't many opportunities to lecture English-speaking youth about the importance of Indian culture in India, though, so for a while, public speaking remained a part of my life only when we traveled abroad.

CHAPTER 29

"You're Going
Somewhere Beautiful"

JANUARY 1998

As my parents and I got into the car at Los Angeles International Airport, my mom called her voicemail to retrieve messages. There was one from the nurse at my grandmother's nursing home. "Sue, please call me right away," the message said. "It's about your mother." I had met my parents in London to spend a few days together over the Christmas holidays. We hadn't seen each other since the Dharma Yatra tour had left LA in July.

It was now ten months since I'd taken a one-year leave of absence from Stanford and nearly five months since I'd been back in India after the Dharma Yatra. I hadn't wanted to come back to America yet; I had planned just to see my parents in London. But I had to deal with my university status and tend to my belongings in storage.

I knew when I first took the leave of absence that it was a ruse to ease into the truth that I was moving to India. Keeping up the myth of moving back to California felt like a comedy routine in which a man is standing with one foot on a dock and the other on a boat, and the boat starts to drift to sea. Inattentively straddling the dock and the drifting boat, he ends up in the water. I couldn't keep one foot in California and the other in India without eventually falling into the ocean of my own consciousness. I had to take my foot off the dock and put it into the sailing boat, so I planned to drive to the Bay Area to empty out my storage unit. It made no sense to keep paying monthly rent to store items I wasn't coming back to.

My mom picked up her car phone (at that time, she had one of those phones that attached to the console between the front seats) and called the nursing home. "We're coming now," she said and hung up. Grandma was in a coma, and they said she likely wouldn't live for more than a few days.

We drove together down to Laguna Hills in what was by our internal clocks, still on British time, the middle of the night. My mom had been diagnosed with virulent breast cancer a few months earlier and had undergone aggressive chemo and radiation that autumn. Now her mom was dying. My grandmother had been dying for several years, it seemed. She had had colon cancer, then two or three heart attacks, each leaving her weaker and weaker. Despite her failing body, however, her mind had remained sharp, and she had refused to loosen her clenched grip of control. The story is still told today of how she corrected the nurses on one wrong digit of her Social Security number while being wheeled into surgery.

Now, she lay in bed, all but her face covered with a white sheet, her thin, gray hair pulled away from her face, her eyes closed and her head drooping loosely onto the right side. The nurses gave us the details of her lapse into incoherency. We stood silent, each of us reaching out to touch a part of her through the sheet.

"You should get home," I told my parents after we'd stood for a while at my grandmother's bedside. "I'll stay with Grandma."

"There's no need," the nurse said. "There is nothing she needs, nothing to be done. She probably won't wake from the coma." We stood over my grandma's bed, her already tiny frame appearing to disappear beneath the sheet. She seemed to be in a deep sleep.

"I want to stay," I told the nurse. "Can I?" After unsuccessful attempts to convince me that I didn't really want to stay, they made arrangements for me to sleep in a room across the hallway. After my parents left, I closed the door to my grandma's room and crawled into bed with her. The hospital bed was large and her frame was tiny. I got in on the far side of her bed, away from the door, so it might not be so obvious should someone look through the window of her room. My grandmother was on her back, and her head dropped away from me. I reached out and stroked her face, pulling soft gray hairs off her forehead and smoothing them back with my palm.

"It's OK, Grandma. Don't be afraid. Where you're going is beautiful. You will not disappear into nothingness. I promise. You're just going to be without the pain of this body. You will still be here. Nothing is happening to *you*. It's just happening to this old and sick body. Please don't worry. I promise where you're going is really, really beautiful."

I spoke from a place in me I didn't know existed. Since when was I so sure? How did I know? The "I" with which I identified didn't know. Yet there was an absolute *Knowing*, and the Knowing spoke. The Knowing resided within me, although it didn't feel like "me." Slowly, over the years, this Knowing would begin, gently and almost imperceptibly, to take over my identity, like an unevictable tenant slowly occupies one apartment and then, day by day, all other units as well.

I kissed her face. Her skin felt like delicate sheets of lace beneath my lips. My grandmother had been mostly touch-averse. She loved deeply and fully but did not express her love through physical contact. I am not sure if she had lived behind this wall of protection while still married to my grandfather or whether she had constructed the wall after he had left her for a woman my mother's age. Either way, she was not a cuddler.

I was always a hugger, though. As I was growing up, I would come into our living room, where Grandma was knitting one of her intricate argyle sweaters or afghans, the patterns of which she solved mathematically in equations beyond the capacity of my schoolteachers. I'd leap onto her lap from behind or from the side, throwing my arms around her neck and planting kiss after kiss on her face. "Enough, enough," she'd say as she pushed me away lovingly. "Enough, enough." But that night, she just lay there and let me kiss her.

I chanted Sanskrit mantras for her, the few that I knew, the ones we sang in morning prayers and the evening aarti, over and over:

Om Sarve Bhavantu Sukhinah

Sarve Santu Nir-Aamayaah

Sarve Bhadraanni Pashyantu

Maa Kashcid-Duhkha-Bhaag-Bhavet

(May all beings be happy. May all beings be healthy. May all experience that which is auspicious.
May no one suffer.)

Om Tryamlakam Yajamahe Sugandhim Pusti—vardhanam

Urva—rukamiva Bandhanan Mrtyor—muksheeya Ma—amritat

(O Lord, who sees not only with the two physical eyes,
but He who sees with the third, divine eye, O Lord who
sustains and nourishes the world, O Lord, please release
me from the bondage of disease and death and grant me
divine immortality. Let me become One with You so that
I am free from the disease and death of this world.)

I rested on my side, next to her, my right hand on her head and my left hand on her leg as I mixed mantras with wet kisses.

Suddenly, my grandma turned her head toward me with her lips puckered up. None of the rest of her body moved, and her eyes did not open. Her puckered lips led the way and carried the rest of her head a full 180 degrees to her left side, where I lay. After more than an hour of stroking, kissing, and singing to a body whose life force was departing, I was face to face with a pair of plump, eager, puckered lips! I gave her a big kiss, moistening her dry lips with my tears, and a few moments later, her head returned whence it had come, again hanging limply on her right side. She never moved again before passing away the next afternoon.

"She waited for you to come home," my mom told me as we drove together back to Los Angeles. "She waited to say goodbye." I believe that, but not for sentimental reasons. I do not think my grandmother waited for a hug or a kiss.

I do not believe she waited to hear my voice or to "see" me one last time without opening her eyes. I do not believe she waited to say goodbye. Rather, I believe she waited because she needed to hear what only I could tell her—that it was OK to let go.

American Jewish culture, and particularly the American Jewish upper-class and upper-middle-class culture—and, even more particularly, the culture of my family—has perfected the art of control. We're micromanagement experts. There is a right way and a wrong way to load the dishwasher. At 6:45 p.m., it is already late for a 7 p.m. engagement. The ringing phone in the middle of the night is the police calling to tell you that your child is dead. The sky is falling. Some of this anxiety stems from a very real and deeply serious history of persecution. The sky did fall on the Jews.

However, the science of anxiety perfected by many American Jews is one that tragically kills us psychologically long before the things we fear kill us physically. I'm not sure about the horse/cart sequencing of American Jewish anxiety and whether it is caused by or simply coexists with a history of persecution. It is, however, very common. As there is usually no tangible, specific threat in our daily lives, the anxiety in my family and many other people I know gets projected onto the nearly absurd: The grocery store is out of what we want; we're late for an appointment; the person we're supposed to meet is late; there's unexpected traffic on the freeway; the neighbor's dog is barking and keeping us awake. We grasp desperately for a semblance of control over our immediate world and everything that gets eaten, drunk, purchased, worn, or said within it. It is a sincere, albeit misplaced, attempt to not have to feel our own deep fear 24/7.

My grandmother was a master at the fervent attempt to control the uncontrollable, to know the unknowable by holding tenaciously to each thread in the tapestry of her own life. She was brilliant, and, at a time when only 3 percent of women completed college and barely 20 percent entered the workforce, she got two master's degrees and started her own business. We used to joke that we'd be billionaires if only Grandma would be a contestant on *Jeopardy*. She knew every single answer to every question, and the ignorance of the contestants drove her crazy. "Oy vey!" I would hear her say from the living room as I did my homework upstairs. "They are idiots! Doesn't anyone know anything anymore?"

In the nearly ninety years of her life, she taught herself to succeed, thrive, and then survive when Grandpa left her. She was a warrior, a woman I never saw cry even once. But she didn't know how to let go. How could she let go of things she had spent almost ninety years holding together? How could she relinquish control after holding tightly for so many decades? How could she loosen the vise grip and breathe into the universe?

This is, of course, an affliction that not only burdened my grandmother, that not only burdens Jews in America, but burdens most Americans as well. We cling tightly to things we believe we can control in order to minimize our anxiety over the things we know we can't control. Unfortunately, this technique doesn't work. Controlling my weight or my spouse's driving or how the dishwasher is loaded does not resolve our fear of loss and change. Amassing great wealth or fame or beauty or trophy partners cannot overcome the fear of ego-self dissolving.

Nonsolutions though they may be, we all pursue them. We build security towers in our castle of the self, while the whole thing sits on shifting sand—to be called back into the ocean with the next incoming tide.

So, all my grandmother needed to hear was something I had to go to India to learn: It's OK to let go. Where we are going is beautiful. Nothing will happen to the true Self. It is only the old, ill, or broken body that is changing. She needed me to sing her clenched fist open, to kiss her as she let go of her death grip on the threads of life. I closed my eyes as my mom drove up the 405 back to LA, and gave thanks for the Knowing that had come to reside in the complex of myself, and that spoke through me to my grandmother.

She had insisted that there be no funeral. She didn't want to be buried. She didn't want people to come and cry over her grave or feel guilty for not coming. She wanted to be cremated. Scriptural injunctions, augmented by visceral memories of the Holocaust, have made cremation anathema in Jewish culture, but my grandmother wanted to be cremated.

When we got her ashes back from the crematorium, I prepared them in a box to carry with me back to India to offer to the waters of the Ganga River. In a special ceremony, my grandmother would, finally, with assistance from the goddess Ganga, be free.

After the cremation, I went to the Bay Area and emptied my storage unit. I sold almost everything I owned, gave away most of the rest, and drove back to LA with the remaining possessions in the back seat of my Honda, with plenty of room for me to see out the rearview mirror. I sang at the top of my lungs along with Cat Jinns one minute and along with Hindu devotional singers the next.

I returned to Los Angeles for the two final days of sitting shiva (a weeklong period of mourning in the Jewish tradition, not connected to Lord Shiva in Hinduism). When her yahrzeit candle finished burning in our living room, I returned home to India, carrying her ashes.

Pujya Swamiji and I decided that the best date to immerse Grandma's ashes in Ganga would be Maha Shivaratri, the day dedicated to worship of Lord Shiva. In Hindu tradition, Shiva is the Destroyer, but not a destroyer in the negative sense of razing all that is good. Rather, Shiva destroys, dissolves, and dissipates to make room for the new creation of Lord Brahma. On Maha Shivaratri, devotees stay awake all night with prayers that Shiva should remove from them all that is keeping them from enlightenment, all that is blocking and thwarting their path. It is, next to Krishna Janmashtami (the birthday of Lord Krishna) and Diwali, probably the holiest day of the Hindu calendar.

In February, the river Ganga runs low. Mountain glaciers are frozen and the weather is dry. Without rain or melting glaciers, the flow is calm and relatively shallow compared to the fullness of her movement in summer, when she overflows her banks.

Typically in the winter months, the riverfront was flanked by fifty to a hundred feet of rocks. One had to walk far out onto the rocks just to touch water. However in 1998, unseasonal rain began the day before Shivaratri and didn't let up until late that afternoon, by which time Ganga had risen, submerging the rocks and touching the foot of our marble platform. "She came for your grandmother," Swamiji said with a smile.

I walked down the steps to the riverbank, holding most of my grandma's ashes in a bronze *kalash*, or pot. The rest sat in the original box from the crematorium in my closet at my parents' house, adorned with my own necklaces as substitutes for flower garlands. We decided to keep some of her ashes in case any of the other family members later felt that they wanted them. In the twenty-plus years since, no one has. Still, today, Grandma's remaining ashes occupy a special place in my closet, my faux-amethyst necklace draped adoringly over the brown box.

I walked alone, holding Grandma with both hands, careful not to trip, lest she fall out of the pot. A group of yellow-clad young priests joined me and chanted the appropriate Sanskrit mantras. The ceremony had to be official, I felt, and it wouldn't be without the proper chanting of Sanskrit mantras.

In the last year, Grandma had asked me endlessly, "Why India? Why not Israel? You can find a good rabbi in Israel." Thus, the irony of sending her off into eternity in a Vedic ceremony wasn't lost on me. But it felt important. It was the only way I knew to properly honor her life and her death. "I love you, Grandma," I whispered as I knelt and poured her ashes into the flowing river. "Ganga has come to take you. It will all be so beautiful for you. I promise."

I rose from the banks of the river and, following the compulsory shower and hair wash after coming into contact with ashes, served dinner to the saints and priests in the dining hall. Walking up and down the long rows, I respectfully put a red tilak, the Hindus' ornamental red spot, on their foreheads, between the eyebrows, and handed each fifty rupees.

According to Hindu tradition, feeding religious people is considered not just a generous act but also an auspicious one, particularly in memory of a loved one. I smiled to myself and shared a private laugh with my grandma as I bent low and handed round, sweet balls of flour, sugar, and ghee called ladoos to the saints. *I bet you never imagined this! A send-off with lots of food!*

My grandma had been on strict diets as long as I had known her. Rice cakes, chicken broth, Bieler's broth (a nauseating, nearly calorieless soup made from blended string beans and zucchini), and other inedibles constituted her food intake for the last decades of her life as she tried fervently but unsuccessfully to rid herself of a few unwanted pounds.

All the saints and priests, draped in orange, white, and yellow robes, offered a prayer for my grandmother as I bent to serve them.

Later that night, when I left my office to go back to my room, I went back to Ganga to say thank you. In the few short hours since the ceremony, she had receded into the middle of the riverbed, exposing a hundred feet of rocks between the water and our ghat.

CHAPTER 30

Lessons of a
Tibetan Pilgrimage

In June 1998, we were in Kathmandu, heading to the sacred Mount Kailash, a 22,000-foot peak towering above the high Tibetan Plateau. Mount Kailash is said to be the home of Lord Shiva and His divine consort, Parvati. Circumambulating the mountain by foot, a treacherous thirty-two-mile journey, usually takes three days, but we did it in two. It's a pilgrimage that adherents of Hindu, Buddhist, and Bon-Po traditions believe absolves the participant of lifetimes of sin.

Now, more than twenty years later, the Chinese government has developed the route to Mount Kailash and the sacred Lake Mansarovar, a crystal-clear freshwater lake at a 15,000-foot elevation that is believed to have flowed from Lord Brahma's mind. There are asphalt roads nicer than any in America, marked by drainage every hundred yards or so. Proper bridges now span the rushing rivers, tributaries of the Brahmaputra and the Ganga, and gas stations, restaurants, and hotels have sprung up from soil more friendly to tourism than agriculture. But in 1998, when we were there, there were no bridges or roads, or places to buy gasoline or bottled water.

We arrived at Lake Mansarovar from Nepal in a caravan of Range Rovers, plowing across the barren, roadless land. I was lucky to enter Kathmandu at all, as my passport and I had arrived separately. In order to travel to Mount Kailash and Lake Mansarovar, one had to be part of a tour group and obtain a group visa to Tibet. Mainland China visas are not sufficient for travel in Tibet, nor could individuals receive a Tibet visa. Nepal-based travel companies that specialize in group tours process all passports together for the Tibetan permits.

Indians don't require visas or passports to enter Nepal. A driver's license or other photo ID is sufficient. Hence, our tour organizers, to save time, sent everyone's passports in advance to Kathmandu so our Chinese and Tibetan visas could be processed and ready by the time we arrived. They overlooked the fact that there was an American citizen ostensibly subject to different rules and regulations than the 200 Indians I was traveling with.

On the day we departed, I asked the organizer for my passport. "You'll get it tomorrow at the hotel," he said. "How am I supposed to travel without it?" I asked. His face fell. "Oh, no!" he exclaimed. "We forgot you are American and need your passport to enter Nepal. We'll think of something."

That "something" was to have me go through the Nepali immigration queue in a thickly packed group of Indians who merely waved driver's licenses and voter ID cards in the faces of disinterested immigration officials. Whether a hundred IDs were shown for a hundred people or not, no one noticed. A group passed through; some ID cards were held in the air. No one even looked at me. The thrill of committing an international felony surrounded and protected by my new family was exhilarating.

Two days later, we left Kathmandu at sunrise, led by three masters: Pujya Swamiji; Pujya Swami Gurusharananandji Maharaj, a revered and renowned saint from Mathura, the birthplace of Lord Krishna; and Pujya Sant Shri Rameshbhai Oza (also known as Pujya Bhaishri), a world-famous *kathakar*, one who delivers, over a period of seven or nine days, a devotional rendition of the holy epics of Hinduism—the Srimad Bhagavatam, the Mahabharata, or the Ramayana. In their company, we were a village of more than fifty Range Rovers, four trucks filled with tents, food, and water, and two tankers of gasoline, as there would be no place for more than 300 miles to refuel.

We traveled through the lush Himalayas from Kathmandu to Nyalam at the border of Nepal and Tibet, then from Nyalam to Saga, a Chinese military town where photography of any sort was prohibited. In Nyalam, rows of holes in the ground served as toilets. There were neither walls nor doors separating one from the other. Pujya Swamiji joked about "toilet conferencing."

In Saga, we slept in the deserted rooms of a military compound on the hard, cold cement floor, fitting together like pieces of a jigsaw puzzle beneath two raised cots given to Pujya Swamiji and Pujya Bhaishri. Icy winds blew in all night through shattered glass windows, and, wearing all of the clothes we'd packed, we huddled into our sleeping bags.

On our second evening in Saga, I went into the room of Swami Gurusharananandji Maharaj, with whom I'd fallen completely in love. Maharajji, as everyone calls him, was the mother of my dreams, the one in whose lap you just want to sit forever while he gently strokes your hair. From his eyes flowed a divine motherly love that embraced all his glance fell upon. I tried to position myself in his field of vision as much as I could, and each time our eyes met, I felt I was being reborn, resuckled, and reparented.

"Ao, beta" (Come, child), Maharajji said as I entered. "He sat on his cot, propped up with pillows carried from India, with a cup of hot soup in his hands. His disciples had found some cardboard and newspaper to cover the holes in his glass windows, so only sunlight streamed in and onto the long, white beard flowing from his chin to the middle of his chest.

I sat on the cement floor near the bed and lay my head on his soft blanket. He gently and rhythmically patted the side of my face as though I were an infant he was putting to sleep. After a few minutes, he spoke. "Beta," he said as I lifted my head, "how much soup is too much soup?"

I wasn't sure I'd heard him properly, as I was still swimming in the effects of his touch. "Ji, Maharajji?" (Yes, Maharajji?) I asked.

"I said, how much soup is too much soup?" I had no answer—and wasn't even sure I had understood the question. There was, of course, no such thing as too much soup.

"Beta, I have had three cups of soup. Do you think that is too much, or do you think I might be able to have another cup of soup?" Suddenly, I realized that in the midst of pouring forth divine love, he was asking me a logistic and pragmatic question to which he actually wanted an answer.

"Maharajji, I think you can have as much soup as you want," I cooed in response. Truly, what was a bit of extra soup in the presence of an ocean of love?

"OK," he said matter-of-factly, "then tell them to give me another cup—if, of course, you think it is not too much."

It was years before I fully realized the depth of what had happened in that room. It wasn't a Zen-like koan about soup that needed deciphering. Rather, it was a realistic question about the physical body asked by one who lives not in the body, but in the soul. It was the equivalent of me asking a gas station attendant, "Is there a difference between the 87, 90, and 92 octane grades? Isn't the 87 just as good, and cheaper?" Maharajji, in complete identification with the Soul, the Divine Self, was actually asking me about the working of this vehicle: How much soup is too much soup? What is the right grade of gas?

After two days in Saga for high-altitude acclimatization, we departed for Paryang, the last stop before reaching the crystal waters of Lake Mansarovar, nearly three miles above sea level. The guesthouse we stayed in was a series of mud-walled, mud-floored rooms with no doors. The walls and roofs kept out rain and snow but did little to insulate us from the icy winds that filled our lungs with air but little oxygen. Breathing—something I had always taken for granted—suddenly became a gift to which I clung on this high-altitude plateau.

The dearth of doors brought not only wind but other guests as well. In the morning, I opened my eyes to a group of Tibetan children standing in our doorway, pushing each other out of the way to squeeze to the front. When I made eye contact with them, they started poking themselves in the middle of their foreheads.

"What are they doing?" I asked the woman lying next to me, whose eyes had also just opened. "I have no idea," she said. "I wonder what they want." We had heard that the children ask for pens, so we'd brought bags of pens and packs of cookies and other treats.

"Pen? Pen?" I asked and mimed someone writing. They shook their heads feverishly and kept poking themselves in the forehead. Suddenly, one of them leaped through the doorway and onto the sleeping bag of a woman who was applying a bindi with her hand mirror. She had peeled off one of the thin, round, red circles from a sheet of about twenty and was gingerly sticking it between her eyebrows as the young boy motioned excitedly toward the rest of her pack.

She looked up at him, and again he began poking himself between his eyes and then pointing at the pack of round, red, sticky bindis. "Oh, you want a bindi?" she asked incredulously, and we all watched in awe.

She peeled off another and stretched her hand out to him. He grabbed the bindi from her finger and immediately stuck it on his forehead. Without the aid of the woman's hand mirror, it wasn't quite in the center, but it seemed he found it satisfactory. The rest of the kids piled into our makeshift room and, traipsing over those still sleeping, made a beeline for the woman with the bindis.

Within a few minutes, they all had bright red circles between their eyebrows at the agya chakra, or third-eye center. (Hindus apply the tilak or kumkum [vermilion powder] or bindi sticker as a reminder that we must use our third eye rather than our two physical eyes to see the world. As Pujya Swamiji explains, "These two eyes are the cause of all our problems. Everything we see makes us angry or jealous or greedy. So, we apply tilak to remind ourselves to use the third eye, the inner divine eye, the eye that sees not separation but oneness, not objects but essence.")

Why these young Tibetans wanted bindis is something I still don't know. It touched me deeply, though, because they are not Hindu or Indian and probably don't know anything about the connection of this red sticker to the opening of the third eye. But there are things that transcend religion, that know no borders or boundaries. There are practices that are rooted in a truth beyond teachings, so the truth is apparent even in the absence of the teachings. Tilak and bindis seem to be one of these practices.

I have low blood pressure. It's not dangerously low, but new doctors always check it twice until I assure them, "Don't worry. It's always low." I suffer no ramifications of this in my life other than needing to keep my head down a bit longer than most when coming out of headstands or backbends while doing yoga. If I come back to the upright position too quickly, I get a head rush.

The only other occasion that this impacts my life is high-altitude trekking. When I trekked in the mountains of the United States or Europe, or in Ecuador, I knew that I could go to about 12,500 feet before beginning to hallucinate. Once, while hiking in the mountains around Baños, a few hours south of Quito, Jim and I walked a bit higher than that and the trees started gesticulating to me. The lack of oxygen at high altitude, coupled with already low blood pressure, turns lush mountaintops into my own dizzying *Little Shop of Horrors.*

Lake Mansarovar sits at more than 15,000 feet. The trek around Mount Kailash begins at Ashtaput, crosses through Dirapuk at about 17,000 feet, and finally crosses the Dolma La Pass at nearly 20,000 feet before descending to Zuthulpuk and finally back to Darchen. I had told Pujya Swamiji in advance that I likely would not be able to make it all the way due to the altitude.

"No problem," he said. "We'll send a vehicle back with you, and you can wait in Kathmandu or return to India. Just come for as long as you feel comfortable, and the moment you don't feel well, let me know."

That moment never came. Maharajji's question about soup symbolized the distinction between vehicle and driver, between body and the soul. These saints live as their souls, not as their bodies. That grace was somehow contagious, and I stayed near enough to them to catch it.

On future trips, I learned about Diamox, a medicine that mitigates the effect of altitude and is recommended by doctors for people going to high altitudes. However, on this journey, I knew nothing about it, only that I was carried by One for whom altitude is irrelevant. I was blessed to rely not on my own legs and lungs, but on the arms of the Divine, in which I rested easily, to carry me.

Here are some excerpts from the journal I kept on yatra:

> *Here on yatra, looking out over the incredible mountains, stretching out as far as you can either see or imagine—reducing you, your van, your entire life into nothing more than a grain of sand, blowing by the side of the road. The mind, eyes, ears, and senses just dissolve into thin air, burning one minute and freezing the next.*

> *"We're on yatra" is the motto, making anything else seem like superfluous gibberish. Even my fears, tears, etc., dissipate into the clouds as they embrace the mountaintops, obscuring from our view the true height of their majesty.*

> *The quiet—of my tongue, of my mind. The voices around me just swirling above me, to my sides, but unable to penetrate inside to disturb the incredible stillness.*

"We're on yatra." Yatra to what? From what? Yatra from a life of petty concerns, overestimated needs, empty words, excessive reliance on others, and external focus. Yatra to a mountain that will make us realize the simultaneous nothingness and everythingness of our beings. Nothingness: the futility of our attempts to exercise control and power, for who could so much as leave a lasting footprint on the sands of Shiva's mountain? The superfluity of our endless obtainment of material possessions . . . who could carry a mansion to Lord Shiva's feet? We can barely carry our bodies. The irrelevance of the concerns that saturate our daily life . . . now, it is simply a matter of food, water, sufficient oxygen, and a prayer against rain.

Yet, with this ego-annihilating nothingness, there is a simultaneous ecstatic realization of our oneness with the sands of which the mountain is made, of our inextricable link to the glorious height of the mountain—why else would we be so compelled to come, in the face of such hardship—of our brotherhood with the never-washed faces and empty bellies of the people whose lives begin and end in this vast sea of simultaneous emptiness and overflowing abundance.

Car rides, through roads that aren't. How do they know how to go over so many miles of open space? Do they have a sort of homing instinct? Simply driven to Lord Shiva?

Finally, after days of endless driving, roads winding on and on, we suddenly come upon a view that can only be the grace of God. The sand-and-tumbleweed landscape suddenly gives way to a lake of majestic proportion—crystal clear, tinged with purple and blue hues as the evening sun casts its last rays upon the waters. The lake seems a mirage—a vast pool of lush beauty in this arid land, a gift sent from Heaven as we get closer to the abode of God.

We are, at the moment, at the peak of a high hill, almost a gentle cliff of sorts. The lake was a sudden gift as we ascended, as though we were granted a divine vision simultaneously. The sun is setting on the far shore, casting a brilliant halo around the lake as well as filling the lower sky with wisps of gold.

We are a fleet of Range Rovers, and suddenly we all stop; no one needed to coordinate it. We silently emerge from the vehicles, pulled by a strength and power in the presence of which we are helpless. Some immediately fall to the ground in pranam; others simply gaze into the divine sight. I burst into tears which quickly become sobs, as though wresting parts of my heart from me I didn't even know were there.

I wasn't expecting to be affected in this way. A beautiful lake, beautiful mountains, invigorating hiking, the joy of being on Mother Earth's territory. That was my expectation. Yet, here I am, brought to my knees as I shake with emotion in front of a God I am not supposed to worship. The power of the experience eclipsed any last hold that teachings from Sunday school and synagogue against the manifest presence of God may have had on me.

I fall in pranam at Swamiji's feet, my tears unstoppable. If I could just stay there, forever, at the feet of the man who has done this to my soul . . . . I look back and forth: his face, glowing in the light of the setting sun; the holy waters of this lake formed of Brahma's mind; the distant towering peak of Mt. Kailash, the most sacred of mountains, upon whose peak Lord Shiva resides. Back and forth—Swamiji, the lake, the mountain. It's as though they've merged together into one indivisible, consuming presence of God. I can't meet his eyes; it's too much for me. What will happen if I look into the eye of God? I am too overwhelmed to find out.

When all the Range Rovers arrive, we all instinctively fall to pranam at the lake, the mountain, and our leaders who have brought both our bodies and our souls to God and gather into a semicircle of prayer, with Maharajji, Swamiji, and Bhaishri in the center, facing the lake but clearly seeing beyond it.

A true yatra, a true pilgrimage, a true journey to God. We forsake sleep, food, warmth, comfort in this quest to truly see, feel, and experience God in His holiest manifestation. What are we willing to endure? Ten-hour rides over dirt mountains and through rivers in which our Range Rovers get stuck? Nights without sleeping gear, days without food. Although I say endure, it isn't endurance. Endurance implies a struggle, a battle, a conquest. This is a stillness in the mind, a peace in the heart, and a joy in the soul untouched by struggle or endurance. It's more like separate realities coexisting—one in which we're cold, hungry, exhausted, and feverish, and another in which we simply are . . . . We just sit, walk, and pray in God's land.

Sometimes, on occasion, the first world penetrates the second, but only momentarily. Then, we complain or whine. But just like a wave that seems so big for a split second and then becomes soft white water on the beach, these momentary waves leave no lasting impact on the peacefulness and joy of existence.

It is a true yatra; we are stripped to the core of ourselves and left bare for God. A land with no beginning and no end—the mountains following each other religiously.

This part of my journal describes our trek around Mount Kailash:

A day that has lasted close to fourteen hours—fourteen straight hours of trekking under Shiva's protecting glance; clothes that come off and go on as the weather randomly and radically changes from scorching summer heat to bone-chilling winter winds. Then, a trek up to 22,000 feet—the highest pass (following two other high passes today). We go a few feet, stop, drink water. We offer each other food no one wants. We sit in silence—words defy the experience—and take too much valuable oxygen.

The rain comes, pouring down on us, first in drips, then in sheets. Then, as quickly as it came, it disappears—leaving a sky filled with dark clouds, each lined by the ever-present sun streaming between them. The clouds become lighter, wispier, mistier. As we sit, on the top of the world, peering through the bright mist that envelops the mountains as well as the sky, it seems we are truly sitting in Heaven.

We sit in Shiva's abode, looking down to a ground that cannot be seen, looking up to His mountain. He offers us momentary glances, then covers Himself again in the curtain of clouds. Although the peak of His abode is only visible at times of special grace, His presence is felt continuously.

I had been wanting a new name since a few months after my arrival in India. There was nothing wrong, of course, with my old name, and taking a new name never occurred to me before coming to India. But once I had the inner transformation, it seemed to require a new name. I wasn't the same person who had arrived in India. I needed a new name to mark the new experience.

A woman living at Parmarth nicknamed me Radha, after the sincerest, closest devotee of Lord Krishna. Other devotees named me Priya (the sweet, loved one). I was temporarily named Shakti (divine power), a name I chose because it was one of the only Sanskrit words I knew that was related to women and because the idea of being the embodiment of power—sometimes gentle and sometimes fierce—appealed to me.

"That's not a name," Pujya Swamiji told me. "No one is named Shakti. You can be Shanti, which is 'peace.'" But I didn't want to be peace. I wanted to be power!

So, depending on who I was speaking to, I was either Radha or Priya or Shakti.

The first time I met Swami Gurusharanandji Maharaj was in fall 1996, on the pilgrimage through the sacred area of Vraj. The evening after we had completed the thirteen-mile walk around Govardhan Hill, I bowed in pranam at his feet as he walked out of his room. "Pranam, Bhagawati," he said as he walked by with his hand outstretched in blessing. I had no idea what *Bhagawati* meant, but in that moment, it was the most beautiful word I'd ever heard. I filed that moment away in a corner of my mind and heart.

Now, as our caravan of Range Rovers parked on the ridge overlooking Lake Mansarovar, I told Pujya Swamiji I wanted a new name, not just a nickname or a name chosen by random devotees or a name I had picked because I thought it was cool. I wanted a real name that I could wrap around me as the cloth of my new being. So he spoke with Maharajji and Bhaishri and decided that the three of them would give me the name together. They gave me a few options to choose from—nice names, but none felt exactly right.

In that moment, the experience with Maharajji opened up in the corner of my mind and heart. "Maharajji," I said, "When I first met you, you called me 'Bhagawati.' What does that mean? Is that a name?" He smiled. "Ahh, yes, Bhagawati."

Pujya Swamiji explained. "It means 'the Divine One.' Do you like that name? If you like it, it is perfect."

"Yes," Maharajji spoke again, from a deep meditative state. "Yes. Bhagawati."

So, with our gaze filled by the lake that sprung from Brahma's mind, with the mountain home of Lord Shiva and goddess Parvati towering over us in the thin air of the Tibetan Plateau, I was given the name Bhagawati. I wore it as a shawl draped around me, a new cloth in which I could be cocooned, wrapped, and protected while my former self liquified and re-formed.

For me, it was not just a name. It was an official solidifying of a change that was taking place internally. I was no longer the name of my childhood. My identity was no longer the one given by my mother and Manny. It was the one given here, in the home of Lord Shiva, by the three saints.

I had been through a name change before. At the age of nineteen, after Manny had paid off the lump sum of half of my remaining college-tuition expenses, and after I had to sign away any legal right I might ever have to anything that was his, Frank legally adopted me.

Although Frank had been my "dad" since nearly the day he and my mom had started dating when I was seven, there is something very important about ritual. As I stood in the courthouse in Los Angeles, dressed up for this special occasion, Frank and I each signed the legal adoption certificate. Yes, I accepted and welcomed this man as my father. Yes, he accepted and welcomed me as his daughter. I took his last name legally as quickly as I could, eager to erase any vestige of identification with Manny.

When Jim and I married, I did not take his last name. "I just changed my last name a few years ago," I said. I wasn't ready to change it again.

So, I already knew the power of a name change to effect, solidify, and legitimize a change in identity. When I became Frank's daughter instead of Manny's, I began the journey from an identity as one who was abused and abandoned to an identity as one who was chosen and embraced.

The change to Bhagawati was another shift—from an identity given by my mother, named after a character in her favorite novel, to a woman, a divine woman who was the embodiment of the Mother Goddess.

I opened the door of the white Range Rover, an unlikely venue for the exclusive and special name-giving ceremony, and—careful not to turn my back on the saints—stepped out onto the hard ground. I walked into my new name eagerly, knowing it formed the identity into which I would grow.

On the final day of the pilgrimage, our vehicles descended into greenery as we reentered Nepal. The wet, green vines reached out toward us from the mountains along the road. Suddenly, a hot shower sounded heavenly. Other than soaking in the mineral springs at Chiu Gompa, the monastery above Lake Mansarovar, I had not bathed in almost two weeks. Pujya Swamiji's daily sprinkling of water over my head with purificatory Vedic mantras served for me to remain "pure," but I certainly wasn't clean.

We arrived back at the hotel midafternoon and had a special aarti scheduled that evening. The Bagmati River flows through Kathmandu, right outside the famous Pashupatinath Temple. Pujya Swamiji had decided we would start the Ganga aarti on the Bagmati River.

Ever since Pujya Swamiji had left his family to meditate in the forests in his early childhood, nature has been his mother. When he came to Rishikesh at the age of seventeen, after nearly a decade of silence and intense spiritual practice in the forests, jungles, and Himalayan mountains, Ganga became his mother. He has worked since the early 1970s to keep the banks of the holy river clean. When basic advocacy campaigns didn't work as well as he had hoped, he turned the rocky shores of Ganga into a beautiful marble ghat, or platform, and instituted daily worship ceremonies on the ghat. He knew that no one would poop in the morning where they pray in the evening, so he began the evening Ganga aarti at Parmarth Niketan as a way to rekindle people's reverence for the river and transform Her banks from being a toilet and trash can to being a temple.

In the decades since, as Ganga's pollution has become even more dire, he has started the Ganga aarti in Varanasi, Allahabad, Kanpur, Badrinath, Rudraprayag, Gangotri, and many other places. When the group went for darshan at the Pashupatinath Temple in Kathmandu before traveling to Mount Kailash and Lake Mansarovar, Pujya Swamiji noticed the trash on the banks of the Bagmati. "When we return from Kailash, we will have Bagmati Ganga aarti here and inspire people to keep Her banks clean and green," he said.

I wasn't with him at the time, though; as a white person, I wasn't permitted to enter the Pashupatinath Temple. The temple rules say they permit only Hindus, but after an entertaining debate with the guard, it became clear that the rule is "Only people with brown skin." No one checks religion. No one checks passports to determine place of birth. No one checks race—are you Indian, Pakistani, Sri Lankan, Brazilian, Latino, or Puerto Rican? No one cares, as long as your skin is brown. Placing me in the midst a large group of Indians worked to slip me into the country, but not into the temple.

"Her!" the guard shouted as the amoebic mass of our group pushed through the gate, hiding me from view, my head covered with a scarf and eyes to the ground. "Her! She is not allowed!" the guard bellowed. I wondered what training they'd undergone to learn to smell white skin. The guard's position was ridiculous. We grilled him with questions that began, "Well, what about . . . ," but he never wavered. The absolute absence of logic in his position did not disturb him. So I meditated in the gardens outside the compound while the others went in for darshan. The aarti was going to take place on the steps across the Bagmati River from the temple complex, so I would be permitted to attend that, at least.

After a long shower, I sat in the hotel lobby with Pujya Swamiji and Dorje, the Tibetan tour guide.

Pujya Swamiji had been struck by the lack of proper facilities along the five-day pilgrimage route and especially at Lake Mansarovar and Mount Kailash, where so many pilgrims flock each year. As we'd entered the area of Mansarovar on the third or fourth day of our pilgrimage, we encountered a group from England who were on their way out. They recognized Pujya Swamiji and, descending from their vehicles, fell at his feet to receive blessings for successfully completing the pilgrimage. Their exuberance was tempered, though, as they told of the pilgrims who had returned early due to altitude sickness—especially one they feared may have passed away before she got back to Kathmandu.

So, from that point on, Pujya Swamiji spent much of the rest of the trip meeting with local leaders, trying to ascertain who owned this land—who was in charge of it? Who would he have to apply to for permission to build something here? "Swamiji, forget it," everyone said. "This is China. There's no way they'll give you permission to do *anything* on their land. It's a waste of time."

But Swamiji follows a different inner guidance than common sense. It didn't matter that the task was unlikely to succeed. It had to succeed. Properly insulated rest houses needed to be built, and there had to be a medical clinic for those who fall ill. It needed to be done, and therefore, he would do it.

So, prior to the Bagmati aarti, we sat with the tour guide, discussing how to proceed. Dorje had obtained the names and addresses of the Chinese officials responsible for the Ngari Prefecture of the Tibet Autonomous Region of the Republic of China. Our letter-writing campaign to them began a few weeks later, and culminated with the construction of three ashrams/rest houses—one on the banks of Lake Mansarovar, one at Dirapuk, along the Mount Kailash parikrama route, and one in Paryang, land of the children with bindis.

Where they had never seen running water, we constructed an ashram with hot showers by boring wells in the ground, and provided a generator for electricity. The former prime minister of India, Shri Atal Bihari Vajpayee, summed up the achievement by saying, *"Jo Bharat Sarkar nahiy kar pai, ek sadhu ne kiya"* (What the Indian government could not do, a sadhu has accomplished).

That evening, after sitting with Dorje to plan our campaign to petition the Chinese government for land to construct a rest house, we left for the Bagmati aarti. The saints and other yatris headed back to the temple for darshan and would walk across the river for aarti. I, still being white, and uninterested in another round with the temple guard, took a different route. I rode in a taxi to the edge of the Bagmati, and the driver pointed upriver toward the temple on the opposite bank. "Fifty meter you walk," he said. I walked up the edge of the river as the sun began to dip behind the shikara, the highest dome of the mandir, towering regally above the rooftops of neighboring homes and shops.

Across the narrow river, cremations were underway. In Hindu tradition, cremations are performed on the banks of sacred rivers and the ashes duly immersed into the waters, a practice believed to bestow liberation on the soul of the departed, freeing it from the cycle of birth and death.

Raised cement platforms dotted the river's edge, and on each a body lay engulfed in flames. A few family members and friends sat on benches behind the burning ghats. The rest stood near the body. The flames rose high, carried on the afternoon wind, filling the air with a stench from which my heart and my nose both withdrew. I had never been to a cremation, and I'd never smelled the last moments of someone's existence. As I walked upriver, the smoke followed me, wrapping itself in my hair, across my face, and into my eyes.

I could hear the sounds of the jubilant pre-aarti songs coming from the steps ahead. What must it be like, I wondered, to watch fire consume the last bit of your mother, father, child, or spouse? To know, to see, that they will not, cannot, come back into their body, to have to stand calmly as flames rip into the hands that held you, tear through the lap you sat in? And what must it be like to hear people rejoicing while she on whom your identity was based, he who was the container for your love, is rendered into nothing but smoke and ash?

The mourners must be livid, I thought, as we sang the aarti and waved oil lamps from damp stone steps along the banks of the narrow Bagmati River—incensed at the audacity of us celebrating, dancing joyously. When a loved one dies, even the sun seems rude for rising. The world should stop, as our world has. It must be so hard for them, I thought, to be grieving while others are celebrating.

As I looked up at the smoke rising above the river, I realized that I would be irate because I live in a world where mourning and celebration are seen as inherently separate and distinct from one another, where there are places for mourning and places for celebrating, times for mourning and times for celebrating. Life and death are packaged nicely and neatly into boxes, each tied with a different ribbon. Indians and Nepali don't live like that. Life and death are in the same box, and the bows tie life to death, and death to life.

Mourning and celebration are sunset and sunrise, each following the other religiously. The flames of cremations seem separate from the flames of aarti only on the lowest level. The moment the flames rise in the air, the wisps of smoke merge one into the other, death embracing life and life embracing death. No, our aarti wouldn't upset them, just as the cremations across the river wouldn't bother the Indians performing aarti. The jubilant dancers could dance as flames of death consume a body, for they danced knowing fully that someday, the burning body would be theirs.

By the time our aarti finished and we walked down the steps to the banks of the river to perform the *achamana*—the drinking of holy water—the pyre directly across from us had mostly burned down. The crackling logs reminded me of bonfires at summer camp. The flames of the pyre subsiding, the family sat on the steps leading into the water, near where their loved one continued to burn.

Suddenly, the tender of the fire, the one in charge of keeping it hot and evenly spread so the body would burn fully, took his wide, hoelike tool and started to push the red logs and unburned bones into the river. They sizzled as they made contact with the cool water. From one side, then the other, the fire tender pushed the remains of the fire into the river. The logs crackled one by one as they splashed and were carried quickly downstream, along with any remains of the loved one.

Family members turned their heads to watch the current as the now-extinguished logs bobbed on top of the water and the ash spread out in the current's wake. They sprinkled their heads with drops from the holy river while the fire tender threw bucket after bucket of cold water onto the ghat, washing away any last bits of wood, ash, and bone. The platform was still burning hot; the fire had raged for hours. As water was splashed on it, steam rose thickly into the night air.

Wafts of gray smoke overlapped the blackness of the evening. Only death cast a shadow on the night. The family turned from the river and left, their loved one dissolved into steam rising off a cement platform, dissipating into the darkness.

As we walked back down the river to the taxis, another body was being carried to the ghat. The next body, and the one after that, were lined up around the corner, fastened with rope to wooden platforms, awaiting their turn. The families of the ones to be burned after them were still dancing and singing on the steps, knowing not which number they would be. This intermingling of life and death—the palpable impermanence of our existence seamlessly woven into day-to-day life, the ability to dance and celebrate while knowing that someday it will be your body burning on the pyre, the undeniable presence of a Truth from which we cannot escape (nor did they even feel an urge to escape)—was *so* different from the way I'd been raised and had always felt about death. The impact of this night has continued to ripple through my awareness since then.

CHAPTER 31

"When Are You Going to Stop Talking About That?"

After the pilgrimage to Lake Mansarovar and Mount Kailash in June 1998, we undertook another Dharma Yatra, across the United States. This time, we were accompanied by Amardas Bapu, an elderly saint and renowned leader from Gujarat, whose love for God made him giddy. He broke into spontaneous, infectious laughter even as he lectured. Again, I was given the task of speaking at almost every event. By now, I had learned some stories from the epics and scriptures I could use to illustrate my points. I also told stories I'd picked up in English books or in the rare, precious moments when Swamiji leaned back in his chair and said, "There once was a king . . ."

In late summer, we returned to Delhi, where work on the *Encyclopedia of Hinduism* was in full swing. Still headquartered in Columbia, South Carolina, with satellite offices in India, Canada, and England, all were working full tilt. Delhi was the main office for India.

The office was in our small Delhi ashram, in a single-story block of rooms that bordered a green garden. There was a satsang hall, where, each day, the priest gave talks on the Bhagavad Gita, the Ramayana, or the Vedas, and where—twice a year during the nine-day celebrations of Navratri—local women would come and sing from 4 a.m. onward. Not one among them could carry a tune, but it made no difference. I've always envied the Indians for their absolute lack of self-consciousness about bellowing far out of tune or clapping vigorously to a beat that is not the beat of the song. Whenever I was in Delhi, I was awakened by their devotional screeching.

Next to the hall was a small kitchen used only for Pujya Swamiji and the three or four guests the ashram could accommodate. Adjacent to the kitchen was a line of adjoining rooms. The first, Pujya Swamiji's, was a small, bare chamber with simple carpeting on the floor and paintings of Lord Krishna on the walls. At night, the boys would come and roll out a thin mat for Swamiji to sleep on. Each morning, they'd roll it back up again. Next to Pujya Swamiji's room was the guest room with two beds and a small table between the beds, and an attached bath. Next to that was the office for the *Encyclopedia of Hinduism* project. Behind those three rooms were three smaller rooms: Pujya Swamiji's office, a tiny one-bed room where I stayed, and the project's computer office.

Typically, Pujya Swamiji conducted meetings sitting on the floor of his front room, but when someone couldn't sit on the floor or when there were lots of files and papers to view, the meeting might take place around the table in his office. Scholars sat, met, read, and corrected entries in the encyclopedia office. I usually worked in the computer room along with the guys inputting corrections and changes using the mammoth computers and saving everything on floppy disks.

One afternoon, I walked from the computer office to the kitchen to refill my water glass. Pujya Swamiji was sitting at his desk, immersed in files relating to eleven schools we'd recently adopted in Gurgaon and an upcoming multidisciplinary medical camp at Parmarth. As I walked by his desk, I quietly picked up his empty water glass so I could refill it, along with my own, in the kitchen. "We will go to Gurgaon tomorrow," he said without looking up from his desk. "There is a meeting at 10 o'clock."

Gurgaon is now a metropolis, home to the best hospital in India, the largest hotels and shopping malls, sprawling housing complexes that are like entire cities. Twenty-five years ago, it was a slum. After our first visit in August 1997, I wrote in my journal:

The laundry lines hang low, and clothes are draped a few feet above the dirt. Goats, mangy and not much more than skin and bones, sleep piled on top of one another. A dog barks in the background, although the cry sounds more like that of a child. Occasionally, a cow will wander lazily to the laundry lines to make lunch out of the drying clothes. Children run and chase each other, like children everywhere. However, these children are half-naked, and it's December. Infections cover their bodies, and they are hungry.

Here, a room has been built out of scraps of wood, sheets of metal, and clothes that have finally been discarded. The room has no light other than the sun rays that trickle in from the narrow doorway or the holes in the imperfect walls. The floor is damp, as it has recently rained, but none of the children seem to mind, even though many are without pants.

Outside the doorway of this ramshackle room, the shoes of those fortunate enough to own a pair lay neatly in rows. In India, you always remove your shoes before entering a holy place, and to these children, this shack that serves as a school is a temple.

At the front of the room—a maximum of ten feet by ten feet, stands a young girl, perhaps six years old. Her eyes are closed, her hands are in prayer. She says a verse, and the rows of children at her feet repeat it back to her. Those on the floor are in three rows, nine or ten children per row. All are sitting cross-legged, arms stretched out on their knees, thumbs touching the first two fingers—the classic meditation posture. As the morning prayer ends, the young girl's voice breaks into an exhilarated cry: "Bharat Mata Ki!" (Mother India!)

The children shout, "Jai!" (Glory to Her!), eyes opening and filling the room with their innocent sweetness.

Then, she calls, "Daish ki seva, quon karega?" (Who will selflessly serve the people?)

"Hum karengay! Hum karengay!" (We will! We will!) comes the exuberant response from the children, filled with angelic optimism and faith.

"Hum karengay!" Here are children with nothing vowing to give to others, children the world has forgotten joyfully, gleefully pledging to serve that very world.

"Oh, and don't cry," Swamiji said as an afterthought, still without raising his head from his desk, as I walked into the kitchen. I had been able to control myself during the first visit, a year earlier, shutting off the part of me that feels deeply, while we surveyed roofs, floors, and walls for renovating the slum schools, and handed out fruit and cookies to the children. But on the car ride back, I cried nonstop—not the soft, gentle tears expected when one comes face-to-face with abject suffering, but near-hysterical, breath-stealing, uncontrollable sobs. It was hours before the tears subsided—that too only with Swamiji's intervention.

When we arrived back at the ashram after visiting the eleven schools, that first night, I couldn't eat dinner. "Those kids haven't had dinner," I wailed. "They won't have blankets tonight. How can I eat?" Swamiji looked straight at me, unmoving, while rivers of tears streamed down my face. Finally, he asked, matter-of-factly, "Are your tears helping them?"

"No, but, oh, my God, I can't stop crying, Swamiji. It's so unjust, so horrible."

He continued to look at me. He didn't reach out a hand to comfort me or say anything soothing. He just watched.

Finally, he said, "Your tears are only helping your ego. You think, 'Oh, I'm so compassionate and caring. I am so upset, I can't even eat my dinner.' But your tears are not giving food or shelter or an education to those children. No one benefits except your ego. If you really want to help the children, eat your dinner, sleep early, and get up at five o'clock tomorrow morning and figure out how to raise enough money to sponsor all eleven schools."

That had been a year earlier. Since then, we had raised the money and adopted the schools: We had built roofs and floors and proper walls, supplied books and other school supplies, and taken over paying the teachers' salaries.

I filled our glasses with water and walked back to Swamiji's desk. As I put his glass on the desk in front of him, I said, "Don't worry. I'll be fine. I was just overwhelmed the first time to see such suffering and pain. As an abuse survivor myself, I tend to identify so much with other children's suffering."

I walked back toward the encyclopedia office, my water glass in hand, and heard him ask behind me, "When are you going to stop talking about that?" I turned. He had not lifted his head from the desk.

"What?" I whispered, unsure I'd heard him properly.

"When are you going to stop talking about that? The abuse."

It had been nearly two years since I had arrived in India, nearly two years since I had stood knee-deep in Ganga and, with the moonlight reflecting in Her rushing waters, given Her my pain. For the first several months, I had searched for it. I had done whatever I could to try to trigger the suffering I'd become accustomed to. I had tried to trigger feelings of being a victim, a child, small, and helpless. I had tried to trigger feelings of abandonment, to pull forth tears. They hadn't been there. There had been no memory, image, nothing I could pull forth that triggered the pain, fear, longing, and vomiting I'd been habituated to. Ganga had taken them; I was free. I had not vomited or dissociated since.

Yet it was clearly ingrained in my identity. It was present even at this moment, when my childhood was far from my mind, a moment when I was happily walking back to work, focused on the schools, women's centers, and medical camps, along with my first editing job—an encyclopedia on the teachings of the Mother of the Aurobindo Ashram. I was not rehashing or wallowing in my past. I wasn't suffering from or affected by it in any conscious way. Yet it was still a deeply present part of my identity.

I stared at Pujya Swamiji. He continued to write notes in his small pad, one of dozens he carried around with him—filled with perfectly organized notes on each project, each place. He had asked a simple, matter-of-fact question. It had no more emotional affect than a query about who was coming to meet him tonight or what time we'd leave in the morning. It was process and form, not content.

I was free, by Grace, from the cellular suffering, from the identification that smothered my heart and my lungs, rendering me breathless. I was free of the content. The inner knowing, the inner awareness, the inner experience of self was free from what had happened two decades earlier. But in form—my habits of speech, in my unconscious, involuntary casual identification—I still had "abuse survivor" written all over me.

"Swamiji," I said, and was about to jump back into the worn-out costume and role I knew so well. "Swamiji," I repeated, and almost began to recite the lines of the drama and turn his small room in Delhi into the stage of my childhood—and then I stopped before saying the next word. Something inside felt forced, unreal, scripted by someone else; the set of the stage seemed two-dimensional rather than three. Unconsciously, I was erecting thin, flat fronts of the past on the stage of my present, trying to squeeze into a costume I had long since outgrown, to say words that were no longer my own.

Although I tried to get back in character, to be outraged at the callousness with which he'd referred to the very real pain of my childhood, it didn't work. I couldn't squeeze into the costume or remember the lines of the script. I couldn't generate any genuine feeling of hurt—neither at what had happened nor at my guru for speaking about it so callously. He knew, I realized much later, that it was no longer part of my present existence.

There was no "I" in that sweltering room in South Delhi in 1998 who had been abused. No "I" who had been abandoned. No "I" who was a victim. There wasn't one cell of my body that stood, steel glass of water in hand, that had even laid eyes on the monster of my memories. Scientists tell us that the cells of our body regenerate quickly. Skin cells slough off every few days. Organs take longer. Within seven or eight years, every single cell of the body has regenerated.

"I" had been abused. Who? Which "I"? Certainly not the "I" who stood before him, not the twenty-seven-year-old. A young girl had been abused and abandoned. But that girl was no longer here. She was not the "I" who stood before her guru on a sweltering September 1998 day in New Delhi. I could no longer squeeze into her clothes or speak her lines convincingly. I could no longer play her on the stage of my life.

"Now, I think, Swamiji," I said, finally answering his original question.

Yes, now I would stop talking about it, because it was not the truth of my present moment. It was a vestige of the past that I carried around in a suitcase that I never let out of sight. All the clothes, makeup, and script of the identity were heavy, but had until then seemed to be crucial luggage for my journey through life. But in that moment, he gave me the opportunity not only to be free on the deep emotional, psychological level—not just a freedom of content—but also to be free in process and form. There was no need to carry around the old suitcase of clothes that no longer fit.

In that moment, as the summer sweat ran down from my scalp onto my face, as the heat drew the water from my cells in the streaming river of perspiration, caked-on makeup of roles played long ago was finally washed clean. I picked up a washcloth from my bed in the tiny room on my way to the encyclopedia office and wiped my face dry.

CHAPTER 32

Challenges and Prayers

My days at the ashram were filled with seva. Correspondence, preparation of brochures and newsletters, follow-up with important people regarding important projects—the chief editor of the *Encyclopedia of Hinduism* and the administrator in charge—to be sure that assigning, writing, editing, and receiving articles was all on schedule, following up with local government officials on various environmental projects we undertook in the area: land to put the wandering cows on, land for a trash dump so it wouldn't go into the Ganga, land for tree plantations.

I also ghostwrote articles and books for Pujya Swamiji, channeling his words in my head. So many people were thirsty for this wisdom; it had to be put down and published in book form. I closed my eyes at my computer and typed as he dictated soundlessly into the space of my own brain.

I oversaw our burgeoning educational programs, raising funds from devotees to build and renovate schools and women's vocational-training programs.

We formed the Youth Education Services (YES) project, a precursor to the Divine Shakti Foundation that included the schools and women's programs.

And I prayed. A lot. To be worthy. To be worthy of the life that was given to me. To be divine. To expand into the space created by my name, Bhagawati.

And I struggled. I struggled with Indians doubting me, being suspicious of the white girl who clearly was up to no good. At one point, a journalist published an article stating that I was a Jewish American spy sent to dismantle one of India's largest and most renowned spiritual institutions, and criticized Pujya Swamiji for his inability to see the obvious and throw me out.

I struggled with people's inability to understand that, really, all I wanted was to give back to this place, this land and the culture that had given me so much—and, yes, I was aware of my inadequacies. I was unworthy, yes, but a spy, no. I struggled with people assuming I was Pujya Swamiji's mistress, people who projected their own impression of men onto my guru, who actually knew neither man nor woman, but only soul.

"Don't worry about them," he would say. "They will understand one day."

"But I can't bear that my presence is bringing you or the ashram a bad name," I would respond, crying. "Just send me back. It will be so much better for you." He would hear nothing of it, and chastised me for being so affected by gossip.

"They just don't have any other work to do," he told me, "so they gossip. You are here for something much greater. Do not waste your time."

Pujya Swamiji runs a huge risk by opening the doors of Parmarth Niketan to Western women. The Indian religious world of renunciates prides itself on the distance it keeps from women. "There are no women allowed here at all" is often stated with an air of superiority. It's a world in which male leaders judge themselves and others by the distance, or lack of distance, that is kept from women. "He roams around with women" is the worst insult one could make about a spiritual leader. Whether or not one is insinuating a physical or sensual relationship, the simple act of "roaming around" with a woman is in and of itself cause for censure.

The fallout that Pujya Swamiji has faced over the years due to my presence and the presence of a large number of Western female sevaks cannot be overstated. And his answer is always, "I see only the heart and devotion, not the gender. If God keeps sending me devoted sevaks who want to serve selflessly for humanity in the form of women, that is who will do the seva. When God sends men with that much devotion, we will take them too."

For me, it's always been a struggle, hearing that I am, simply by my existence in a female form, already defective and a liability. A renowned saint once said to me, "I will pray for you that in your next life you may be born as a boy so you won't have this difficulty." I was touched by his intent, but the comment was infuriating.

I don't want to be a boy in my next life, I seethed to myself after our meeting and my blessing. *Why can't you pray for a culture that sees girls as being as inherently valuable as boys? Why can't you pray for a culture that isn't suspicious and judgmental? Why can't you pray to purify people's eyes?*

CHAPTER 33

Mantra

NOVEMBER 1998

I woke early, long before the alarm went off at 4:30. The excited beat of my heart, despite the early hour and despite the fact that I'm not a morning person, reminded me of waking up on Christmas mornings. Having and decorating a Christmas tree and surrounding its base with presents is an inextricable part of American life, regardless of whether one is Christian. Only by Christmas 1983, when I was twelve years old, three months before my Bat Mitzvah, did I question whether observant Jews should be celebrating Christmas with such vigor. Till then, it had been an unquestioned given. The excitement of knowing that the new day would be filled with gifts pulled me from slumber at dawn.

Today, in India, while the sense of excitement was similar and my heart beat with the same anticipatory joy, the presents wouldn't be wrapped in paper and tied with bows. Today, I was receiving a mantra.

It was Thursday, November 26, 1998, Thanksgiving morning. The auspicious date was chosen not by the science of Vedic astrology but by my Western sentimental sensibility. Also, Thursdays in the Hindu tradition are dedicated to the guru. Each day of the week is named after and dedicated to a particular manifestation of the Divine. Thursday is called Guruvar in Hindi—the Day of the Guru. Thus, Thanksgiving, always celebrated on a Thursday, seemed the perfect day to get a mantra.

I had been asking Swamiji for a mantra for nearly two years, since I had heard him speak about its power—that a mantra is the master key to stilling the mind and achieving an expanded state of consciousness. I wanted a mantra immediately, but he wouldn't give me one.

"Just wait," he said. Would the alchemical power of the Sanskrit sound be too much for my consciousness, the boundaries of which were already melting into the world around me? Was my experience still too fragile to be able to handle the additional energy? My psyche was a crucible, already cooked and cracked by the fire of the experiences I was having. Would a mantra shatter the vessel irreparably? Or was he worried about what my parents would think?

I'm not sure why it took him two years to agree to give me a mantra—whether it was careful deliberate titration of my spiritual progress or whether he was simply hesitant to initiate an American Jewish girl into the rites of ancient Vedic culture. My inquiries into the reason for the delay were no more successful than my entreaties for the mantra itself had been. The answer, however, went from "No" to "Yes" around the twentieth month of asking.

I did not allow Swamiji's withholding of my mantra to prevent me from trying to reap its benefits. If he wouldn't give me one, I'd make one up. After all, Swamiji always emphasizes the importance of devotion and sincerity over rote recitation. His lectures are filled with stories—scriptural, historical, and apocryphal—of God's preference for sincerity over expertise, for love over ritual, for spirit of the heart over spirit of the law.

His favorite story is of a boy who, not yet knowing the complex invocations, recited the alphabet during the time of silent prayer in the temple. "God loves that boy," Swamiji whispered, tears filling his eyes despite the number of times he'd told the story before, "for his sincerity and devotion more than all those who could recite the prayers perfectly but whose minds were at the office or in the shopping center."

So, I made up my own mantra. "I love you, Krishna. I love you, Krishna," I chanted, carefully turning the beads of the rudraksh mala I'd received along with members of Jacqueline's group of Americans my first month at the ashram nearly two years before. After Swamiji's talk about mantras and the power of japa—repetitive recitation—they all requested sacred mantras. They fared no better than I.

"Just chant whatever name of God appeals most to you," he told them. "It could be Christ, it could be Adonai, it could be Buddha, it could be the word God. Don't worry. God recognizes all names." On the day of their departure, he blessed them all with a string of 108 rudraksh beads. As I had become an honorary member of the group, I received one as well.

"I love you, Krishna. I love you, Krishna." I moved the beads one by one between the thumb and ring finger of my right hand. "One should never use the pointer finger to do japa," Swamiji explained as he showed us in slow motion how to turn the beads of the mala, "because that is the finger we use to scold. So, we use the middle finger instead."

Sure, one should not admonish God, but one probably shouldn't flip Him off, either. So, without telling Swamiji about my adaptation, I began turning the beads of my mala with my thumb *and ring finger.* It required more dexterity but soon became automatic. For nearly two years, I had done japa with my homemade mantra. Today, I would receive a real one. I bathed and washed my hair.

In India, bathing has a significance far greater than physical cleanliness. We bathe not just for physical attractiveness or to spare friends our body odor, but also to purify ourselves—inside and out—before approaching God. No traditional Indian would enter even a small temple in their home, let alone take part in a ceremony, without first bathing. To bathe is to prepare oneself to encounter God.

On our pilgrimages to the sacred areas of Mount Kailash and Lake Mansarovar in Tibet, I marveled at the ability of Indian women to bathe from a bucket of ice-cold water in a makeshift, open-to-the-sky tent in the subzero temperatures of predawn darkness. Not bathing was as unthinkable to them as stripping off five or six layers of thermals and woolens and pouring ice water over my naked body was to me. Finally, on the third or fourth day of unobtrusively disappearing at the time the other ladies were bathing, I went to Pujya Swamiji and confessed. "I can't do it," I said. "I will die of pneumonia. Surely, God won't want that."

"Stand here and close your eyes," he said in yet another instance of what I discovered to be boundless compassion for those of us who had been touched by Grace due not to discipline, not to austerity, not to worthiness, not even to conscious seeking, but simply due to the amazingness of Grace itself.

Soon, I heard him chanting verses in Sanskrit I didn't know or understand except for the word *pavitra* (purity). Then I felt a light drizzle of water over my head. When I opened my eyes, he was gently splashing the final drops on me. "Now go."

Each day on the pilgrimage in the morning, I would come to him, bow at his feet, and receive my shower in the form of Vedic mantras and a gentle sprinkling of water from his hand, a special ritual for his only devotee who couldn't brave an ice-cold bucket bath. That particular privilege was reserved, however, for frigid Tibetan mornings. On all other days, I had to actually bathe.

After my bath on Thanksgiving Thursday morning, I lit the oil lamp on the temple in my room and began my japa. "I love you, Krishna," I chanted, knowing that within a few short hours, that mantra would be replaced by one with true Vedic power. Krishna, of course, would still know that I loved Him, but now I would have an official way of saying it.

After my meditation, I put on my new saree. It was a delicate golden silk, gifted to me several months earlier by a devotee of Swamiji's from Varanasi. With uncharacteristic restraint, I didn't wear it immediately, but put it away for a special occasion. The following February, in 1999, at an event with the Jain community in Singapore, I learned how silk is made, about the torture and death of the silkworms, and swore off silk forever. However, in this moment, before the Singapore trip, oblivious to the violence woven into each thread of my garment, I draped it over myself with joy.

The sun rose around 6:30, and I followed the first rays of her light down to Ganga. As I stood with my feet in Ganga's waters, the sun climbed over the Himalayas behind me and the moon descended into the sacred river before me. How had I ended up here? "Thank you, God," I whispered. It was not, of course, an answer to the question of how this had happened, and yet it was.

I would not have coffee this morning, as I needed to fast before receiving my mantra. Fasting before certain rites and rituals is not obligatory but is recommended. It is said that in lightness of body, we're more receptive to the Divine. Weighed down by food, our body is less available to subtle energies, and our prana, our life force, the river of grace as energy flowing through our physical and subtle bodies, gets diverted into the process of digestion. Hence, there's an emphasis on fasting in Hindu tradition.

Fasting, though, in modern Indian culture is quite different from both the Western concept of living on water or juice and the traditional Hindu emphasis on being light and focused to sit with God. The Sanskrit word for fasting, *upwas*, literally means "sitting near to." Near to what? Near to God. So, traditional Hindu fasting is not about dietary restrictions for health or weight loss, but about forgoing food in favor of sitting with God.

As the traditional has given birth to the contemporary, fasting in India has undergone great changes. In autumn 1996, during one of my early months in the ashram, I sat in the dining room eating the regular fare of boiled yellow lentils, lightly cooked *loki* (a zucchini-like squash), and a dry chapati. The man next to me had a plate full of deep-fried potato *pakoras* and puris—fritters and fried bread—still glistening with ghee and a bowl of potato stew, the surface layer of which looked like clear ocean water in which an oil tanker had spilled its cargo.

He looked down at my plate and disparagingly said, "It's Ekadashi, the sacred eleventh day of the month. You're not fasting?" I felt for a moment like I'd been transported to an alternate reality. Were the piles of fried goodies on his plate a hallucination? Had too many months of simple food driven me to become delusional and manifest pakoras on my own retina?

"Uh, no," I responded, as I could think of nothing else to say.

"Umph," he retorted and looked at me with such disdain that I felt like I was sinfully drinking wine with my meal.

Phalhara—essentially, "a diet of fruit"—is the term used to describe food that is permitted on a fast in India. It can be anything that is not made with grains or legumes and, in some cases, any salt other than rock salt. It is meant quite literally to be a diet of fruit, something to lightly sustain the body while one engages in deep spiritual disciplines, while one sits near to God.

However, human nature is undaunted by semantics, and while necessity may be the mother of invention, hunger is the mother of rationalization. So, over the years and decades, the definition of *fruit* has expanded and now includes a wide variety of substances that are not grains or legumes but are also far from the raw, simple juicy nectar blossoming on trees and bushes. There is now phalhara dough for pizzas, phalhara batter for dipping and frying pakoras, and phalhara flour from which to make fried puris, all of which count as "fasting." But this morning, about to receive my mantra, I really fasted. No fruit. No coffee. Only water. However, given that I was meeting Pujya Swamiji at 7 a.m., my abstinence was not, it must be noted, that impressive a feat.

I sat on the cool marble steps and closed my eyes into the wind. It blew from the tops of the Himalayas into the valley through which Ganga flows and across the rushing waters onto my face. The sun rises over the mountains to the east of the ashram, so in winter, it's midmorning before any rays fall onto the river. I sat in the first light of dawn as the dew of the pine trees mingled with the wet mist rising over Ganga and anointed my closed eyes and bare cheeks.

In other months, the banks are filled with families bathing, splashing themselves and each other with exuberant cries of *"Jai Gange! Jai Gange! Jai Gange!"* Children run and play, followed closely by their parents' reprimands. Priests gather the devoted and offer prayers for health, happiness, and prosperity. In winter, though, Indians tend to stay away from the mountains. I looked up at the clock tower that sits on Parmarth's marbled platform lining Ganga's banks. It is a landmark that has been there since the 1950s, decades before any of the shops, restaurants, or cybercafés mushroomed along the riverside. The clock said 6:45.

I bowed down onto the chilly marble platform lining the banks of Ganga. Through my shawl, I could feel the chill on my chest and belly. I stretched out my arms, palms down on the slightly damp stone, pressed my nose and forehead onto the ghat, and prayed. "Thank you, God. Thank You. Please make me worthy. Make me worthy of this place, worthy of Your presence in my life. Make me Divine." I raised my head and let my gaze merge with the rushing river. The wind reached into my unblinking eyes and brought forth tears. I rose, smoothed my now faintly wrinkled, slightly damp saree, and walked up the steps into the gates of the ashram.

The sun appeared in the dip between mountain ranges and was beginning to fall on the benches that line the central ashram pathway. I walked past the hand pump and gave it a slight bow. I pass it several times a day, oblivious to our special history, but today I remembered that it was here, just next to the hand pump, where the very ground had reached up and grabbed my feet. I smiled at the hand pump as though it were an animate, conscious coconspirator in God's plan for me to live here.

I had to find an offered flower—one that had of its own accord fallen from a vine and landed softly on the Earth, still fresh and beautiful. "God does not like us to pluck flowers," Swamiji explained. "He put them on the vines and trees for a reason. We must leave them there." I scoured the flower gardens along the central walkway until I found the perfect one, a pink blossom with large, soft petals that seemed to have floated to the dirt effortlessly, its petals still perfectly curved, with no tears or frays. I bent over the top of the bench to reach into the dirt and carefully scoop it up. There wasn't a speck of mud on it, and it seemed to have fallen from the vine just moments before, fresh and moist with morning dew.

I opened the screen door leading to the room where Pujya Swamiji gave daily darshan and sat on the thin orange carpet. My saree and the petticoat beneath it prevented me from doing *Badokanasana* or other yoga postures while I waited. So I just sat cross-legged, my back against the wall the darshan room shares with Pujya Swamiji's meeting room, drawn to the place closest to his energy. A short while later, the magic middle door opened and, rather than the young boy who usually appeared, Swamiji stood before me. I jumped up, then dove down to bow at his feet.

"Come," he said, and led me through his sitting room into his personal prayer room. The room was sparse, with a low bed in the center. A long sheepskin rug ran parallel to the bed. "I usually sleep on that," he explained. "I like to be closer to the Mother." A few feet from the rug was his temple.

He had brought me here once before, in December 1996, on the day before I had to leave India to go back to school, to seek the Mother Goddess's blessings for a safe journey and a fast return. "Why?" I asked Her repeatedly. "Why bother sending me back with your blessings for a safe and quick journey when I'm already here, safely. Why not just keep me here?" Now I was back at his temple. A large, ornate image of Ma sits in the center, with images of Bhagawan Krishna on both sides. In front of the temple, on the floor, is another, smaller, sheepskin. Pujya Swamiji sat on that.

"Sit down," he gestured. There was a thin, square mat on the ground next to his sheepskin. "Sit on that," he said. I sat slowly, careful not to show my feet to Ma in the temple. I crossed my legs under my saree and folded my hands in my lap, still holding my pink flower.

"Give the flower to Ma," Pujya Swamiji instructed. I placed the flower on the base of the temple, next to the silver oil lamp with a thin, cotton wick burning in it, casting the only light on the room other than faint rays of sun coming through the blinds of the adjacent room.

Pujya Swamiji began to chant Vedic mantras. I closed my eyes and held my palms against each other in front of my heart. "Oh, God, how am I here?" The divine craziness of it all washed over me, and I smiled into the sound of the prayers. Although I didn't know the mantras or understand the words as Swamiji chanted them softly, I could feel them resonating in my own head. They had a physical presence, not just the vibration of sound waves. Each word, each phrase, appeared in my mind as he chanted it as though he were literally blowing the words through my ear into my brain.

After a few minutes, he said. "OK, now I will give you your mantra. Repeat each word after me."

"Om."

"Om," I whispered.

A mantra given by the guru is never supposed to be shared. It is said that the spiritual power gets diluted if the formula is spoken aloud to others. The mantra's shakti is maintained when it exists as a cord between guru and disciple. For this reason, I won't share the actual words of the mantra he gave me—only that it, like all mantras, begins with "Om."

He chanted slowly, careful to enunciate so I could repeat it without a mistake. I felt each word resonate inside the cells of my brain. This was more than an experience of tiny hairs in my ear canal vibrating with the frequency of the sounds he made, bouncing off my tympanic membrane and getting relayed through the inner ear into the temporal lobes of my brain. He was not merely speaking these words. He was placing them, one after the other, into the crevices within my brain matter, weaving them into the web of neurons with their axons and dendrites, wrapping each word up in the nerve fibers along which consciousness is carried.

After he placed the mantra in my brain, he reached over to the image of Gayatri Ma, touched both her feet, and then touched the top of my head. Like a soldering iron, he burned the mantra into place, the energy pouring from his hand through my skull and into the electric wiring of who I am. The stuff that held me together chemically and electrically within the cushion of my skull had been reset. It was as though all the neurons had dumped all their neurotransmitters into my synapses simultaneously. My brain felt like a swirling pool of energy. The ability to open my eyes, to move, or to speak was gone. I heard Pujya Swamiji rise and felt the slight shift in the air as his dhoti brushed over the sheepskin carpet next to me.

I have no idea how long I sat in the pool of my own mind matter at his temple. The mantra seemed to be the only solid, stable presence. Slowly, my neurons managed to regather their chemicals and realign themselves for normal functioning. I was again aware of my breathing and opened my eyes. I rose from the temple and went through Swamiji's empty sitting room, through the daily darshan room, back into the ashram courtyard, and into the rising rays of the sun. My mantra chanted itself.

Since that day, my mantra has been a rope that carries me into a state, an experience of presence and truth. I chant it on my prayer beads each morning and evening, and during the day whenever I have free hands. When I feel myself getting stressed or upset, I reach for it and hold on for dear life as though I were drowning and it was my life raft. Most of the time, it runs in the background of my consciousness, an anchor connecting me to the depths of my existence.

CHAPTER 34

Gallstones? The Miracle of Ayurvedic Medicine

For the first few years at the ashram, I ate my meals happily in the *bhandara* (the large main dining hall). Bells rang twice a day, and I took my place cross-legged on the thin mat and ate whatever was scooped onto my metal tray. Occasionally, spontaneously, Swamiji would ask, "Would you like to eat chocolate?" Sometimes it was after a meeting about seva. After clearing a full file of work, he'd say, "Maybe there is some chocolate for you."

Sometimes, in seemingly random moments, he would say, "Chocolate? Would you like a chocolate?" How boxes of Belgian, Swiss, German, and Austrian chocolate appeared in the small refrigerator of the tiny kitchen Swamiji used for heating water to gargle or drink in the winter was beyond me. "Yes, I know you like it," he'd say, sticking one piece in my mouth and another into my hands.

"You must feel bored with the food being the same-same all the time?" he asked one day. How could I explain the gift of never having to think about what to eat? How to explain the gift of chanting while everyone's plates were being filled, then eating boiled potatoes and lentils in silence flanked by fellow devotees? Bored? Never. For the first time in my life and perhaps for the first time in generations of women in my family, food had become a friend. I didn't miss anything.

But chocolate was never to be refused. And it wasn't just any chocolate. He never fed me Cadbury or Nestlé or any generic variety. It was as though the Exotic-Chocolate Fairy paid a visit to his fridge every week and left a box for his American secretary.

Sometimes, after meeting with group after group of devotees in his garden, he would rise from the grass and we would all rise with him. I always tried to stay back to see if there was any important seva or anything Swamiji needed, or so I told myself. Actually, it was to linger for an extra glance, an extra smile, an extra energetic transmission of the grace that flowed from his eyes into my cells. As I'd lose awareness of where my body physically ends and the universe begins, as I melted into the jasmine-fragranced evening or the sun-soaked afternoon, as I bowed low at his feet and then rose to meet his eyes—to swim again in an ocean without a shore—Swamiji would say, "Chocolate? Would you like a chocolate?"

Then, one day in April 1999, a devotee arrived with a basket of baked goodies. Bringing food items to the guru is standard fare. Each day, as lines of devotees wait on benches in and near the reception area for the two open darshans, their hands and laps are full of fruit. But Swamiji long ago announced that he would not accept any gifts. "I don't need anything. Bring only your pain. Bring only your obstacles. Bring only your anger. Give me that as your guru dakshina [gift from disciple to guru]. Do not bring gifts."

Then people tried bringing large bouquets of flowers or intricately woven garlands. "Please leave the flowers on the bushes, where God put them," he would request. "I appreciate and accept your devotion, but please offer me the flower of your heart, the flower of your service for humanity. Do not bring bouquets of God's children who have been ripped from their stem."

Later, he acquiesced to accepting a single flower. "OK—as our tradition of offering flowers to the guru is so strong, you may offer just one flower," he amended the instructions. "But it must have fallen from the bush or vine," he emphasized. "Do not pluck any flowers."

So, devotees were left with the possibility of fruit. Swamiji had instructed specifically what he wanted—our anger, our pain, our obstacles, our temptations, to offer these to him so he could give them to Ganga or to God and we could be free. He wanted our devotion and our commitment to serve humanity. He did not want gifts. But tradition is strong and the grip is not easily loosened, and fruit became the gift of choice. Fruit he did not refuse. It could always be used. With so many people eating every day, fruit at least could be shared and could benefit everyone. It didn't harm the Earth; the bounty was provided by Mother Nature.

But one day, some devotees came from Australia with a basket of egg-free cakes and cookies. That evening, Swamiji took me into his small kitchen. "This has come," he said, pointing to a large wicker gift basket filled with more than a dozen boxes of Western baked goods. "They are very nice items. You can enjoy them." Within the next two days, I had eaten nearly everything in the basket.

Until then, I'd had no craving. I never found myself thinking, "Oh, I'd love a cookie." But once I beheld the beauty of these Australian goodies set artfully on fake grass, I could think of little else. I became a marionette with strings being pulled by a part of me I'd forgotten was there. I opened the first box and put one cookie into my mouth, and my taste buds kicked right in. I finished the whole box without even realizing what had happened.

Each box was a different variety, and so they all had to be tried. Whenever I went back to the kitchen for another (I couldn't very well move the basket to my office, even though I was the only one eating it), if Swamiji was in his sitting room alone, I would ask him, "Would you like one?" I knew the answer would be no, but, just to be polite, I asked. He had granted me the freedom to access his kitchen, and I didn't want him to think I was ungrateful or took it for granted. "Are you sure you wouldn't like even one?" I asked. "They are really nice. You were right."

"No," he said without even looking up. Then, as I moved past him into the kitchen, he continued, "We don't just keep eating." In Hindi, *mein* (I) and *hum* (we) are used interchangeably, so Swamiji and other Indians might say *we* when they're actually referring to themselves in the singular. It's possible he meant the plural *we* to refer to the true yogis or spiritual people, or to those who have a grip on their impulses or who are not slaves to their senses. He didn't elaborate, and I was too embarrassed to ask. He felt me pause and said, "No, no. It's OK. Keep enjoying."

Whereas most spiritual teachers give both instructions and injunctions, Swamiji's way is to remove obstacles between us and our growth. He doesn't change us, but, rather, encourages situations through which we will experience what we need for personal change. He had intuited that I still was under the thumb of my taste buds and that parts of me still craved the numbness of a carb hangover. Until those parts were brought into the light, they couldn't be healed. So he handed me a monster basket of cakes and cookies.

For two days, I was intoxicated—and, other than a bit bloated, not unpleasantly so. I skipped most of the meals in the bhandara and fed myself chocolate-filled cookie sandwiches instead. On the night of the third day, after having finished off most of the basket and given away everything else for fear I would eat it, I woke up feverish and trembling. I shook to the core not just my arms and legs, but the muscles that held my organs in place. This went on all night long.

The next morning, I called the ashram doctor, who said it sounded like malaria. He gave me some medicine for fever and said to watch it another day. The same thing happened the following night. "It's definitely malaria," the doctor pronounced, even though the blood tests came back negative.

Then the diarrhea started. By this point, the gift basket was far from my mind. It had been nearly two days since I had finished my last cookie, and I figured the diarrhea was related to the fever, not the pastries. And the diarrhea was white, like someone had simply poured a glass of milk in the toilet. I spent the next two days doubled over in pain with a fever that finally broke on the third day. But the diarrhea didn't go away with the fever. The doctor gave me a variety of medicines, but none of them worked.

Finally, Swamiji called an Ayurvedic doctor he knew, a renowned specialist in the traditional, ancient Indian system of medicine. The doctor did not need a stool sample or even to feel my distended stomach. He looked at my tongue and held the wrists of both hands gently while taking the pulse of my inner forearm with different fingers and pressure. I felt like the strings of a guitar on which he played a very slow, deliberate melody. Finally, he asked, "Have you eaten a lot of medha recently?" *Medha* is the Hindi word for the Wonder Bread variety of refined white flour. It had now been five or six days since my binge, and I actually hadn't connected it with malaria, a mosquito-borne illness.

"Well, yes," I admitted. "I ate a lot of cookies and cakes just under a week ago."

He explained that the sugar in the flour had taxed my internal organs (he didn't specify anything more) and that it would only get worse and could create a lifetime of difficulty for me if I didn't follow his instructions exactly.

He sent a young boy out into the market to get a variety of herbs he crushed by hand over the following hour. Finally, he handed me three or four bottles, each containing what looked like dirt from different flowerpots. They were each brown and finely ground—some a bit darker and some a bit lighter.

"This one, you take before each meal. One spoonful in the mouth, followed by freshly churned buttermilk. This one you mix into the buttermilk. One half spoon. This one should be eaten with papaya first thing in the morning. This one, take twice a day on empty stomach, followed by one glass of warm water."

"And," he said as he stood to leave, "no more medha."

Since the cookies, I had barely eaten anything. I had no appetite at all, and between the pain and the fever, it was all I could do to get down some fruit or thin soup.

Within twenty-four hours of starting the medicinal regime, I was starving. I walked into our kitchen and asked the cook, "Please make me a full meal. I am so hungry." The fever ended without ever actually breaking. There were no sweaty sheets or wet shirts from the perspiration of a fever breaking. This one just went quietly away. As did the diarrhea. After two days, it was as though the entire experience had never happened.

When I was back in Los Angeles a few months later, I mentioned to my doctor what I had been through, and he asked me to come in for an ultrasound. "It seems like you had gallstones," he said. "The cookies probably pushed them into the duct, which is why you had such pain and the fever. This doctor seems to somehow—" my doctor paused for a long moment. "He seems to have just melted them."

The science of Ayurveda (literally, "the science/scripture/wisdom of life") is based on balance—balance of hot and cold, light and heavy, energies and characteristics. Its goal is not to treat symptoms, but to restore balance to the system. Through feeling the pulses of the body—not just the speed of the heart but the flow of the different energy systems—and looking at the health of the tongue, the doctor gets all the information needed to know what's out of balance.

I was out of balance both physically and mentally. The baked goods had thrown my digestive organs into a frenzy, leading perhaps, as my LA doctor hypothesized, to gallstones getting pushed into the duct. But it was a systemic imbalance in the first place that had led to me being unable to stop eating something so detrimental to my own health. Self-sabotage, on any level, is an indication of a system gone awry.

His treatment not only cured the diarrhea and fever, it not only dissolved the gallstones (if there were gallstones), it also rebalanced my system such that since that moment more than twenty years ago, I have never been tempted to eat a cookie or cake, even if it's vegetarian!

CHAPTER 35

The Greatness of Forgiving

About two and a half years into my stay in Rishikesh, I got a fax from Manny, my biological father. We'd been out of touch for many years; I'd seen him only once since I was seven. I referred to him as "the sperm donor" to distinguish him from Frank, my true dad, who raised me, taught me, guided me, and loved me. I hated Manny. He had given me more than his genes.

In September 1979, when I was eight, as I was preparing to visit him in Colorado, where he'd moved after divorcing my mother, he called her to cancel. He had canceled my last several scheduled visits as well for one reason or another. This time, my mother said, "I cannot do this to her again. If you want to cancel, you tell her." As I sat on the edge of my parents' bed, the man who had gifted me his DNA told me that he did not want to see me again. He went on to explain that I wasn't really his daughter. The biological connection did not inherently create an emotional one.

The science of attachment is fascinating. I had no positive memories of any time spent with him since he had pulled out of the driveway when I was three. Weekend visits while he still lived in Los Angeles included emotional and sexual abuse and pathological behavior that I interpreted as just his personality. But my psychological attachment was stronger than reason, and I was distraught. How could he not want to see his own daughter? How could he not want to see me? For a full decade after that phone call, I wrote him poignant letter after poignant letter, begging to know why he wouldn't see me. What had I done? I sent him photographs of me as I grew. There was never any response.

The first communication I received, after that September phone call as I entered third grade, was at the beginning of my freshman year at Stanford in 1989, a full decade later. The divorce agreement with my mother compelled him to cover a portion of my college education, and Stanford had a policy whereby it would accept tuition payments only from students directly, not from their parents or guardians. Therefore, he needed to communicate. His letter mentioned wanting to reconnect. It was neither apologetic nor tender, but it was an opportunity for which I'd been yearning for ten years, so I responded, albeit trepidatiously.

I visited him once, in Denver, during spring break my first year at Stanford. He opened the conversation—the first one we'd had in a decade—by explaining that if I was looking for apologies, if I was looking for repentance, I was looking in the wrong place. He continued by telling me that having me was the second-biggest mistake of his life. Marrying my mother was the first.

The rest of the evening is a blur. It faded quickly into the comfort of dissociation, that special place where I could be in the world but not of it, physically present but untouchable. Dissociation had been my friend for years, ready to rescue me from any painful situation and take me into the playground of my mind, where I could run freely in the grass.

I was in the first of three hospitals less than a week later, a few days after arriving back at my college dorm. I vomited so much blood that the doctors thought I might have ruptured my esophagus. *You cannot vomit up your father. You cannot feed yourself his love. Neither is he present in what you take in, nor is he present in what you force out.* I knew the truth of what I was doing, I knew how to talk to myself and others about it, and I knew the absurdity of it. But I couldn't stop.

Our only communication during the next year—which I spent in and out of hospitals and eating-disorder units—was through doctors and lawyers. His legal obligation to pay for my college had one stipulation: I had to stay continuously enrolled full-time. This clause was to protect him from having to pay for a degree in which I took only one or two classes at a time and ran up bills year after year. It was not intended to absolve him in case of a medical leave of absence. However, after my first semester spent in a hospital rather than in class, he sent my mother a letter saying he would no longer pay, since I had violated the terms of the agreement. They finally agreed on a settlement in which he gave a lump-sum payment and would be responsible for nothing else again, ever. At nineteen years of age, I signed papers legally absolving him of any further paternal responsibility. A month later, Frank legally adopted me.

Then, suddenly, eight years later, after I'd moved to India, this fax arrived. My family doctor had contacted him for medical-history details. In his reply, he requested my contact information, so I gave the doctor permission to provide him my fax number in Rishikesh. Manny's letter was sweet, kind, caring, and interested in my life in India. It did not include apologies or repentance; he had long since told me I would never get that. It seemed, however, genuinely nice.

Hesitantly, I wrote back. I was not willing to turn my back on this opportunity for a relationship with a man I knew only through the ways he had hurt me, but whose presence and acceptance had felt so vital throughout my childhood. We exchanged a few faxes. I shared details of my life in India, the schools we were building, the medical camps, and the women's vocational-training centers.

I said nothing of my spiritual experiences or the depth of openings and awakenings. I said nothing about the ceremony I had done to forgive him and give my pain to Ganga. His letters were filled with questions, wanting even more details about my life in India, and appreciation for the good work being done. They were superficial but perfectly normal and innocuous.

The sweetness of his letters unraveled me. *Who is this man?* I had such a complete picture of him as a terrifying, haunting monster. Now, more than two decades after violating the very body he'd given me, after attempting to rub out, to smear away, to extinguish the very life he'd created, after turning the tools of his profession—of medicine, of psychiatry—into tools of torment, now he wanted to be friends.

There would be, it was clear, no discussion of anything that had happened in the last nearly thirty years—not the abuse, not the abandonment, nor any ramifications of it. Now, we would just chat lightly about academic curricula in India compared to America, about whether sewing or embroidery was more of a useful skill for women in the Himalayas.

My head spun. I looked deeply into each mirror I passed. *Who am I? What really happened? Is this the man of my nightmares? Are these letters from the Monster? Could a man capable of what he'd done just turn around and become "normal"? Had he ever been anything other than normal? Had I made it all up? Were my memories figments of my imagination, projections of my doctors and psychologists?* The foundation on which I understood my life was coming apart.

I finally reached out to Swamiji. "I need to ask you something important. I have never asked you to use your magic powers, but I need you to use them now."

He smiled at me. *"Bolo"* (speak).

I took a deep breath and tried to keep my anxiety under control. "I have, as you know, vivid memories of horrendous abuse at the hands of my biological father. I have spent decades of my life suffering—and healing—from the abuse and all the effects it has had on my life. Now, this man is sending me faxes that are so nice, so sweet, that they don't seem like they could have been written by a man capable of inflicting the pain of my memories. I need you to use your magic and tell me whether the abuse I remember really happened. Was it fact, or did I make it up?"

Swamiji was silent but kept smiling at me. "Please tell me," I begged.

My guru rose from his chair and began to organize files on his table. They were already in immaculate order—files dedicated to the cleaning of Ganga in one group, others on new technologies for river rejuvenation, meetings with government officials, papers to be followed up on, options for solid-waste management with the pros and cons of each for rural India. As he stood, he straightened the piles, already far neater than anything on my desk had ever been. He moved his pen from one edge of the table to the other, threw away a scrap of paper on which there was no more room to write notes.

We had already had a prior conversation about the use of what is known as the siddhis (magical powers). These are abilities that come through deep and intense spiritual practice, sustained over many years and typically under the direction and grace of an enlightened master. Some may have siddhis from early childhood or even birth, marks of a soul that has done great sadhana (spiritual practice) in a past life and took another birth just to finish up some specific karma. Or, in the case of the saints and enlightened beings, there are those who come back after death and, out of compassion and grace, take a physical form to help others.

Siddhis are also gained through continuous recitation of certain mantras along with esoteric yogic practices. These powers are, however, seen as distractions from the path, by-products of intense sadhana—a temptation along the way, not the goal. There are, in fact, many stories of religious figures who, distracted by the siddhis, ended up going astray and losing their way. So, while some may use them consciously and judiciously in order to increase faith in followers or convince a hardened scientific mind of the miracles of spirituality, typically, masters avoid using the siddhis they have or even speaking about them.

In the first few months of my time at Parmarth, when I originally began helping Swamiji with correspondence, we would go through letter after letter quickly. I took notes in my own scribbled version of shorthand. One day, toward the end of 1996, he received a letter from a young girl in Fiji, filled with questions. She was paralyzed by anxiety, and her letter was a plea for help. I went through the questions one by one, reading them aloud to Swamiji and noting his answers:

"I worry about falling sick," she wrote.

"Take care of your health, serve others with dedication, and have faith in God," he responded.

"Should I focus on my studies, or try to find a husband?"

"Study, my dear. You are still young. Enrich your mind so you may better serve the world. You will find a good husband in due course."

"I find myself panicked with fear about whether my parents will die in an accident or by natural death."

"Natural death."

The pen dropped from my hands, and I froze. I raised my eyes to him. "Swamiji, this girl may be only a teenager now, but she trusts you so fully. If, even forty years from now, her parents die in an accident, she will remember what you told her and she will lose her faith. Are you sure you want me to write this?"

"Natural death. Move on. Next question." I couldn't move or lower my eyes from his face.

"Do you know this, Swamiji?" I whispered.

"Next question. Move on."

It was the first time I had ever seen him uncomfortable, not at full ease with the present moment and situation. He clearly did not want me to keep questioning him on how he knew or what he knew. But I couldn't stop myself: "Swamiji, please tell me. Do you really know this?"

He stood up. "We'll finish the letters tomorrow. Go now."

That was my introduction to the concept of a siddhi, explained to me later by one of the elder devotees, a woman from Jaipur. "He knows everything," she said. "However, he does not use these powers. He wants to keep us focused not on his miracles but on the miracles of the Divine, focused not on him as the doer, but on God."

I said nothing more about the questions of the girl from Fiji and simply mailed his letter to her as instructed. I did not mention the powers again until this day, a few years later, when I could not help myself. "You must tell me," I pleaded desperately. "It is really important for me to know if this all happened or if I just made it up in my imagination."

Finally, amid arranging papers on his table, without looking up, he said, "You have forgiven him—that is your greatness."

Swamiji turned and walked into the other room. I followed in close pursuit, blinded by everything other than my need to know.

"But did it happen, Swamiji? Did it actually happen? Are my memories correct?"

He ignored me and repeated, "You have forgiven him—that is your greatness."

"Swamiji, please," I begged. I was stuck. I was not interested in the subtleties of different levels of existence. I was not interested in the truth of our oneness and the illusion of separation between people. I was not interested in anything other than knowing, on this very physical, "real" plane of existence, had it happened or had it not? Relentlessly, I followed my guru from room to room as he moved about, picking up a file here, folding a shawl there, anything to avoid my pursuit.

Finally, after the fourth or fifth time I asked the same question, "But did it really happen?" in an increasingly obsessed frenzy, Swamiji turned around—in a moment of great compassion mixed, I am sure, with great exasperation—met my eyes and, through my eyes, bore into the deepest corners of my being. Matter-of-factly, he said, "To forgive something that did not happen is not so great."

So, that was it. The full lesson in two short sentences. It had happened, but that was not the important part. My lesson was not about what he had done, but about my own forgiveness. My lesson was rooted in forgiveness and greatness. I was not a victim. I was someone who had, given the opportunity, expanded enough to forgive.

He neither condemned nor condoned my father's acts. He offered no sympathy, no process, no lap in which to cry or work out the turmoil of my mind. Nothing was relevant, save my forgiveness and the way that seed of forgiveness was blossoming into a tree of greatness. The greatness of which he spoke was not a greatness of separate achievement. It was simply an opening, an expansion into a place where two becomes one—where the strong lines between him and me, between perpetrator and victim, between doer and do-ee, between subject and object dissolved, and I was able (most of the time) to live free in each present moment, not as the victim of my rehearsed history.

The teaching regarding forgiveness is complex and fraught with many "Yes, but"s. Yes, of course we should forgive as spiritual, compassionate beings, but doesn't that make us weak? How many times? Should we just keep forgiving while the world, or specific individuals, trample over us time and again? If we forgive, who will right the wrongs being done to us?

We forgive because we need to be free. We forgive to expand the space and consciousness within ourselves. Holding onto pain, holding onto grudges, constricts us. It defines who we are by thick lines: *I am the one who was abused. I am the one who was wronged. I am the one who always gets the short end of the stick. I am the alcoholic, or I am the child of the alcoholic.*

The greatness of which Pujya Swamiji spoke was not an ego-defining greatness of me as a separate, "great" being. It was an acknowledgment of what is able to flow through me when I surrender my attachment to the story, when I loosen the grip on my identity as victim. Into the space created by surrender, into the space created by awareness of the perfection of the universe, grace and greatness flows.

CHAPTER 36

It's Only the Body,
Not the Soul

CHRISTMAS 1999

"I found the perfect dress for you!" my mom exclaimed triumphantly as she walked into my room, the bedroom in which I'd grown up. "Come, come see it." It was December 1999, and I was in LA on a visit after being in India for nearly three years. My parents had decided to have a Christmas party, as it had been so many years since I'd been home for the holidays. I followed her into her bedroom, confused, as I didn't wear dresses anymore.

"It's absolutely perfect. You'll love it!" She put the treasures from her shopping trip onto the bed. "I can't believe I found something so perfect at the last minute." She pulled a gift box from a large Ann Taylor shopping bag. "It covers your arms all the way to the wrists and your legs all the way to the ankles. It has fully covered shoulders too. It's perfect!" She was beaming from ear to ear.

In the early years, before I officially took sanyas, Pujya Swamiji always encouraged me to wear whatever my parents wanted when I was in Los Angeles. "Make them happy," he would remind me. "They've given you the freedom to move to India. At least you can dress how they want when you are together in LA. And anyway," he always emphasized, "it's only your body that's wearing the clothes. Not your soul. They can't dress your soul."

In those early days, before saffron robes became the extent of my wardrobe, when I was with my parents, I wore long skirts with loose, flowery tops or *salwar kameezes*, traditional Indian long cotton tops over matching pants cinched by drawstring. My cotton skirts and salwar kameezes were not, however, dressy enough for a Christmas party. I'd assumed I would just wear a saree.

My mom was excitedly pulling the pink tissue paper off my perfect new dress. She lifted it out of the box, shook it loose, and held it up in front of me. "Isn't it perfect?" It was black.

Los Angeles December evening wear was, in 1999, black by default. But I was a renunciant, a nun, about to be ordained into saffron-robed sanyas. In traditional Hindu lineages, renunciants wear white prior to ordination and saffron/orange after (although I wore white for many years after ordination as well). Yellow is also acceptable; it is the color of brahmacharis (religious students). But black? No one spiritual wears black, I thought.

"Try it on," my mom encouraged me. She had no idea how not perfect the dress was. I pulled it over my head, sliding my arms into the tight black sleeves. As I smoothed the dress over my torso, I realized that yes, quite literally, my mom was right. It did cover my whole body—arms, legs, wrists, ankles, shoulders.

However, that which is acceptable by the letter of the law is not always acceptable by the spirit of the law. The dress was skintight. It looked as though someone had painted it on me with a black acrylic brush. Neck to hips, it was tighter than the leotards I'd worn in my failed attempts at childhood gymnastics. It hugged my hips in a drop waist and then flowed out to the floor.

I dug my fingernails into the palms of my hands and bit down on the side of my tongue to fight back tears. "It's only your body, not your soul, only your body, not your soul, only your body, not your soul," I chanted to myself desperately, clinging to the words as though they were a life raft in the ocean about to swallow me.

"Oh, you are gorgeous! You're like a model. You have such a beautiful body. I don't know why you don't want to show it more." A river of compliments gushed from my mother's mouth. "Look in the mirror. You are so gorgeous," she cooed in that way that only mothers can while beholding their daughters dressed for special occasions.

I couldn't look. It was all I could do not to collapse in tears on the floor of her bedroom. Did she really understand so little? My mother's a smart woman—not just book smart but also deeply insightful about other people's lives and psychology. How could she think I would be happy in skin-tight black Hollywood wear?

"Come on—look in the mirror," she said, oblivious to the struggle I was going through. She had spent hours of her otherwise busy day shopping for me, searching, I am sure, with great frustration for something that fulfilled all my criteria. In a well-intentioned effort to prevent any last-minute conflict over what I'd wear, she had shopped in advance.

I had to raise my gaze from the Oms I was drawing on her carpet with my eyes, trying unsuccessfully to meditate myself out of the current situation. I glanced quickly into the mirror next to my parents' fireplace, and the tears finally rushed, unabated, into and through my eyes. The woman in the mirror was not me.

"Why are you crying?" my mom exclaimed, more a statement than a question. "How could you possibly be upset with this? It looks gorgeous, and it covers everything. What is wrong with you?"

Rhetorical though I knew her questions had been intended, I finally spoke: "Look, Mom, if you want to go downstairs to the party and tell your friends a lie about who your daughter is and what my life is about, that is absolutely fine. I will stay in my room and meditate, read, and work. I will be very happy to do that. But if you want me to go to the party and speak the truth about who I am and what my life is, then I cannot wear that dress. That dress is a lie. I can't wear a lie and speak the truth."

"Fine," she pronounced with less anger than I'd feared. "Wear a saree." She walked straight out of the room and down the stairs, leaving the Ann Taylor gift box and delicate tissue paper strewn on her bed.

Later that evening, a close friend of my mom's, who knew what a powerful will she had, asked me how I'd managed to wear a saree to the party. I told her the story and brought her upstairs to see the dress. "Oh, God," she said, laughing. "In that dress, you would have looked like the hors d'oeuvres."

We are not our bodies, of course. That is the bottom line of Eastern spirituality. You can imprison the body, but not the soul. You can burn the body, but not the soul. You can cut the body, but not the soul. This is the core of the teachings of Lord Krishna in the Bhagavad Gita.

We are, however, connected to our bodies. To deny the impact that the body has on our experience is to cut ourselves off from a powerful aspect of our sense of self. The body may not have any impact on the Divine, Eternal Self, which is untouchable, but it certainly affects our individual self and our experience of that self. From landmark studies on the impact of simply holding a pencil between our lips versus our teeth, mimicking the physical musculature of a smile or a frown, to recent research regarding "power stances," psychological research shows clearly that our felt sense of self is deeply impacted by even superficial variations in expression and posture.

What we wear and our experience of ourselves impact and inform each other. We dress according to how we feel, and we feel according to how we dress. Dr. Phil Zimbardo's famous Stanford prison study, and his later research into the Abu Ghraib prison scandal, emphasized the importance of the uniform worn by the guards and prisoners in cementing their identification with their roles: Otherwise well-adjusted young men and women became vicious and punitive in their identification with the guards' uniforms they wore.

So, what does the saffron color of the sanyasi's robe signify? "It is," as Swamiji explains,

> *the color of the sun at sunrise and sunset. The sun gives and gives all day long with no vacation, no hesitation, no expectation, and no discrimination. The sun doesn't wake up one day and say, "I don't feel like shining today." The sun never takes a break. When it is night for us in India, it is daytime for those in the US. When we have the short days of winter, our friends in the Southern Hemisphere have long days of summer. The sun does not discriminate. It does not shine on Jews and not Christians, or whites and not blacks, or Hindus and not Muslims. The sun shines for all and with no expectation. The sun does not shine more for those who do sun salutations or perform sun worship in the mornings. That is the way a sanyasi should live. Giving and giving to all with no expectation, no hesitation, and no discrimination.*

Saffron is also the color of fire, the ultimate purifier. Prior to taking sanyas, the initiate performs a yagna, or fire ceremony. I performed one for seven straight days. Into that fire we offer all that is keeping us from being a pure vessel for the Divine will. The fire purifies our desires, our attachments, our very selves, so that on the day we enter Ganga to emerge naked into a new birth, it is not only the clothes that have been removed, but all vestiges of the former self as well. It's not only the physical body that is purified but also the longings and attachments of the emotional self.

So, wearing saffron is not just something the sanyasis do because it's a uniform. The color has a deep and ancient meaning. Every time I drape myself in the saffron robe, I am reminded about who I am and what my life is for. A skintight black evening dress would have been a vivid reminder of who I am not.

CHAPTER 37

Sanyas

JUNE 11, 2000

The moon hung low in the sky, as though perched on the ridge of the Himalayan foothills. Slightly bigger than a half moon but far from full, she illuminated the morning into which twilight was now emerging. It was just past 3:30 a.m. I had been awake all night. That morning, as the sun would begin its ascent over the mountains, I was going to be initiated into sanyas. Layers of false self would be washed off me, and I would emerge from the waters of Ganga as a newborn child from the womb of the mother—untouched, untainted, unafraid. I would emerge as the unclothed fullness and truth of my Self—whole, complete, pure, divine, a vessel through which God's will would flow unencumbered by ego.

I sat on the cool marble steps. The ghat was still mostly empty, but today being Ganga Dussehra, the day that the goddess Ganga descended from heaven in the form of a river, the crowds would come earlier than usual for a ceremonial bath. For that moment, though, I sat alone, my back against the round pillar at the water's edge, the same spot I'd sat nearly four years earlier, when Ganga flowed not only beside me but also from my eyes.

It was here I had come to put my feet in the water the day that Jim and I had arrived in Rishikesh. It was here, looking out over the river I didn't even know was sacred, that I had had the first vision of the Divine. It was here I had already been given a new life. Now, it would be ceremonially sanctified.

I closed my eyes and chanted my mantra in my mind. The only sound was that of the waves of Ganga, rising slowly with the melting glacial snow, breaking on the steps and occasionally splashing over my bare feet. As I sat there, the waves began to flow not only in front of me but also through me, crashing on the steps of the marble and on the edges and corners of my being. I could hear and feel the water rushing into my mind, coursing through my thought patterns, loosening my hardened reactions and identities.

As wave after wave broke inside me, each carried away a part of my identity, ebbing from the shore of my awareness into Ganga's waters, to be dumped into the ocean past the Bay of Bengal. As I sat, the sloshing and breaking of the waves within me got louder, and I realized that the space had increased. As each wave carried another part of me out to sea, the emptiness inside grew. I sat. The water flowed over my toes and, just as palpably, through my mind and through the container of my self. The gong of the clock tower at four o'clock pulled me back to the present moment.

Pujya Swami Gurusharananandji Maharaj, the saint who had inquired, "How much soup is too much soup?" and who had first pronounced me as Bhagawati, told me I could come get him after four and we'd go together to Pujya Swamiji. I rose, then dropped again back onto the marble steps. Ganga had reached beyond her banks, into my chest, and pulled my heart. I lay with my face on the wet step and stretched my arms out in front of me, my legs behind. I lay flat on the step, the water seeping through my thin white cotton gown and soaking my face. "Just take me into You," I prayed. "I am already Yours."

I stood and wrapped a cotton shawl over my chest and shoulders, covering my now-wet white cotton gown, and walked up the steps toward the room in the ashram where Maharajji was staying. He had come especially for my sanyas initiation, graciously, when I told him that I really, really wanted him to be there and to do the rites with Pujya Swamiji.

Sanyas is an ordination passed down from guru to disciple. Pujya Swamiji is my guru. But the moment I met Maharajji, my heart leaped out of my chest and threw itself at his feet. He is also my guru, and I wanted to take this step by his hand. As Frank had held the back of my first two-wheeled bicycle while I cycled around the lot of a vacant gas station, releasing it only briefly until I was strong and steady, I wanted Maharajji to be there for my sanyas, along with Swamiji, to have them both hold me, carry me, and guide me into this new life.

I knocked on the door of Maharajji's room, and his disciple answered. "Wait here," he instructed and went into the back. I stood, vacillating between breathless excitement and breathful stillness. A minute later, Maharajji appeared, the clank of his thick wooden sandals announcing his presence before I could see him in the darkness.

I bowed at his feet and he said, *"Ao, Rani"* (Come, Queen). In his presence, I felt less a queen than an infant, but by using nicknames like that, Maharajji continually reminds us who we really are—not queen of some finite physical kingdom, but Queen of the Divine Universe.

He walked past me regally, and I stood and followed him up the central ashram pathway to the front door of Swamiji's room. The priest was already there, and, upon seeing Maharajji arrive, he gently rang Swamiji's bell. Swamiji walked out into the twilight of breaking dawn.

I fell to the ground and bowed at his feet. This incredible being had carried me from the life I knew into a new world. By his gentle yet powerful presence, the curtain had dropped on Part One of my life, and the whole drama—all the actors and the entire script of my first twenty-five years—had faded into darkness.

Now, being ordained into sanyas, the curtain rose on My Life: Part Two. This time, I was to step onto the stage with no costume or script or role—just naked, as only my Self.

Swamiji walked out silently. He moves with an unusual grace; I frequently find myself checking the ground to see if his feet are really touching, rather than gliding a few inches above, the pavement. He and Maharajji bowed lovingly to each other and walked side by side out of the ashram and down the marble steps to the water.

Swamiji observes silence fourteen hours every day, a practice he began about twenty years ago, when his former practice, since childhood, of several months of silence each year was no longer feasible given the intensity of his many service projects. He now observes silence from 10 p.m. to 10 a.m. daily and for two hours each afternoon. So that morning, like all mornings, he did not speak, and Maharajji led the proceedings.

Maharajji and Swamiji sat on the steps at the water's edge. "Hold the chain and take a dip," Maharajji instructed. There are thick metal chains a few feet long attached to the bottom step for people to hold on to while they bathe, as the current is so strong. I did as he instructed. Holding tightly to the chain, my feet buried into the rocks and sand of the riverbed, I squatted low so the water would rush over my head. However, Ganga wasn't interested in gently washing over my head. The swift current swept my feet out from beneath me, and I had to pull hard on the chain to stand back up.

"Again," he said as I surfaced. It was an invocation, not a command. Maharajji wasn't simply instructing me to dip in the water. His words, the actions that followed, and the prayers that he and Swamiji chanted silently, their lips moving, were part of an ancient, intricate initiation ritual. I wasn't just dunking my head in a river. I was being ordained. Through the words, the prayers, the chants, and the blessings of these two saints, the goddess Ganga anointed me, purified me, washed over and through me, extricating all that was not conducive to a life of renunciation from the crevices of my being.

At times of emergency evacuation, when one is given only a few moments to gather up precious belongings and rush out to escape fire, flood, or storm, one has to decide, instinctively, what matters most, what's worth holding onto. As Maharajji instructed, "Again," "Again," "Again," each time I emerged from the current, the self with which I had always identified, the personality, the identity of whom I thought I was, let out a subtle evacuation call within me.

My ego reached out its arms and tried to grab hold of anything it could. Fear. Abandonment. Abuse. Desire. Longing. The suction cups of its octopus arms scraped against the inner walls of my self, grasping unsuccessfully for something to hold onto. Again and again, I dipped and let the waters carry me. Again and again, the current pulled me until I was horizontal in the water, arms outstretched toward the waning moon as she dipped behind the mountains, the top of which is the glacier from which Ganga descends onto Earth.

"Again," he said, no longer speaking to me but incanting the words of an ancient rite.

Eighteen times, I dipped in Ganga. Eighteen times, She pulled me until I was bowing, face down in the water, toward Her source, toward the womb of the Mother.

"*Ao*" (Come here), Maharajji said as I emerged the eighteenth time. "*Beto*" (Sit down). I sat on the step just beneath him. In his hands was a small bowl of black sesame seeds. "With each *sankalp*, each vow, offer the seeds in your right hand to Ganga. Each phrase I chant is another vow. Vows of renunciation. Vows of celibacy. Vows of simplicity. Vows of nonattachment. Vows to live only as an instrument of God. The sesame seeds are the medium of offering and promising."

I poured a small number of seeds from the steel bowl into my right hand. In Indian tradition, everything sacred, or even respectful, is done with the right hand. The left hand is used to clean oneself after using the toilet. Therefore, regardless of the copious amount of soap and water you may use to wash your hands after the toilet, that hand is considered impure. Whenever taking or offering anything, it is always done with the right hand. Eating, even with a utensil, is done only with the right hand. Religious rites and rituals are always done with the right hand.

Maharajji spoke the Sanskrit lines softly. They were not meant for my comprehension. I already knew what I was vowing. They were recited as prayer, as a bridge of sound connecting the three of us on the water's edge to the fullest, highest spirit of the Divine. They were a bridge to the source of shakti, the power with which I would be infused. They were a bridge to God, to whom I was surrendering. Handful by handful, I offered the seeds as Maharajji gently rocked back and forth, eyes closed, chanting. Beside him, Swamiji meditated—eyes sometimes closed, sometimes open, locked with Ganga, the lover and the beloved swimming in each other's boundless gaze.

When the ritual vows finished, Maharajji and Swamiji both rose silently and stepped down to the edge of the water. They took water in their right hands and each chanted silently to himself, holding the water in an outstretched cupped palm. Not a drop of water fell from either of their hands. After a few minutes, they both extended their fingers, tipped their hands, and offered the water back to Ganga, then bent down again and took more water, which they poured into their mouths. The third time, they bent, took water in their hands, and held it there.

"Come here," Maharajji said. I walked toward them as they turned to face the first rays of sun reaching over the Himalayas. I stood before them and brought my hands together in prayer. Maharajji hadn't told me to pray, but as I beheld these two masters' faces lit by the rising sun with Ganga flowing behind them, I could do nothing else.

Maharajji chanted in Sanskrit, and they both splashed the water from their cupped hands onto my head. I was still dripping wet from the eighteen baths in Ganga, so I was surprised by how strong these drops of water felt. A light spray of water on a soaked head should be barely perceptible, but these drops landed with such force that each of them seemed to pass through my skull, past the spongelike gray-and-white matter of my brain, and into the presence of my mind. These drops splashed onto the energy patterns from which my thoughts arose. With each drop, another thought pattern was washed away, like water bombs destroying the enemy's reserve banks.

When the spray ceased, I bowed low on the wet marble steps facing my two gurus. Then I sat up and opened my eyes, looking up at them. Maharajji took Swamiji's hands and placed them on my head, covering them with his own—their four hands on my head. My eyes closed from the weight of the energy. The physical mass of their hands weighed next to nothing, but the energy was so strong, I felt the roof of my skull crumble under the pressure. The energy poured, unencumbered by the bones of my skull, into and through my brain and mind.

My thoughts just stopped. I wasn't frozen or dead or comatose. I was fully alive, awake, and present. But my mind no longer moved, and where frenetic thoughts had previously raced, now there was space. It didn't feel *empty* empty It was a full emptiness, an empty fullness—a spacious vista opening onto the landscape of stillness.

I was still. Kneeling at their feet, I could hear Ganga flowing and the voices of people beginning to come to the water for their sacred bath. But these sounds did not enter me. I felt like a structure in one of those snow globes I had as a child—the New York skyline, or a house, or a snowman standing still while, with each shake of the dome, snow flurried around it. The building (or snowman) stayed unmoving no matter how hard I shook the globe.

My Self felt that stable. The world swirled around me, but nothing budged inside. There was a tight chain—not one I had to hold onto with my hands, but a heavy, steady anchor that seemed to go through the center of my self, from their hands on my head to the waters of Ganga beneath me: the energy flowing downward, the energy rising up, and an axis of still, spacious energy running through the center of myself.

"*Sadhvi* Bhagawati," Maharajji pronounced and then said it again, emphasizing the word *sadhvi* to the priest standing beside him. I opened my eyes. I did not realize they had removed their hands from my head, for even with open eyes, even seeing their hands back at their sides, Maharajji's right hand now on Swamiji's left shoulder, I could have sworn their hands were still there. They left an energetic impression on my head that is so strong, I still feel its presence today.

Swamiji, ever the mother, signaled for the priest to hand me a towel. I forgot that I was dripping wet. "Go and change," Maharajji said. I would not wear any clothes I had previously worn again. A new saree, blouse, and petticoat, with—very thoughtfully—new undergarments, were in a bag with the towel. The priest handed me the bag, and I walked toward the private changing area on the ghat.

As I peeled off my wet long robe and dried my body, my mind remained spacious—opening to vaster and vaster landscapes. The landscapes of my mind were not filled with artistic panoramic vistas; they were just space. It was not an absence of anything. The space itself was a presence, and it got wider and wider.

I put on my new clothes, smiling at the embroidery in my new white saree. I had just renounced all attachment to form, all identification with the body, but the sweet woman from Delhi who bought me the new clothes to wear had known it was a special occasion, and so she assumed it deserved a special saree, one with delicate patterning and embroidery.

Although sanyasis wear saffron, I continued to wear white. First, Swamiji worried that saffron robes would push my mother over the edge. She said as much: "I associate orange only with Swamiji, and I know he doesn't speak to his parents at all. So, in my mind, I associate orange clothes with not speaking to your parents. I think my heart will stop every time I see you in that color."

Swamiji had insisted that I get my parents' permission before taking sanyas, regardless of what color I was going to wear. So, on my visit to California the previous winter, I had sought their blessings. Outwardly, they had seemed fine with the decision. I had been living in India for nearly three years then, and they had probably expected some such turn of events. When one is initiated into sanyas, it is considered a new birth. Traditionally men emerge from Ganga naked, like a newborn babe. Prior to the ordination ritual, a soon-to-be-sanyasi performs several days of sacred fire ceremonies, including the literal "cremation" of one's past self. The birth name and all ties to that former self are burned in the sacred fire, and it's understood that the initiate will not be going back in thought or deed. In my case, a few exceptions were made due to my gender and culture. They had me emerge from Ganga still in my clothes and remove them only in the privacy of the changing room. I have also been permitted to share my story, to share my past, in order to inspire and help others, and for people to understand that I am not somehow different or holier or better.

So when I spoke to my parents to get their blessings on my decision, I assured them that I would still be able to be in touch with them, but that I was not permitted to use my birth name anymore. That would be burned in the fire. I was truly taking a new birth. It was okay with them, except the color. "Just please don't wear that color," my mom said, "or I'll keep dreading the day when you call and say 'I'm not going to talk to you anymore.'"

I also was not eager to wear orange. Orange is the color of pumpkins, and pumpkins are conspicuous. I believed I blended more into the background in white. It was simple, subtle, and, I thought, unobtrusive. As a foreigner, I already stood out more than I wanted to. To add orange robes would be too much. So, for ten years, I wore white, believing I blended in inconspicuously. But in April 2010, a few months shy of the ten-year anniversary of my sanyas, Maharajji and Swamiji gave me saffron robes during the Maha Kumbha Mela (after clearing it with my mother, of course, despite the fact that I was by then nearly forty).

In the saffron robes, I was too embarrassed to walk outside. "I feel like I am wearing a neon sign," I told Paavani, a close friend. She laughed and said, "Neon sign? Not at all. Now you'll blend in. In white, you stood out."

"What?" I couldn't believe it.

"Of course," she said, as though it were the most obvious thing in the world. "Here in India, everyone wears bright colors. Saffron looks just like another color, so you blend in. White is unusual. You really stood out all those years in white. Now you'll blend in nicely."

CHAPTER 38

Motherhood—
Even for a Sanyasi

NOVEMBER 2002

"I need a baby—I have to have a baby," I half-begged, half-panted. It was 2002, and I was thirty-one. I had been celibate since my experience on Ganga six years earlier. Even while I was still married to Jim, before I had realized our marriage was really over, I couldn't have sex anymore. Having been touched by something that permeated and filled me so much more deeply, my interest in sex was gone.

When desire did rise up in the years that followed, typically unexpectedly, catching me so off guard that I almost didn't recognize it, I practiced a meditation that Pujya Swamiji had taught me, allowing the energy to rise *within* me rather than clamor to be released. The initial urge is for climax and release, but yogis and sages, practicing austere celibacy along with fasting and silence, tapped into the energetic channels and chakras of the body so perceptibly that they realized that this energy has three potential outlets.

One is sexual release. The second is repression. It's simply pushed down and suppressed, like the pressurized containers we used in physics lab. But how much pressure can be exerted in a closed environment before it starts leaking out the corners or, if the box is airtight, explodes in an eruption of fiery fury? As so many of the masters of both spirituality and human psychology emphasize, we cannot suppress aspects of ourselves without having them leak out, or explode like volcanos. So, option number two doesn't really work, and it leads to frustration, restlessness, and belligerence as the building pressure escapes out the sides.

Yogis and sages, in their intense spiritual practice, developed a third option— recognizing the energy, welcoming it, neither denying nor repressing it, but containing it within the body. So, on the thankfully rare occasions when sexual desire would visit, I learned to sit down, wherever I was, close my eyes, put my hands on my heart, and use my breath to carry the energy upward into my heart and then into my third eye. If I could keep my mind on the practice rather than on the object of desire, in a few moments, my heart would begin to pulsate beneath my hands as the energy literally seemed to fill it.

As time went on, I learned to carry the energy even higher to the third-eye center, called the agya chakra. As I brought this energy of desire for communion and connection up to the energy center of divine sight, I could feel it tingle under my skin and begin to expand even though my physical eyes were closed. By the time I opened my eyes, whatever I saw was infused with divinity and I felt physically, energetically, and spiritually connected to everything around me. The urge for release of the self into a communion with another got transformed into an experience of communion with all. This meditation usually takes about ten or fifteen minutes, although sometimes I had to do it two or three times if the object of desire continued to appear in front of me. So, through a grace that I had neither earned, worked, expected, or even requested, most of the desire dissipated of its own accord, and my meditation was able to take care of the rest.

That took care of desire for physical connection. But I hadn't anticipated the power of the hormonal urge to propagate. While I was firm in my vows of celibacy, I needed a baby. Every time I saw a baby, my head would spin, pulled like iron to a magnet, my eyes glued to its pink cheeks. *Baby—I need a baby!* the cells of my body were screaming.

So, finally, I told Pujya Swamiji. "I need a baby."

"You what?" he asked.

"A baby—I have to have a baby, Swamiji. I am going crazy."

He looked at me and laughed. "OK—no problem. It happens. You should do whatever makes you happy. You do not have to stay as a sanyasi if that isn't what you want. If you say, I will find someone for you to marry. We can find you a nice Indian boy."

"No, Swamiji!" I moaned. "I don't want to get married. I don't want to give up being a sanyasi. I don't want to have sex. I just need a baby." He looked at me as though he might be thinking, "And who is the scientist around here?"

"Anyway," he said, amused and perhaps exasperated by the problem I had presented, "you decide. If you want to get married, no problem. You can stop being a sanyasi. Just tell me what you want."

I investigated the possibility of adoption but was informed that no adoption center would give a child to an unmarried foreign woman living in an ashram. Also, I realized that the vows of sanyas probably forbid me to legally adopt a child.

The waves came and went. Weeks would go by when this desire simply didn't arise, and then I'd be in an airport or in the aarti and see a mother holding her child, and the wave would rise and drown me. *A baby—I need a baby!* my body would scream into my brain.

"God will provide you," Pujya Swamiji always reminds people. Whatever the need, whatever the lack, whatever the concern, Swamiji's answer is the same: "God will take care. God will give you what you really need." He frequently shares stories of his days in the jungle, in need of a candle, when suddenly, out of nowhere, a villager would appear at his hut or along the road, candle in hand, and say, "Here—I thought you could use a candle."

God, in Pujya Swamiji's personal experience, is not only the provider of life but also the provider of the smallest things we need to sustain life—assuming, of course, that we're deeply connected to Him and that what we ask for is in accord with our highest unfolding and awakening. So, as I frequently remind people in satsang, God is not a vending machine who gives us what we want or think we paid for; rather, he gives us what we need, including candles for devotees doing intense sadhana in the forest.

And babies?

In November of that year, I was walking on the long, flat ghat on the edge of the Ganga after aarti. It's nearly the size of a football field, a place for thousands to sit and meditate. Barefoot and silent on the cool marble platform in the chilly night air, I walked as an evening ritual, a time of personal meditation, silently chanting my mantra with each step, the only noise that of the waves crashing on the steps.

Suddenly, a young man approached me excitedly. He was in his late twenties or early thirties and had two tiny boys with him, one in his arms and one hanging onto his finger. "How can I put my children into your gurukul?" he asked.

In 2000, we opened the gurukul at Parmarth, a project Pujya Swamiji had dreamed about for many years. It's a free residential program for orphaned, poor, and disadvantaged boys, and they receive shelter, food, and education—academic and traditional Vedic education, including sacred rites and rituals, scriptural study, Sanskrit, and more. Initially, we envisioned it only for orphans, but it quickly grew to include anyone who needed to be there, anyone whose parents could not fully and properly care for them.

The rishikumars, the boys at the gurukul, wore yellow dhoti and kurtas, the traditional outfit of religious men and priests. They led the rituals of the aarti, sat in front, and sang rapturously. Many who came to the aarti shared how touched they were by watching the boys' faces in ecstasy.

This young gentleman repeated himself, his fair skin flushed with excitement. "It is so beautiful to see these young children singing so divinely. Please, will you accept my children? I want them to receive the same opportunity for such a divine life."

"Where are you from?" I asked.

"A small village about an hour from the city of Jammu," he said. "It is far, but I came here because there is a Gita Bhavan temple branch in our local village and I knew they have a branch in Rishikesh also, so I came here with my children in search of a better life for them. When I saw these young boys singing and chanting so beautifully and I saw the smiles on their faces and the glow on Pujya Swamiji's face, I knew this is the right place for them."

I looked at the two tiny children with him. Our gurukul accepts five- and six-year-olds. We don't have the infrastructure for those who need assistance going to the bathroom, bathing, or brushing their teeth. These children looked too young.

"He is two," the man responded to my unasked question, nodding toward the young boy in his arms. "And she is four." The child on the end of his fingers had black hair cut close to her face and wore the same gray shirt, black pants, and solemn expression as her brother. They had both appeared to be boys.

"I am so sorry," I said. "Two is much too young, and our gurukul doesn't take girls. We are planning to hopefully open one for girls soon, but at the moment we have only boys. However, if you stay here and they stay with you, then I am sure we can arrange for her to study in the gurukul in the day and stay with you in the night."

He was ecstatic. "This is a dream come true," he gushed. "I will do whatever seva you say. I cannot believe we are so fortunate, so blessed, to be able to stay in such a holy place."

Each day, they came and spent time in my office. The father, Rameshwar, gushed effusively about his joy of being there and the possibility of a better life for his children, free from the difficulties they faced in their home and village. The two children were mostly silent and stoic.

Slowly, I began to get a half smile from the young girl, Shivani. As the days turned into a week, she began to crawl into my lap as soon as they entered my office, feeling somehow entitled to occupy that space and push onto the keys of my keyboard, clearly a device she'd never seen. Tap-tap-tap, she would push.

When I drew her attention to the monitor to show her how what she tapped was appearing on the screen, her mouth opened wide and she exclaimed, "Ah, Daddy, come see!" And she tapped and tapped, pointing to the monitor. She couldn't, of course, read, but simply the fact that this device responded to her taps in such an obedient way thrilled her to no end.

From then on, I had to make sure to close out all programs I was working in whenever she entered my office, because inevitably, if I merely took a breath, or a sip of water, or sneezed, she would tap-tap, push-push, wreaking havoc on any document or file. But it was worth it. As she sat in my lap, folding her legs between mine, tapping the keys and touching everything within arm's reach, I knew I loved her.

After they had been at the ashram for about a week, Rameshwar came in one day and said he needed to go back to Jammu. His wife had found out where he was, through connections between their local Gita Bhavan center and the one next to our ashram, and she insisted he return home. He was a clerk in a local government office, and government jobs are hard to come by. Even in a small town, as a clerk, the perks and benefits outweigh any other potential employment. To lose that opportunity at such a young age would not be wise.

"I will take Shivam back with me," he explained, "as he is so young. I can protect him and care for him properly. But I am worried about Shivani. I cannot properly care for her. Can she stay here with you all?"

The ashram is filled with hundreds of permanent residents. Elderly widows, retired householders, and young seekers who are more eager to delve into the depths of spiritual practice than into married life fill ashram rooms and pathways, and meditate on benches in the sunshine.

There was a young woman living at the ashram at that time named Vasudha, who had come from a city on the outskirts of Delhi. She was in her early twenties, well educated and cultured, and spent her days in prayer, meditation, and worship of a small image of Lord Krishna she had installed in her room. She would be perfect to care for Shivani, as she had the time and the youthful energy, as well as the culture and values needed to raise a young girl.

I spoke with Pujya Swamiji, and he agreed, given the circumstances of Shivani's home situation, that despite her father having to return, she could stay and Vasudha would be perfect to care for her.

However, at that moment, Vasudha was away for a few days. It was Kartik Purnima, the full moon of the month of Kartik, which falls during October and November and is very holy for worshippers of Lord Krishna. She had gone to Vrindavan, the city where Lord Krishna had lived, to dance and pray in the moonlight as the gopis had danced with Krishna on this same night so many thousands of years ago.

"No problem," I told Rameshwar. "She can stay with me for a night or two until Vasudha returns." His eyes filled with tears as he bowed low to touch my feet in gratitude. "I cannot believe how God has sent you to us," he said.

When the time came for him to leave, Shivani barely noticed. Tap-tap, push-push on the keys of my computer. Amid the giggles, there was a "Bye" as he walked out the door, Shivam in his arms, to catch the train back to Jammu.

Shivani spent that night in my bed. She didn't begin there, as my room has two single beds and she had her own. However, a few hours into the night, she awoke with a start and began crying. "Ao, ao" (Come, come), I said. She crawled into my bed, still crying in her sleep. The single beds at the ashram are not like single beds anywhere I've ever been, although the ones in my Stanford dorm were close. These beds are so small that an obese American would spill out over the edges. They are definitely not beds for two. But when one has a four-year-old crying in the night, practical matters are secondary.

She curled up into my body as I held her, her heart beating through her bony back into my hands. I drifted into sweet, albeit short-lived, sleep. Shivani's legs had uncurled and now were attempting to push their way through my abdomen. She had a knee in my ribs, then a foot in my belly button, then an elbow in my chin.

I turned her over onto her other side and held her close from behind, lest she push her way out of the bed. However, her kicks were remarkably adaptable, as now her legs flailed backward, heels planted firmly into my stomach. It was a sleepless but blissful night as I held this beautiful gift of life in my arms.

In the morning, I filled the bucket in my bathroom with warm water and picked up her wriggling naked body. "No, no!" she giggled and shrieked, pulling her legs tight into her body like a turtle, lest her toes touch the water. "It's nice— it's warm," I explained. She didn't understand. Her home must not have had a hot-water geyser.

I took her hand and gently put her fingers in the bucket. Her eyes lit up. "Warm water." She raised her arms so I could lift her and place her into the bucket, bottom first, with her calves dangling over the edge. One plastic bucket. A few gallons of warm water. A bar of soap. These were the only ingredients necessary to turn my small bathroom into her own personal Disneyland.

She laughed and yelped and splashed, scooping water out and throwing it on her face and head. I put a bit of shampoo into the palms of my hands and began to wash her hair. Her arms continued to toss handfuls of soapy water into the air and now into my face as I bent low to shampoo her hair. I filled jugs of water to rinse it, but as I brought each jug close to her head, her hand shot up to block it. No, no—she was not ready to be rinsed off yet. She was not ready to abandon her soapy paradise.

Later that afternoon, Vasudha returned from Vrindavan, and I explained the situation. She happily agreed to the seva of caring for Shivani. I introduced her to Shivani and explained to Shivani that she would be staying with Vasudha from now on. She could come visit me, of course, whenever she wanted, but she was to stay with Vasudha.

She let Vasudha take her by the hand out of my office and back to her room. However, at 10:30 that night, there was a knock on my door. I had not slept the night before, due to the kicking of my beloved bedmate, and I was just getting into bed. I went to the door, and there stood a harried Vasudha with a screaming Shivani in her arms. "She'll only sleep with you, didi," Vasudha said in English. "I tried." (*Didi* is the Hindi term for "older sister" and is used respectfully on its own or as a suffix.)

Shivani leaped from Vasudha's arms and past me into my room. *"Kya hua?"* (What happened?) I asked Vasudha.

"She was fine all afternoon and evening," she replied. "She played nicely in my room and even ate her supper. But when I tried to put her down to bed, she started crying and said she would only sleep with you. I have spent the last hour trying to get her to calm down and sleep, but she will not. I don't know what to do. I am sorry."

"Don't worry," I assured her. "Get some sleep, and we'll sort this out tomorrow."

I walked back into my room to find Shivani asleep, sprawled across my bed.

For many months, she lived with me, slept in my bed, bathed in my bucket, burrowed her way deep into my identity and existence.

She went to school at the free day school we run for children of the ashram as well as local children in need of education. In the afternoons, she played with the rishikumars. I bought her yellow bottoms to match the boys' dhotis, and she wore the same yellow kurta top. She sat on the floor of my office, a small individual dining table as her desk, coloring, cutting, and eating peanuts and popcorn. Each evening at aarti, she lined up with the rishikumars at the very front of the line to escort Pujya Swamiji down to the riverbank.

In the aarti, she sat as near to Pujya Swamiji as possible, watching him closely out of the corner of her eye as she mimicked every motion. When he sang, raising his arms into the air ecstatically, she, too, threw her arms in the air. She swayed when he swayed, clapped when he clapped, and sang only his portion of the call-and-response. Alone in my office, she would repeat the full rendition of aarti, now free to go beyond accompanying Pujya Swamiji and actually be him. "Hare Krishna, Hare Krishna, Krishna Krishna Hare Hare!" she bellowed, her body leaning dramatically, first left, then right. "Hare Rama Hare Rama, Rama Rama Hare Hare!" she threw her arms in the air, eyes closed, pumping the sky with her palms.

One evening in January, at the peak of winter cold, I stayed back in my office during the aarti, finishing up some work. A few moments after Pujya Swamiji left to walk down to Ganga, flanked by rows of yellow-clad rishikumars, led on one side by my adopted daughter, I noticed she had forgotten her shawl in the office. The sun was setting, and it would be fifty degrees and dark by the time the aarti finished. I grabbed the maroon wool shawl, identical to the ones the rishikumars wore, and rushed after her, sprinting down the main ashram pathway in my bare feet. But they were too far ahead and were already descending the steps to aarti by the time I reached the main gate.

Despondent and bewildered, I stood there imagining icicles hanging from her short hair, her lips blue and body frigid. Suddenly, I began to laugh. The sun was setting on the opposite side of the river, the last rays of light dancing on Mother Ganga's waters. The opening stanza of the "Hanuman Chalisa" had begun, and the old ladies sitting on benches lining the pathway beside me began to sing along. Here I was, I laughed, a white-robed sanyasi, a celibate renunciant, racing anxiously—woolens in hand—after a four-year-old girl lest she catch cold near the river. I had become a mother after all.

"Who is she?" people asked, as it was unusual to see a small Indian child on the end of the pinkie finger of an American nun. "She's my daughter," I responded. Should anyone need to verify it, I would ask her, *"Tum kis ki ho?"* (Whose are you?) She would look up at me and smile, *"Aap ki"* (Yours).

Several months later, in the spring, her father returned, along with Shivani's mother. Swamiji spent several days counseling them, trying to bring peace into a marriage pervaded by abuse and blame.

"No!" Shivani cried, flinging herself flat like a pancake on the wall of my office when they tried to take her back to Jammu. As they tried, one after the other, to peel her from the wall, she sank down in a limp puddle of tears. "No, I don't want to go." She cried my tears as well, for I had to keep my face dry. I had to be the adult here and do the right thing. *Of course, any child would be better off with her mother and father, regardless of their circumstances, rather than living in an ashram with someone as busy as I am*, I reasoned to myself. *This is what's best for her*, I repeated as a mantra in my own mind, staving off despair at how God could so cruelly grab back the gift He'd given us both so lovingly.

"You'll come back very soon, my love," I told her, breathing as deeply as I could to keep my voice from cracking. Biju, one of the young men living in seva at the ashram, threw her limp, sobbing body gently over his shoulder and carried her to the rickshaw that would take her family to the train station.

"Maya kaha chele gi?" (Where has Maya gone?) Pujya Swamiji asked me later that day. "Her name is Shiv—," I began to correct him and then stopped suddenly. My words froze in my throat. *Maya* is the Sanskrit word for "illusion." It's used to refer not to literal optical illusions, like the mirage of water in the desert, but to that hypnotic power that wraps its veil around our inner eye, convincing us that the transitory is permanent, that the form is content, that the physical world is real. Maya is that which keeps people living life only on the outermost level, the veil that prevents us from seeing the Truth.

"God has given this opportunity," he continued, "not merely for you to give the gift of love to a child, but also for you to experience the bonds of attachment and how to break through them to the truest, highest love."

He looked at me and shook his head with gentle disappointment. "So far, you have learned only how to be attached and how to give love out of your own attachment. Go beyond this. Learn to love without requiring her physical body in your lap all the time. Learn to love bigger than just feeding her peanuts and popcorn."

Shivani returned before the heat of summer, brought by her father into my open arms. "We are so blessed," he said, "that she has you, that we all have you." For the next several years, she traveled back and forth between Rishikesh and Jammu, spending most of her time in Rishikesh, whenever I wasn't traveling abroad.

Shivani's parents responded to this new turn of events in Shivani's life with gratitude and deference—deference to my role as a religious leader and to my background academically, economically, and culturally, and effusive gratitude for the inexplicable blessing their young daughter was receiving. Their own personal circumstances and the difficulties therein occupied most of their mind and attention anyway.

I tried not to let my tears of joy show upon her arrival, nor my tears of sorrow upon her departure. I tried to focus each day on loving her essence, not only her form, of loving the divine content of her being. As I held her tiny body in my arms at night while she kicked her way to sleep, I focused on loving her soul, on expanding my own love from the confines of the heart in my chest to my own boundless soul. This gently snoring being and I merged into an ocean of love where there was no place she ended and I began.

A few years later, when her front teeth fell out, I could focus only on how cute she was. I couldn't look at her without laughing joyously. Then her permanent teeth grew in, and I could again focus on loving her soul.

Our years together passed in much the same way as normal parent/child relationships go—minus, thankfully, any teenage rebellion. I sent her to a high-end all-girls boarding school about two hours from Rishikesh in the city of Dehradun, the famous former British hill station with schools that count former prime minister Rajiv Gandhi among their alumni.

In India, students are required to choose their academic path much sooner than we are in the West. I remember letters I got during my third year at Stanford that began, "Dear undeclared junior" and proceeded to give me a deadline by which I needed to make a decision—sometime during the junior year of college. In India, from tenth grade on, the streams separate—science or humanities or commerce.

Humanities and commerce are the common choices. Science is, as I remember from college days, chosen only by the crazy few who are (*a*) driven enough to truly live, breathe, eat, and sleep schoolwork for the next God knows how many years of life and (*b*) endowed with ability and intelligence to speak the language of numbers foreign to the rest of us.

I had excelled in math in high school and on standardized tests. Scoring near the one-hundredth percentile on my SAT math and having completed college-level Advanced Placement math in high school, I expected to walk into freshman math at Stanford and continue to excel—except that I couldn't understand a word the teacher said. "Is this the right class?" I wondered. Alas, it was, and I quickly realized I would need to take it pass/fail rather than for a grade. To pass, in itself, would be a miracle. Those who stayed in the sciences were those I believed to be masochistic, unbelievably dedicated, or outrageously gifted, none of which was I. But now my daughter wanted to do science. Out of her class of about twenty students, only two chose science. "What do you want to do as a scientist?" I asked her.

"Go into outer space," Shivani said. *Oh, my God*, I thought. *I've raised an astronaut!*

"Do you like physicals lab?" I asked.

"No."

"Do you like chemistry lab?"

"No."

"Do you realize that astronauts spend much, much, much more of their time in laboratories than in outer space?"

"Oh." Her face fell. "Well, then, I will do computers. I like computers." Still, science.

"Are you sure?" I asked.

I tried to stay present with my commitment to support and nourish her every step of the way and to make sure she knew that all doors of life were open to her. Just because she had come from a village, just because her family wasn't well educated, there was no reason she could not reach the stars. I had been emphasizing this since she was four years old. However, her grades were fine but not fantastic. She consistently scored well above average but not at the top. She was not a born academic.

One day, she told me, "My biology professor is crazy. He expects us to learn too much. I mean, OK, there is a cell. Then, inside the cell, there are so many things. Then, inside that, there is a nucleus. Inside the nucleus, there are so many things. And then, inside that and inside that and inside that. Doesn't it end? How much can we really learn?"

She had to reaffirm her commitment to science in her tenth- and then twelfth-class exams. I continued to open doors for her, as every time we spoke, her only stress was her science classes. "Are you still sure you want to do science? If not, there are many other possibilities open to you." She was always sure. She was even sure when, having been so confident that she would get into one of the top science institutes in the country, one of the Indian Institutes of Technology, with a cutoff at the 99.97 percentile, she applied nowhere else. When she didn't get in but received offers to study humanities or commerce at other universities, she turned them down and enrolled instead in an intense yearlong computer course to prepare for retaking the science exams the following year.

In the debate of nature verses nurture in child development, I think they left out a third variable: Whether you call it karma, destiny, or out-of-the-blue greatness, not everything can be explained by nature, nurture, or the overlap between them.

Shivani's academic tenacity, her willingness to stay awake night after night studying, to take not what came easily but what needed to be worked for, was not in her DNA or her home or ashram environment. It grew in fertile soil that seemed to be from another garden altogether, one I had never visited, but marveled at constantly. She excelled in her exams the second time around, got her first choice of campus and degree, and has now completed her bachelor of technology (B.Tech.) degree in software engineering and has been hired by a well-reputed multi-national company.

As nearly all marriages in India are still arranged by the parents, I find my mind floating toward young men her age I know who would make good spouses in a few years.n a recent conversation we were discussing her parents, who finally, albeit temporarily, took some time apart from each other after decades of mutual abuse. They both called us frequently and begin their conversations asking whether we'd heard from the other: "Has he called you?" "Has she called you?"

Shivani said to me during that time, "I've told my mother that I will not answer that question, because it is of no benefit to her to know whether he has called. It has no relevance to her life, and she should not be asking things like that. She needs to get herself involved in some good work, because she overthinks everything and this causes her to suffer."

She said it very casually. We had been laughing about the silliness of them splitting up, only to constantly try to monitor each other's actions. We were chatting about her upcoming internship. She did not warn me that she was going to make a brilliant spiritual pronouncement. She did not say, "Sit down, because this is really going to excite you." She just said it as though it were the most obvious thing in the world. Of course, to me it was. To me, at forty-six, having dedicated nearly half my life to spiritual practice, this was obvious. But to her? At nineteen? At nineteen, I had my head in toilets, throwing up Twix bars and Häagen-Dazs as a poor substitute for throwing up feelings that could not be felt.

"I am so proud of you" was all I could muster, my voice choking with gratitude for the gift of mothering this incredible being.

CHAPTER 39

Monkey Face

2004

It doesn't happen so much now that I'm a middle-aged woman, but in the beginning, when I was a vibrant twentysomething, people would ask me, "Don't you ever think about romance or sensual pleasures? Do you really want to be celibate forever?"

In the beginning, the ecstasy of the spiritual experience was so overwhelming that it didn't leave space in my psyche for anything else. Hunger, fatigue, and discomfort slipped from my awareness. I ate when the bell rang for meals. I slept in the night because it was dark, we had no TVs or internet, smart phones didn't exist yet, and I could meditate only for so long before slumber dragged my body onto the bed. None of these was an internal call. I had no experience of hunger—not in my stomach for food or for physical or sensual pleasures.

Those internal biological mechanisms had been flooded into stillness by the waves of spiritual experience.

This absence of physical desire—whether for bagels or for sex—lasted even after the initial ecstasy waned and my spiritual experiences became more internal and less as though I'd been swept up by an ecstatic tornado. The fulfillment that my new spiritual life provided, the deep inner connection I'd been gifted on the banks of Ganga, removed the longing to reach out and fill myself with either food or a relationship. On the rare occasions when these urges did arise, as explained in the previous chapter, I learned to meditate and channel the energy upward.

That was until a particular famous actor came to the ashram. On the second day of his visit, we sat in my office talking about my spiritual life and his movie career. Suddenly, he said, "I'm very attracted to you." I froze. I was supposed to be a spiritual teacher, not a love interest! I carefully deflected the comment without blatantly ignoring it, and our conversation regained its former flow. Neither of us ever mentioned or hinted at it again.

However, his comment, natural coming from a thirtysomething unmarried man to a thirtysomething unmarried (albeit celibate) woman, was a match reigniting a fire that had long ago been extinguished. I couldn't stop thinking about him.

He left Rishikesh the following morning, but our friendship continued, and each time we met, I felt a surge of excitement. Romantic fantasies brewed in my mind. I found myself daydreaming about him in the midst of work. Finally, I told Swamiji. "I have a confession to make," I began, my face flushed and my eyes looking down at my fingers in my lap as though the secret of how to share this confession lay in careful examination of my fingernails. He said nothing and waited for me to continue. I couldn't speak.

"Yes?" he finally prompted. I hated myself. How could I possibly admit this? What had I gotten myself into? Now he was waiting for me to speak, but of course, there was nothing I could say. "Yes?" he repeated a few minutes later, as though I had simply forgotten that I had come in with an announcement.

"It's about [I'll call him] Tom."

"Hmmm?" Swamiji responded and picked up a file on his table. If I was going to take all day to spit it out, he might as well peruse some of the papers on his desk.

My face felt so hot, I thought it would melt off my skull and drip onto my lap. It was not from shame, but from embarrassment that I had to tell my guru about what I felt. Yet, in an odd way, it felt good. Giddy good. I giggled a bit as my face got redder. Swamiji looked up from his papers at my red face and into my eyes, which, despite all my willpower, I could not raise to meet his. "Oh, no," he said, laughing. "Really? Come on."

"I don't know what to do," I said, and I refocused my deep concentration on my fingers fidgeting in my lap.

"Do? There is nothing to do. Ignore it, and it will go away. Work harder. Do your japa, your meditation practice, whenever the thought comes, and don't pay attention to it."

"But . . . ," I stammered. How to explain that I was enjoying the experience?

Swamiji gently put down the paper on his desk and looked at me with loving pity. Just as a mother explains to her child after they come home from the Arctic exhibit at the zoo that no, a polar bear cub would not be a good pet—yes, it's cute, yes, it's cuddly, but polar bears do not belong in suburban homes—in that same voice, he explained to me that, no, fantasies of Tom did not belong in my celibate life and could come to no good conclusion.

"One day," Swamiji began as he sat back in his chair, "the great sage Narada was visited by a king and his daughter. The king asked Narada to look at his daughter's palm and bless her future, as the day of her *swayambara* was approaching. On this day, she would choose her groom from among a castle full of eligible bachelors. Narada—a holy rishi, a brilliant spiritual guru, and the author of the Bhakti Sutras—took the young girl's hand in his. However, rather than reading her palm, he became intoxicated by its softness. He could see only his own yearning in the delicate lines running along her pink, silky skin. As he raised his eyes and beheld the princess's beauty, Narada was transfixed.

"Quickly regaining his composure before the king noticed, Narada told the king that his daughter was the embodiment of goddess Lakshmi and that no one less than Hari—Lord Vishnu—would be her groom. The king was thrilled to receive the sage's blessing and requested that Narada grace the swayambara with his presence. Narada agreed, planning not just to grace the event but to be the one chosen by the princess.

"Narada knew that he had the wisdom and greatness to marry the princess, but not the beauty. So, he rushed to Lord Vishnu and begged him, "O Lord, please bestow upon me thy glorious face of Hari, the effulgent face of the Divine." Lord Vishnu, knowing all that transpired, told him, *'Tathaastu'* (And so it is).

"Narada strutted into the swayambara, ecstatic in his confidence that the beautiful princess's hand would be his, for he now had the face of Hari, the glorious, divine lord. As the princess walked up and down the rows and aisles, surveying one potential groom after another, Narada waited patiently, knowing that the moment she came upon his divine greatness—both in wisdom and in beauty—she would put the flower garland upon his head, symbolizing her selection.

"However, when she came to Narada, she looked at him and, with a slight smile on her lips, continued to the next man in line. Narada was incensed. How was it possible? He stormed out of the castle and found a river in which to behold his reflection. As soon as he knelt down at the river, he understood. Lord Vishnu had given him the face of a monkey. One of the meanings of the word *hari* in Sanskrit is "monkey." Lord Vishnu had fulfilled his promise to Narada. He had given the sage the face of Hari.

"Lord Vishnu knew that Narada was not meant to run off with the princess and live in a castle. He was a great, unparalleled sage and rishi who was needed for humanity. Narada was meant to write the Bhakti Sutras, a unique and sacred treatise on devotion. His life was not fated to be running after sensual pleasures with a beautiful woman. So, when asked for the face of Hari, Vishnu gave him a face that would teach him a lesson, a face that would make him face himself and understand who he really is and what he is meant to do and to be, not a face that would win the princess's hand."

"*Samje?*" (Do you understand?) Pujya Swamiji asked me after concluding the story. "You are not meant for that life either. You are meant for something deeper, for something more. To run off with Tom is not your dharma."

"OK," I ceded, but I probably didn't sound as convinced as he would have liked.

"If you continue this nonsense, I will have to give you a monkey face. Now go."

CHAPTER 40

In the Womb of the Mother

Less than 200 miles north of Rishikesh, high in the Himalayas where India meets China, lies a sacred area known as Char Dham (Four Sacred Abodes). There, each of four holy pilgrimage sites is home to a sacred temple at the source of a sacred river. Three of these rivers join at Dev Prayag (Divine Confluence), and it's here that the river Ganga is born. From this point, it flows 1,500 miles to the sea.

Even though she is formed by the merging of three rivers, one of these—the Bhagirathi River—is worshipped as the Ganga, and the source of the Bhagirathi/Ganga River is the Gaumukh Glacier. This is the place where, according to legend, the goddess Ganga came down from heaven in the form of water and, by Grace, stayed on to uplift and free the hearts, minds, and lives of those who come to her.

Ever since I had first stood on the banks of the Ganga, I had yearned to bathe in the waters of her source, the Gaumukh Glacier, the sacred womb of the Divine Mother and the womb through which she came. The mere mention of Gaumukh caused my cells to rearrange the way iron filings act in the presence of a magnet. Gaumukh was due north for every molecule in my body. It called to my heart.

Eleven miles from Gaumukh Glacier is the Gangotri Temple, situated at 10,000 feet. Originally, the temple was much closer to the glacier—perhaps at its perimeter—but global warming has caused the glacier's tragic erosion, and it recedes by a depressing number of meters per year, farther from the temple erected in its honor. One must now trek eleven miles through high-altitude forests to reach the glacier beyond the town of Gangotri.

The town lies 150 miles north of Rishikesh, but due to the narrow, winding, frequently jammed mountainous roads one must travel to reach it, the journey takes an entire day. After I arrived at the ashram, Pujya Swamiji traveled there twice to attend events and invited me to join him, but I declined. I couldn't bear being close to the Mother's womb, the glacier so near the temple, but unable to make the pilgrimage due to time constraints. So, I waited till I could have it all—see the temple and immerse myself in the source of the Mother.

Pujya Swamiji's birthday is on June 3, during the hottest time of the year in India. The Indian "summer" is considered to be May and June, with school and government holidays and a tenfold increase in Indian visitors to Rishikesh. In May 1997, my first summer there, I sent my parents a David Letterman–type top-ten list titled, "You Know It's Hot When . . ." The list included:

- At 4 a.m., when you walk out of a cold shower, you need another cold shower.
- Your toothpaste melts in its tube and pours like water onto your toothbrush.
- The candle you light for morning prayers and then extinguish before leaving your room does a full backbend during the day, so that by evening, both the base and the wick are stuck to the fabric of your shrine.

During my first experience of Indian summer, all I could do was laugh. Could it really be this hot? I was sweating in places I didn't know could perspire. Sweaty shins? But the Indians seemed not to mind enough to keep from flocking to Rishikesh for the holidays.

Swamiji does not permit pomp and show for his birthday. Except for the epic celebrations we threw him—surprises up to the last minute—for his fiftieth and sixtieth birthdays, he prefers we treat his birthday like any other day. It is foolish, he teaches, as many of the great saints do, to celebrate the natural process of age and decay of a vehicle. The body, he says—as much as we revel in its beauty, as much as its voice carries us to heaven, as much as a smile and the love pouring forth from its eyes wipe clean our slate of self-hatred, worthlessness, and insecurity—is "just form."

In May 2007, a decade after I compiled my top-ten list, Pujya Swamiji agreed that I could plan a yatra, a sacred pilgrimage, for his fifty-fifth birthday. We had been to Badrinath and Kedarnath in the previous few years. We had trekked the wooded dirt path to Gangharia and from there to the Valley of the Flowers and Hemkund Sahib. We had been to Mount Kailash and Lake Mansarovar three times. But we had never been to Gaumukh.

"Can we go to Gangotri?" I asked, nearly breathless with excitement.

"Sure," he said.

"And," I said, then paused. What if he said, "No"? Would I burst into tears? Would I be able to see the perfection in that too? Probably not. I was attached to getting out to the Source of the Mother. "Can we trek out to Gaumukh?" The moment passed gently, and he said, "Sure."

So, on May 30, 2007, a fleet of cars departed Parmarth Niketan for Uttarkashi, the halfway point between Rishikesh and Gangotri. Uttarkashi lies, geographically, more than a hundred miles from Rishikesh and only thirty-five miles from Gangotri. But the upper Ganga Basin, the pristine, fragile, sacred ecozone between Uttarkashi and Gangotri, is so mountainous that the drive takes as long as the one from Rishikesh to Uttarkashi.

We reached Uttarkashi by late afternoon. Pujya Swamiji had organized a special aarti there on the banks of the Bhagirathi. In addition to Parmarth's world-famous aarti, this sacred ritual, the evening "Happy Hour," he has begun aartis in more than a dozen cities along the banks of Ganga—including Gangotri, Uttarkashi, Rudraprayag, Jwalapur, Kanpur, Allahabad, and Varanasi.

My mind was focused on only one thing—getting to Gaumukh. The aarti was beautiful, extraordinarily so, as the priests and residents of this sacred town joined together in waving oil lamps, a ritual usually performed only in temples. "Ganga is our temple," Swamiji always says, "a 1,500-mile flowing temple."

That evening, post-aarti, local leaders came to meet with him to request that he adopt the local gurukul, a Sanskrit residential school that had been horribly damaged in the earthquake a decade earlier and had never been rebuilt. The roof was collapsing, and most of the premises were unusable. It was only the devotion and tenacity of those in charge that kept it open, but now they were out of funds. If they did not secure help, the Veda Shala (home of Vedas) would have to be shut down. "Of course we'll adopt it," Swamiji told them.

We left early the next morning for Gangotri, hairpin turn after hairpin turn up the Himalayas. I'm convinced that only a strong belief in reincarnation permits people to drive on these roads. Ganga rushes through the steep valley below while cars and buses in both directions vie for the narrow roadway perched between steep mountainsides to one side and a sheer drop to the other. Because the Himalayas are young, what locals call *kachha* (not really firm), they are prone to landslides and avalanches, and the roads to any of the four Char Dham yatra sites are often blocked for weeks, especially during the rainy season.

The local solution is to dynamite the mountain, then clear away the rubble. Boom! The road is wider—a temporary success—but the next mudslides are usually worse, because the mountains have been destabilized by the dynamite. And the boulders and dirt fall into the rushing waters of Ganga, choking the narrow river. And each time tourists complain about the landslides, the officials decide to blast more dynamite to make the road wider. As we drove through these mountains, I laughed at the bureaucratic and engineering absurdity, and I cried at the ramifications this has for the sacred mountains and those who live here.

Finally, we reached Gangotri, and I ran down from the guesthouse to the rushing, icy waters of Bhagirathi Ganga, a mere eleven miles from her source. Promises to my mother not to drink the water were long forgotten, made in another time and place. I scooped it up by the handful, raising my cupped palms to eager lips. I could not get enough. Palmful after palmful I drank. It was the sweetest nectar I'd ever tasted—and so cold, my teeth began to throb. The water quenched not only my tongue and throat but every yearning I had ever known as well.

Early the following morning, June 2, as I laced up my hiking boots, the adrenaline rush began. I had spent many blissful weekends and vacations hiking, trekking, and backpacking through the mountains of California, Wyoming, Montana, and other parts of the United States. Trekking on dirt paths through winding redwood and pine forests was by far my favorite way to spend free time. Since moving to India, however, I hadn't done any hiking except for our pilgrimages to Lake Mansarovar and Mount Kailash in Tibet, and trips to Badrinath and Kedarnath. In ten years, I'd laced these boots just a handful of times.

There were two distinct yet intermingling levels of my adrenaline rush that morning: first, just to have those hiking boots on and know that in a few hours, I'd be far from cars, roads, and buildings, and would be walking farther and farther into the woods. My companions would be the trees; my vision would rest only on the path ahead and the wide, dense forest surrounding it. When I raised my eyes, I would catch glimpses of deep blue sky—ever still and present as the canvas for the forest and mountains. In a few hours, my breath would draw more quickly, and my lips would part gently as my lungs filled with high-altitude mountain air—rich with sacred energy but low on oxygen. In that slightly oxygen-deprived state, my mind would become deeply still.

In years long before I had ever heard the words *mantra* or *japa*, I experienced their power hiking in the mountains. As I climbed the Grand Canyon as a teenager, we trekked from the river up to the canyon ridge, up hundreds of switchbacks to where our cars were—an elevation gain of almost 5,000 feet. We began in a group and seamlessly paired off into twos and threes based on hiking speed, but all I wanted was to be alone. I hiked more and more quickly to leave the chatty groups behind so I'd be surrounded only by the emptiness of the Grand Canyon and the heat rising from the sandstone. Soon, I couldn't see anyone ahead or behind me.

Oh, wow, oh, wow, oh, wow, I found myself saying over and over in my mind. Over the six-hour hike, I sweated and became breathless and lightheaded, while something inside kept repeating, *Oh, wow, oh, wow*. Right left right left right left—*oh, wow, oh, wow, oh, wow*. It stayed with me until I drifted off to sleep that night. By morning, I was left with the memory and a permanent impression on my seventeen-year-old psyche that I had *merged* with the Grand Canyon.

Today, we would trek eight and a half miles to Bhojwasa, a tiny hamlet only a few miles from Gaumukh, the only place between Gangotri and the glacier where one can stay the night. There is a threadbare government tourist bungalow there, at which we'd be staying, and a simple ashram—Lal Baba Ashram—where some of our yatris would stay. Eight and a half heavenly miles in my beloved hiking boots, no task except to breathe, no sights except the winding path, no sounds but the rush of the river far below. I so longed for the silence into which I could merge with the pulsing of the trees, the crashing of the river against her rocky banks, and the songs of the birds.

The second reason for my adrenaline rush was that each delicious step, each exquisite moment of merging with the mountains themselves, would bring me closer and closer to Gaumukh, closer and closer to the sacred womb of Mother Ganga.

As we began the trek through the ranger station gates bordering Gangotri, the path narrowed and I wanted to sprint ahead to fall in tears at the feet of the trees, lie in the comfort of the pine needles of the Himalayan chir pine trees, roll and fall in prayer on the earthen path as it rose above the narrow river below. But I could not. The pull of the role I play in a pilgrimage, the responsibility I had internalized in a decade of living in India, held me back. Sadhvis, renunciants, spiritual leaders do not run ecstatically on mountain paths in hiking boots and plunge themselves facedown into the wet, grassy root of the trees. They do not sob with each step. They walk agreeably, smiling, with the group. They make sure everyone has water bottles. They stop for breaks when the group stops. They lovingly answer questions asked by fellow travelers as they walk. They pause so people can take photos with them along the way. But I yearned desperately to burst forth, throw off my clothes—not just the robes, but every stitch of clothing as well—and merge into the mountain, just as Meera had merged into Krishna.

Thankfully, after a few miles, the group organically thinned out. The athletes among us moved quickly, while those with knee and back issues, the overweight and the out of shape, lagged behind. Pujya Swamiji was surrounded, in front, behind, and on each side, by the smartest, strongest, and most responsible yellow-clad rishikumars who had been chosen to join the yatra. Most were from these mountains, and being able to accompany the guru on this sacred journey was the greatest honor.

A small group of devotees, young men and women from around the world who had come to be part of this auspicious pilgrimage, walked just behind Swamiji, interspersed with the rishikumars. One man carried his thermos of warm water and offered it to him every few minutes. Swamiji set a pace for the group that was easy and smooth, yet also fast, which meant he was feeling great. So he was safe.

I allowed my pace to slow ever so slightly, and I dropped back from the group surrounding Swamiji. He was still in easy eyesight—to lose him entirely from view would create a level of anxiety that cut straight through my bliss. The air grew silent, my breath became quiet, and the only noise I could hear save for Ganga's waters below was the sound of my boots on the path. *Oh, wow* had been replaced by a mantra given to me. As I walked alone on the mountain path, firm and stable in my beloved hiking boots, my mantra chanted itself, mile after mile, through my body.

At Bhojwasa, Pujya Swamiji led an aarti on the rocky edge of the Bhagirathi. Zipped into ski jackets with wool hats pulled down over our ears, we sung and meditated as the frigid wind wrapped around us, lashing our noses and cheeks and bare hands.

Our plan was to leave Bhojwasa just before sunrise the following morning and cover the remaining two and a half miles to Gaumukh by 7 or 7:30 a.m. After praying and meditating at the glacier, we'd return to Bhojwasa for a hot breakfast, gather our bags, and trek back to Gangotri. The only thing we needed for the walk to Gaumukh from Bhojwasa was a thermos of warm water, a bit of dried fruit or some kind of snack, and our cameras, of course. As I packed a small bag by flashlight that morning, one of my tentmates looked over. "Why are you packing clothes? We're coming back here on the way to Gangotri, aren't we?"

"Yes," I replied, not in the mood for conversation but trying to be polite. "But I'm going to have a bath in Gaumukh, and so I'm packing a change of clothes."

"You're what?" she exclaimed, breaking the morning silence. "You'll catch pneumonia. You'll have to go to the hospital."

"Possibly," I said. "But I doubt it. I need to take a bath there. There is no question about it. I can't not have a bath."

The idea of not bathing in the womb of the Mother was inconceivable. I was returning to the Source not just to take its picture, not just to pray and prostrate, but to become one with it. Nothing else mattered. My tentmate's eyes widened, and thankfully she said nothing more.

The sun began to rise, casting an orange glow on the east face of the mountain as we trekked one and a half miles on the path, followed by more than a half mile of scrambling over boulders. Due to the fragility of the mountain, the last couple of miles before Gaumukh are a constantly moving glacial zone. There's no set path; each fall of rocks or shift of the glacier changes the route. Some of the group stopped here, satisfied at having arrived, content and blissful. They sat on the boulders and meditated on the banks of Bhagirathi

Ganga while the rest of us continued ahead, with agile rishikumars holding our hands as we scrambled up and over rocks.

As I climbed onto a smooth, oval-shaped boulder, sitting higher than the rest and smoothed by the wet wind and the rushing water during monsoons, I fell to my knees. There She was. About a hundred yards ahead, a small cylindrical opening appeared at the base of a snowy rock-covered glacier from which frothy, foaming blue-and-white water rushed into the world. *The womb of the Mother!* From that opening in the nearly twenty-mile-long glacier, which no longer looks like the cow's mouth for which it is named, Mother Ganga flows onto Earth.

As I focused my eyes on the water pouring out of the glacial source, my peripheral vision faded. The mountainsides, the ground, and the sky all vanished, and only the Source existed. I felt transported back to the beginning of time—to the place, the moment, the state of Creation as it flowed forth from the Creator. It was from here, and it was happening before me and through me, at this moment. The water flowed over my eyes without touching them and pulled down the lids. I sat, still as an unborn embryo, my heart pumping only by the invisible cord that connected me—not through the belly button, but through every pore, every cell of my as-yet-unformed, undifferentiated being. A beating heart, an experience of chilled wet drops being sprayed by the wind, a gentle vibration of energy—this was all I was aware of.

Eventually, the waters pulled my eyelids gently open and I beheld my guru sitting on another rock a few yards away, his eyes closed, surrounded by beatific yellow-clad rishikumars, backs perfectly straight, necks stretched to the sky, eyes closed as well. Into what historic reality had my eyes opened? What did 2007 mean? We were timeless, sitting on rocks, brushed by the breeze that carried drops of sacred birth from the Mother's womb onto our faces. There had never been a time when the water had not flowed. She was eternal, the Creator. I was sitting in the lap of Creation.

Slowly, I climbed down the rocks toward the glacial source. The umbilical cord in which I was wrapped drew me closer and closer and closer. The large boulders gave way to a pebbled pathway lining the narrow riverbed. The waters from Gaumukh are joined along her 1,500-mile path to the ocean at Ganga Sagar by innumerable tributaries, ranging from small local streams to the sacred Mandakini and Alakananda rivers. But here at the Source, she is not yet a wide river. The riverbed is about fifteen to twenty-five feet across. The water is fast, though, being thrust out of the Source by an unseen power, the force with which a Mother births Creation. I bent down and gently put my hands into the water just a few feet from where the Mother Goddess's womb opened. I yearned to touch the Divine. The water was so cold, it burned. My hands felt as though I had thrust them into a yagna fire, the skin melting off them. It did not matter. I would die to be born. I would dissolve into Creation.

I picked up the brass *lota*, a traditional vessel used for bathing. I don't know where it had appeared from; I hadn't carried it with me. I'd planned to dip into the river myself. But unseasonably early rains and shifts in the glacial plates had made the river run even faster and deeper than usual. It was definitely not safe to jump in; yet, there was no way I wasn't going to bathe in Her waters and feel Her with every cell of my being—inner and outer. And now the lota had appeared.

I sat on pebbles at the edge of the water and filled the lota from the rushing stream. Closing my eyes, I poured the water over my body. My senses jumped awake with the shock of the temperature; blood surging to my skin and my racing heart were instruments accompanying the symphony playing loudly within me.

Again and again, I filled the lota and emptied it over my body, dying, being born, and being blessed again and again as the Goddess poured over and through me. Who I thought I was washed off me and into the river. The makeup of my identity, seared off by the glacial water, ran down my body and trickled away, over the rocks, into Ganga. I poured and I poured, the tears from my eyes adding salt to the waters in which I was born.

"Bas Didi. Jal bahoot thanda hai." I heard a faraway voice enter my awareness. "Bas" (Please). "Aap bimar ho jaogay." (Enough, sister. The water is very cold. You will get sick. Enough.) My eyes opened as water was poured over them by my arm, which continued to repeatedly lift to fill and empty the lota on my newly born head. Through the stream, I could make out one of the men who lived and served at the ashram—a close friend, brother, and caretaker—standing over me, his hand outstretched , gently but firmly requesting that I give him the lota. "Enough, my elder sister," he was saying in Hindi. "The water is very cold. You will get sick." He took the lota gently from my hand and wrapped a towel over my shoulders. "Thand lagjaogay." (You will catch cold.)

Still sitting at the river's edge, I allowed him to take the lota and closed my eyes into the strong rays of the midmorning sun. I was home.

CHAPTER 41

Satsang

AUTUMN 2004

As a large bougainvillea in Swamiji's garden grew taller, it began to bend from the weight of its own branches, and the dark and frequently muddy area beneath and behind it encroached on the garden's grassy meeting space. Surveying the tree and the large damp area, Swamiji declared, "We will lift the bougainvillea up and build a hut beneath it. I will have all my meetings in the hut."

"Lift it up?" I asked. "How do you lift up a tree?" Clearly, he had a vision, and once a vision takes root in his mind, it cannot be uprooted. Over the years, I have seen that everything in his mind's eye eventually finds its way into three-dimensional reality.

So, a few weeks later, after consulting with experts to ensure that no harm would befall his beloved tree, a car jack was wedged between the soft ground and the underside of the trunk as it bent heavily from the weight of its branches. Slowly,

slowly, slowly, with instructions on the minute adjustments necessary (Swamiji seemed to be feeling the tree as it was lifted), "a bit to the right, a bit to the left," the tree was hoisted up successfully.

Wooden poles were erected, and the makings of a roof began. A slab of cement was laid on top of the wooden poles, all the while ensuring that the tree was not only untouched but also had plenty of room to breathe. "Come a bit further away," Swamiji instructed when the roof layers got too close.

Then, a floor was laid of *gobar*—a traditional Indian mix of straw and cow dung (I derive great amusement from informing people that they're sitting on cow dung)—and eco-friendly designers covered three walls and the roof with bamboo. Thus, a bamboo-and-cow-dung hut was built with the large bougainvillea and two smaller trees growing through it, exiting through holes in the roof. Their branches now grow comfortably toward the sky, and when they get heavy, they rest on the roof of the hut.

Each evening, following the sacred aarti, crowds gathered in Swamiji's hut for darshan to receive his blessings and, frequently, to ask questions.

Satsang literally means "in association with truth" or "in the presence of truth." This is the unchanging, eternal truth of who we are, the nature of the universe and our relationship to the universe. Why are we here? How do we overcome our egos, fears, desires? What happens after death? How to live a spiritual life in the world with a job and family? These sorts of topics arise in satsang.

On one particular evening, there was a large gathering of devotees in his garden post-aarti, including the regular mix of individuals and families from around the world and a group from the United States that had come for a retreat. I sat next to Swamiji, as was the norm, so I could be available if he needed a quick translation of a question in vernacular English into Hindi, or if anyone requested his presence at an event and he needed to know if he'd be free that day (I carried his calendar engraved upon my brain), and because it had grown to be so. I would be there, next to him, even if he didn't need anything. I'd stopping asking why (I didn't want to jinx it), and my prayers simply continued to be, "O God, please make me worthy . . ."

On this night, one of the Americans asked a question about anger and forgiveness. She hadn't used any unusual words or waxed endlessly or shared her life story to justify her question. She simply asked, "Can you speak on forgiveness and how to be free of anger?"

"Sadhviji," Pujya Swamiji said, followed by a long silence. Was he taking a breath before asking me a question? "Sadhviji," he said again, and closed his eyes to meditate.

When I looked at him, wondering where the rest of the sentence had gone, his eyes were closed and his hands rested palms up on his crossed legs in *dhyan mudra* (the hand posture for meditation), tips of his thumbs touching the tips of his first finger, with the other three fingers—middle, ring and pinkie, stretched straight out over the knee.

My eyes followed the direction his fingers pointed toward the back of the garden, hoping that was a clue—as though my instruction would be inscribed on the wall. There was only a bush of fragrant white jasmine filling the garden. No answers. I looked back at the crowd. It was clear that they were expecting me to answer this question. He had turned it over, fully and completely, for me to handle. The unspoken rest of the sentence was, "You answer this."

Over the preceding decade, I had written several articles on Swamiji's behalf on topics related to anger and other emotions, and on the importance of forgiveness. I had also written two books on his behalf—*Drops of Nectar* and *Grace in the Home*—containing his wisdom, channeled through my slowly improving mind and hands, on aspects related to living day to day as spiritually as possible. I had listened to him give countless responses to such questions in the past: "Do you want to be in peace, or in pieces? Do you want to be better, or bitter? The choice is yours. You can make your life heaven or hell. It is up to you."

As in his teaching to me during my first days in Rishikesh about having to draw the line myself, Pujya Swamiji emphasizes the most fundamental form of self-empowerment: Your own happiness is in your own hands. "No junk mail," he urges. "When junk comes to your email inbox, you delete it. You don't read it or save it. When it comes to your eyes or your life, you must do the same. The fact that someone sends you junk mail does not mean you have to accept it. Just hit Delete and move on." So I knew the teachings. Even if I couldn't implement them all, all the time, I could write about them with ease.

But now I had to answer verbally. I was already doing a lot of public speaking, and I knew Swamiji's teachings well, so I wasn't concerned. I began to arrange the index cards of my brain. What points to start with? What were the main ideas? What order to present this teaching? And as I tried to arrange the cards in my mind, I froze.

I closed my eyes. Maybe if I weren't distracted by their faces, I could get these index cards properly arranged in my mind and give a coherent and appropriate—hopefully, even intelligent—answer. But although I couldn't see their eyes, I could feel them. I shuffled and reshuffled the cards in my brain, but nothing worked. I couldn't arrange them fast enough.

Maybe he's playing a trick on me, I thought. I'd heard lots of stories of gurus doing that—to hit at one's ego, to dissolve illusions, to test one's faith, for all sorts of reasons. Just because Swamiji hadn't played a trick on me before didn't mean he wouldn't now. Maybe it's a mirage, an optical illusion my guru has created to show me how stuck I still am in my own ego. Maybe if I just squeezed my eyes tightly shut, I could make the illusion disappear.

So I tried. I squeezed my eyes tightly shut, wrinkling my face in a way that must've looked really funny to those watching but who had the graciousness never to ask, "What were you doing when you scrunched up your face?" Then I opened my eyes, expecting the garden hut to be empty except for me and my laughing guru, who would say something like, "You're not ready for anything. Look how nervous I made you just by putting you on the spot in front of an imaginary group of people."

But they were still there, still looking at me. No one had budged. I turned to my left and saw Pujya Swamiji, still deep in meditation. He wasn't going to bail me out. So I closed my eyes again. *I'll figure this out—it isn't rocket science. She's asking about anger and forgiveness. I can do this.* I began to search for the index cards again, but I couldn't even read them. My heart beat faster and my palms began to sweat.

Finally, I surrendered. *I cannot do this,* I said to Swamiji in my mind. *I don't have it in me. I am so sorry. You have given me a task and I can't complete it. I don't have this answer.*

My breath slowed. I was no longer stressed. I was, rather, resigned to the deep and painful awareness that I did not have the answer. I could not pull it forth from any corner of my brain. I wasn't up to the task. In my mind, I bowed at Swamiji's feet in my mind and repeated, *I don't have it in me. I cannot do it. I am so sorry.* I gently opened my eyes, ready to sit in my own paucity of intelligence. It would be humbling, but I was resigned to acknowledging my own lack.

I opened my eyes and took a deep breath. And as the breath escaped my lips, my voice poured out along with it. "First of all," I heard myself saying, without knowing where the words were coming from, "it's crucial to remember that forgiveness doesn't mean we condone someone's actions. Forgiveness doesn't mean what they did is OK or right. Forgiveness simply means that I need to move on. We forgive because, regardless of what someone may have done to us in the past, we deserve to be free today. Anger is the chain that keeps us bound to that person and their action. Our forgiveness does not absolve them of their crimes.

"We are not the karma police who get to decide what punishment someone should receive for what action they've taken. Until and unless God says to you, 'Would you mind keeping track for me of who deserves what—I don't want to forget to punish this guy,' unless God tells you that, you can be pretty sure the law of karma will function properly without you standing over it. A seed that is planted does not need us to stand there and remind it what type of tree to become. It knows. That intelligence is present in the seed. The tree and the fruit it will bear are present in the very seed. In the same way, the seed of abuse or betrayal that someone has planted is going to grow into a tree in his or her front yard, the fruit of which they must eat. We forgive because not to forgive is a refusal to become who we are, a refusal to step up to the plate of our own lives."

I don't remember the rest of what I said, but after the satsang, many of them came up to me and said, "We are so touched by your wisdom." Many of the Indians present touched my feet. My wisdom? I asked myself. No, something else had happened. As I stood and folded my hands in namaste to those who came to thank me, I felt as though I had just come out of a deep meditation. It took a while for my eyes to fully focus, and that line of proprioception—where I end and the world—was still blurry. But I hadn't been meditating. I had been speaking. My eyes had been wide open, my lips had been moving, and words had been coming out.

What had happened, I understood later—and the realization has simply crystalized over the years—is that in the very moment of bending low at Swamiji's feet in my mind, in the moment of knowing that I did not have the answer, that it wasn't in me, I created so much space in my experience of self that something divine flowed in. The universe abhors a vacuum, we're told in physics classes. It applies spiritually as well. When we can get our own egos—our own sense of what we know, who we are, what we can do—out of the way, something beautiful can come in to occupy the space.

Long before the energy that flowed in poured out of my mouth, touching others, it touched me. It is the presence of the Divine connecting me fully to the Knowing of the Universe. It was true that day in 2004, and it's still true today.

When I can allow the walls of my "separate self" to be malleable, permeable, and unfrightened enough to be stretched and bent, the presence of the divine world flows in. That is still the way I do all of my speaking, even today. I don't plan in advance. I don't try to figure out what I know on the subject. I focus, eyes closed, breathe deeply, and I just try to get out of the way as much as I can.

Whether it's satsang or a keynote address, the only way what I say touches people is when I get out of the way enough so the Divine flows into and through me, touching and filling me, and then, as my cup very literally runneth over, it spills out of my mouth into the space around me.

Public speaking has become my favorite thing to do. It's an opportunity for me to be bathed by a flow of grace and divine presence that feels distinctly different from how I live the rest of my life. It's as though the "I" with which I typically identify, a spiritually informed but still solid "I," gets put to sleep, and while it's out of commission, my body becomes an empty playground for Grace to come and dance. That it benefits others is a wondrous by-product. The joy of its presence touches and nourishes me to no end.

CHAPTER 42

Encyclopedia
of Hinduism

We sat in an enormous meeting room in a near circle—actually, a sort of square—on couches, chairs, and cushioned footrests in the home of a devotee in Delhi. Pujya Swamiji was on a couch covered by a thin, satiny, peach-colored sheet, draped especially for him, as is traditional for religious leaders so they can maintain the purity of their energy without occupying the same fabric as others. Indians are fantastic entertainers, and many homes have living rooms that can hold dozens of people comfortably.

To Swamiji's left sat the publisher of the *Encyclopedia of Hinduism*, owner of one of India's largest publishing houses. To the publisher's left sat the editor-in-chief, former rector of a prestigious Indian university, a professor of English (as he would remind me pointedly in later conversations) since before I was born. Others who were gathered for our mini-conference included the assistants and editors who were working with the publisher and the editor-in-chief to bring the *Encyclopedia of Hinduism* to completion.

It was the end of October 2009, and this project that Pujya Swamiji had founded more than two decades earlier would finally, and thankfully, be coming to fruition. At this point, twenty-two years in, the encyclopedia team included more than 1,000 scholars from dozens of cities around the world. Each article had been reviewed by eight or more renowned scholars for substantive editing, review, copyediting, and finalization. The illustrations had been painstakingly gathered from institutions as renowned as the Indira Gandhi National Centre for the Arts (IGNCA).

Since not long after the first encyclopedia project board meeting I'd attended in Pennsylvania in 1997, it had been clear to me that this initiative was more of an academic and logistical challenge than Pujya Swamiji had realized when he first suggested it, and perhaps even more of a challenge than he recognized a decade later. To have nearly 10,000 articles assigned, written, collected, compiled, edited, and finalized would be a mammoth enterprise even for an academic institution of great repute with a team of students and professors working on it full-time. To be undertaken by a religious leader who dedicated his life to sadhana (spiritual practice) and service was, many said, impossible. So Swamiji established a foundation with branches in India, the United States, Canada, and the United Kingdom and spent years traveling around the world with the chief editor, a South Indian professor emeritus from the University of Virginia, to handpick the scholars who would form the editorial board. By the time I became involved a decade later, work was in full swing, and I knew there wasn't anything I could do. I wasn't a scholar of Hinduism.

Then Swamiji said to me one day, "You're a scholar. You should go to Columbia and work for the project." So I spent three weeks at the University of South Carolina in the summer of 1998 editing articles, and I vowed to keep my distance from the project after that. It was too big. There were too many moving pieces. It would consume my life. I'd left academia for spirituality. No way was I going back.

"Please don't make me do this project," I said to Swamiji, still unclear that disciples don't get to choose their service. Pujya Swamiji was accommodating. Whether he had no interest in arguing with the daughter of a lawyer or because he had no interest in arguing specifically with me, or if he simply had complete faith in the Divine Plan, he never pushed. My role in the encyclopedia project became simply administrative. I followed up with first the chief editor and then the editor-in-chief in India to make sure articles were being written, edited, and received on time. I handled correspondence with the half dozen publishers we went through, including Indian and internationally renowned academic presses. I handled contracts, memoranda of understanding, and the communication back and forth to agree on terms. I played Sherlock Holmes when one of the early publishers began falsifying bills. But I was determined never to go near the actual content again.

Now, we sat at a great moment in history. The board had made a decision in the early days not to publish the encyclopedia volume by volume, but to wait until all eleven volumes were completed and to release them all together. However, the first volume was ready to be printed, and the publishers came with the editor-in-chief and their teams to hand it over to Pujya Swamiji for his blessing.

The publishers had said that within the next several months, the other ten volumes would be ready to print; it was simply a matter of layout, design, and illustration selection. The editor-in-chief echoed this. His team had gone through all the articles, and the text was complete.

The following spring, in 2010, the Maha Kumbha Mela, the largest spiritual gathering on Earth, would be taking place in Haridwar and Rishikesh, where we live. Tens of millions of pilgrims were expected, and His Holiness the Dalai Lama had agreed to come to our ashram for the launch of the encyclopedia!

There had been whispers over the years that the encyclopedia would never be finished. Having no idea how long something like this could take, Pujya Swamiji thought it would be done in a few years. Then, revised estimates guaranteed it would be done by the turn of the millennium. But by 2004 and 2005, people had begun to wonder whether it could actually be accomplished. Every time I heard these whispers, I felt a pang of guilt. My throat would tighten and my breath would shorten. Was I letting my guru down? Was I avoiding the very project I'd been sent to complete? Who was I to second-guess God? But the pangs, strong though they were, were not as strong as my fear of going near the project. Yes, it was divine. Yes, it was historic and momentous. Yes, it was the compendium of the cultural heritage of India. And, yes, I would drown.

Ganga is divine. She is the liberator, the purifier, the Mother Goddess. And if you go in too deep, or bathe at the wrong spot, you will drown. Her divinity does not preclude the possibility of her killing you. The encyclopedia project felt the same. It would swallow me alive if I went near it. So, as I sat on that October morning with the rays of a still-warm autumn sun flooding the room from high windows, I smiled. The publisher had produced a digital print and wrapped it in decorated cellophane for Pujya Swamiji, tied with a bow. After ceremonially opening the bow and paper, he laid it on the table. *Thank God, finally, it is done.*

As Swamiji and the publisher discussed plans for the launch with His Holiness the Dalai Lama, I reached toward the large glass coffee table at the center of the room to pick up the dummy copy. I opened it carefully, greeted by beautifully golden plates on the inside front pages—"The Encyclopedia of Hinduism. A Project of India Heritage Research Foundation." I flipped through the opening pages—publishers' details, lists of editorial teams and the board of trustees. Then a several-page list of contributing scholars, alphabetized by first name. Who does that? I had never seen a list alphabetized by first name. I, then, skimmed through the articles. The content was rich and deep, esoteric and profound. But in several places, there were grammatical mistakes. The style of writing felt, in some articles, far from that to be expected in a scholarly publication. And in a few places, the content, while factually correct, did not seem it would go over well with the international audience Pujya Swamiji was hoping to touch and inspire.

"Do we really believe that failing to take oil baths properly can lead to a loss of your children?" I asked Pujya Swamiji after the meeting ended and the group left. "Do the scriptures really say that?"

"What are you talking about?" He looked at me curiously.

"It says here," I replied, reading from one of the entries, "that 'our scriptures detail exactly when and how one must take an oil bath, and failing to do so properly can lead to a loss of health, wealth, and children.'" I closed the book. "Really? Children will die because their mom or dad had an oil bath at the wrong time or the wrong way?"

"Of course not," he said. "Show me."

I opened the book and put it on his lap. He read the entry. "Ah, yes, *abhyanga*— they are speaking about the detailed instructions given in Ayurveda for health-inducing practices, including oil massage. If one loses one's health, then usually, one loses financial security as well. Perhaps the original passage mentions children or family as well, but it doesn't actually mean that your children will die. It simply is emphasizing that through these healthful practices, one can safeguard one's health and good fortune. Yes, you are right, though. It should not be written like this. This could be misunderstood."

"Actually," I said carefully, "there are some other places where I'm not sure the phrasing is done correctly."

"You must go through it," he said, no longer paying attention to the ten-foot energetic pole I had erected between me and this project. "I will tell them nothing can be published until you've seen it."

Thus began the next three years of my life, my inseparable marriage to the *Encyclopedia of Hinduism*. I went nowhere without three-inch-thick books, bound by blue plastic spirals, with cover pages reading, "*Encyclopedia of Hinduism*, Volume ___."

As I had done for the *Encyclopedia on the Teachings of the Mother of the Aurobindo Ashram* a decade earlier, I went through the pages line by line, pen in hand. Mostly, it read beautifully. Review by eight top scholars ensured that most articles were ready for publication. But many weren't. In most of those cases, the issue was one of translation from the author's native tongue into English, or untraditional uses of English words: Yes, *ass* is a synonym for *donkey*, but, no, it's not the first meaning that occurs to most English speakers. Better to write *donkey*.

As I spent my days reading every word—and scrutinizing every comma— of what turned out to be more than 7,000 articles, I was often transported to another time and space. The kingdom of the Mainakini, the temples decorated with the Hoysala form of architecture, the grassy fields of Vrindavan, on which Krishna and the gopis danced the *rasa lila*. The challenge was staying grounded enough in my intellectual brain to catch the difference between *its* and *it's* or *their* and *there* while permitting myself to be swept up in the river of wisdom and culture.

I laughed as I removed *the* from places it didn't belong and inserted it in places it did. The sages are right, of course. One can never escape one's karma. I had spent ten years confidently separate from this mammoth project, careful to keep myself from getting swept up in its tide. Clearly, though, it was work I needed to do. The universe had let me feel in control for a while, even to feel that my guru was listening to me and not making me do something I didn't want to do. And now, here I was, not merely reviewing some of the encyclopedia, but reading every word of it. Well, I thought, the illusion of control was nice while it lasted.

And, far from my drowning or suffocating in the project, the river absorbed me. It swept me up, but I didn't drown. I stayed afloat, touched and taught deeply as my eyes ran dry but my heart stayed wet.

The only challenge, really, was the people I had to work with. India is a country that worships the Divine Feminine. Many days a year are dedicated to the celebration of the Feminine: Ganga, Earth, India, Creation, the Cow—it's all mother. Everyone chants, *"Bharat Mata ki Jai! Ganga Mata ki Jai! Prithvi Mata ki jai! Go Mata ki Jai!"* (Glory to Mother India, to Mother Ganga, to Mother Earth, to Mother Cow).

Yet, on the ground, day to day, in the worlds of religion and academia, women are seen as having inherently less value unless a man needs a snack or cup of tea. Yes, there are extraordinary, respected women of both religion and academia, but in general, to be a woman is a liability. To be white and female is a double whammy. To be white, female, and young is more or less equivalent to being an earthworm.

I was white, female, and not yet forty, so there was no way I could know anything. Why, they all wanted to know, "Why, oh, why, is Pujya Swamiji listening to a white girl?" (In Indian culture, regardless of age, one is considered a girl until marriage and childbirth.) An extraneous or missing comma here and there, an omitted footnote indicator now and then, scattered misspellings and occasional inadvertent insertions of some extra letters (*attaineded* instead of *attained*), what does it matter? Why is a saint of such great stature permitting this project to be held up?

I was raised and schooled to believe these things matter. If the project were for an audience of Indians or spiritual seekers only, perhaps these kinds of mistakes wouldn't matter. But my dear, dear guru had spent twenty-plus years working nights, traveling on one-city-per-day tours to raise awareness of a project that was not just preaching to the choir. It was to be the accepted, authentic textual reference for academic and scholastic institutions on all things Hinduism. Every spelling error, every grammatical mistake, undermined the very nature of the project. I couldn't overlook that.

So I edited the articles by hand—for spelling, grammar, and style, and for things that, while present in the voluminous Hindu scriptures, weren't helpful to mention. (For instance, the admonition against taking an oil bath on the wrong day of the week, or a reference to God being strengthened by ghee poured into fire. Really? God needs ghee?)

I also edited some of the word choices, much to the dismay and consternation of our editor-in-chief. "Goddess Sitala, the Goddess of smallpox, roams the countryside on her ass" became "Goddess Sitala, the Goddess of smallpox, is believed to ride her donkey through the countryside, protecting the villagers."

"What is wrong with *ass*?" the editor-in-chief wanted to know. "It is a valid and widely accepted word for *donkey*."

"What is wrong with it?" Pujya Swamiji asked me.

"I can't explain exactly what's wrong with saying, 'The Goddess roams the countryside on her ass,' but please just trust me on this," I begged him. "We can't say it like that."

He did accept my edit, thankfully, but not before the editor-in-chief, not realizing he was on speakerphone during his conversation with Pujya Swamiji, pronounced in dismay, "I've been teaching English since before she was born!"

I had to ask myself, "Who am I to be doing this project? Who am I to have been trusted with such an important task? I thought back to the memos my mom would correct in red pen and send back to her boss during her days in business. I thought back to the innumerable conversations in our car as we drove around LA, with my mom and dad pointing to random billboards and quizzing me on what mistakes were there. I used to roll my eyes and ask, "Who cares?" But now I was thankful for my mom's critical eye, thankful for the gentle chiding they'd give if I dared say, "It's me," in response to "Who is it?" on the phone or in a doorway. "It is I," my dad would say softly but firmly. And now I cared. I was thankful also to have been an avid reader from an early age; Nancy Drew and even Hercule Poirot got their grammar right.

I was not thankful for the stress, though. The only thing that made it worthwhile was the occasional laugh with Pujya Swamiji about the encyclopedia we could write about the making of the *Encyclopedia of Hinduism*. Mostly, the thing that pushed me day after day to write another lengthy email to publishers— who, when a hundred corrections were sent to them, entered only fifty and introduced twenty-five new mistakes—was an inexplicable devotion to a culture that was not mine but had adopted me with open arms.

Why, and how, did I care so deeply about protecting a religion I barely knew? Why was I prepared to lose sleep and sacrifice the time and peace of my days to ensure that this culture and heritage are correctly portrayed—in both letter and spirit? Since the beginning of my time in Rishikesh, I have felt a deep loyalty to the culture and religion of India. It is so frequently misinterpreted and misunderstood, even by its own scholars, particularly those schooled in India in institutions whose classes are conducted in English. There is an ironic and troubling trend among these graduates toward disparaging their own tradition and worshipping all things Western and modern. There is an unspoken but commonly held truth that whatever your grandparents did or believed is backward, and that which appears in TV series and movies and on the internet is progressive and sophisticated and therefore better. Somehow, I became a self-made advocate for India and Hinduism, and editing the encyclopedia nurtured that seed in me.

By the time of the Dalai Lama's arrival in April 2010, only three volumes were ready, so the event was recast as a preview and blessings ceremony. It was historic and exciting, graced by revered spiritual leaders of all the traditions as well as national and political heads, social heads, and celebrities. Watching the Dalai Lama reach out and hug Pujya Swamiji, grab at his beard, and ruffle his hair ("Not fair," he repeated jokingly. "You have much much, and I have little little.") loosened the knots of tension in my mind and shoulders regarding the remaining volumes.

By the summer of 2014, we were done—not only with all the editing and corrections but also with our publishers. After a succession of Indian publishers had breached their contracts in myriad ways, we signed with an international company, Mandala Publishing, based in California. They redesigned the volumes, improved the illustrations, and prepared gorgeous new covers. We now were ready, with joy and pride, to offer these volumes to the world, beginning with the president of India!

As I stood for the national anthem at President House on June 23, 2014, tears streamed down my cheeks onto the table in front of me.

Jana-gana-mana-adhinayaka, jaya he

Bharata-bhagya-vidhata.

Punjab-Sindh-Gujarat-Maratha

Dravida-Utkala-Banga

Vindhya-Himachala-Yamuna-Ganga

Uchchala-Jaladhi-taranga.

Tava shubha name jage,

Tava shubha asisa mange,

Gahe tava jaya gatha,

Jana-gana-mangala-dayaka jaya he

Bharata-bhagya-vidhata.

Jaya he, jaya he, jaya he,

Jaya jaya jaya, jaya he!

(We bow to you, the ruler of the collective
mind of our people
Thou art the Lord of India's destiny!
Thy name rouses the heart of the people and the land
of Punjab, Sindh, Gujarat, and Maratha, of the Southern
states, Odisha and Bengal;
Thy name echoes in the hills of Vindhya and the
Himalayas, mingles in the music of the flowing waters of
Ganga and Yamuna, and is chanted by the rising waves
of the Indian sea.
The people sing thy name and praise.
They pray for thy blessings.
They sing the song of your victory.
Glory to Thee, the giver of good fortune to all people,
Thou art the Lord of India's destiny!
Victory, Victory, Victory to thee)

Fortunately, my speech was not immediately following the national anthem, for it took a while for my eyes to dry.

It was done. It was really done. And it was gorgeous. And perfect. Well, perhaps not exactly perfect, but—by all standards of Eastern and Western perfection—it was close enough.

Later that year, we launched it in the presence of the vice president of India; the head of the Rastriya Sevak Sangh, India's largest national organization; and the prime minister of the United Kingdom, David Cameron. When Pujya Swamiji chanted, "*Aano bhadra krtavo yantu vishwatah*" (May all the noble truths come from all directions), Cameron said, "That's really good. I will use that!"

When the editor-in-chief publicly thanked me for my great role in the project and then clarified that the great role I played was always graciously ensuring that they had a ready supply of tea and snacks during their numerous conferences at the ashram, I smiled. Ah, Mother India.

CHAPTER 43

The Doer Burns Out

NOVEMBER 2012

How to work 7 days a week, 365 days a year, especially if you don't need to? To be impoverished and unable to provide for your family without working seven days a week is a situation too many people around the world face. But how to work constantly if you don't need to? I was not, of course, being paid for my service at the ashram, nor would I ever take any money from the ashram or our foundations. My parents, in one of the great blessings that I don't know how I deserved, support any financial need I have—from a new laptop to travel expenses to toothpaste.

I also knew, after my first several months here, that I wouldn't be kicked out unless I committed a horrible transgression. In the beginning, this all felt like a dream, like I had gone to sleep in the midst of a PhD, a marriage, and a normal life and had awoken in a spiritual wonderland where my tasks were simple yet exhilarating.

Then, over the years, as the quantity of seva grew, so did its importance. We were building schools, orphanages, vocational-training centers for women, ashrams and medical clinics in Tibet, and of course there was the *Encyclopedia of Hinduism*. Plus, whenever any major natural disaster happened, we were right there. My first experience was the earthquake that struck the Himalayan town of Chamoli, a hundred miles from Rishikesh, in the middle of the night of March 29, 1999.

Immediately, before dawn had broken, our ashram vehicles were on their way into the hills with blankets, food, water, and basic medicines. Over the next several weeks, we sent truckloads of supplies along with doctors. Then there was the cyclone in Orissa the same year, then the earthquake in Gujarat in 2001 and the tsunami of South India (and many other countries) the day after Christmas in 2004.

In the wake of the tsunami, we spent several weeks living in a government guest house on the coast of southern Tamil Nadu, in a village called Devanampattinam. There, we set up several large community kitchens providing two hot meals a day, and milk for children and babies twice a day. We provided clothing, food, shoes, and other necessities for thousands of devastated villagers. We built more than a hundred temporary homes and, ultimately, hundreds of permanent ones in Pondicherry. We built an orphanage with classrooms, a computer center, and vocational training for 200 women.

Not working seven days a week would be inconceivable. If only God would give us eight days a week, we'd work eight. If only we didn't have to sleep or eat or bathe, we could get so much more done. And it was rewarding on many levels. To simply finish off a folder full of papers that Swamiji had given me meant I got to go back, sit with him, give these papers back, and receive a new folder of new tasks. I loved finishing whatever was needed as quickly as I could, because the time between our meetings would then be shorter. Once I had no more seva to do, meeting together became a priority so more tasks could be given. And the experience of accomplishment was exhilarating—not just like that of getting an A on an exam or completing a report; these accomplishments were tangible and benefited others.

The time in 1998 that I raised money for sweaters for the children in our schools and placed the order for 1,500 sweaters, I was giddy with excitement. *I did it—I did it*, I thought to myself. It was a high that surpassed anything I'd felt in school, anything I'd experienced, chemically induced or otherwise, and when I got to help distribute the sweaters and see the faces of the children as they came up, one by one, and reached their tiny brown arms to grab a maroon woolen sweater, a perfect match for their brown-and-beige school uniforms, my glee couldn't be contained.

"Don't you ever take a day off?" people would ask. "What do you mean, 'a day off'?" I would ask back in bewilderment. "Do you take a day off from breathing or living? What would I do? Paint my toenails in bed?" Seva—in all its aspects and elements—was my life.

Pujya Swamiji's teaching on service rang constantly through my ears and thoughts. "Give, give, and give," he urged us. "Give like Mother Ganga, give like the sun, give, give, and give with no hesitation, no expectation, no discrimination, and no vacation.

"The sun never takes a vacation," he reminded us regularly. "Mother Ganga never wakes up and says, 'I don't think I'll flow today.' How to become like that? Living on the banks of Mother Ganga, we must take not only her blessings but also her message."

This was easy for me for many years. I remember being at my parents' house in Los Angeles on a short visit in the immediate wake of the Chamoli earthquake. We had found a generous donor from Mumbai who was prepared to donate large truckloads of supplies for the needy villagers. But someone had to send his office a list of what was needed. In early April 1999, I was the only one who could get such a list prepared, typed, and faxed with a nice cover letter before his office opened in the morning.

When I called Pujya Swamiji to tell him I had arrived safely at my parents' house, he explained about the list and letter needed. "Absolutely," I said. "I'll do it right away." Fatigue vanished, and I was exhilarated by the opportunity to, through a few short minutes of typing, be a vehicle for relief supplies to get to the villagers. I pulled out my laptop and sat down at the very desk I had used throughout elementary and high school, and began to work. After a few minutes, my mom came in and said, "Honey, you've been traveling for thirty hours. Go to sleep."

I assured her I was almost done and kept typing. Pujya Swamiji and our team on the ground had prepared a full list of exactly what was needed: blankets, candles, water, biscuit packs, and tarpaulins—and warm clothing, for although it was springtime, the mountains are frigid twelve months a year.

I prepared an effusively grateful cover letter and printed it out. As I stood over the fax machine, my mom came in again. "Sweetheart, come on. It's late. Enough, already. Can't somebody there do this?" How to explain the ashram's digital divide? In one office, work took place on a computer connected to the internet that could send printouts to an HP inkjet, and in the office across the way, work was handled by pen on carbon paper, spun in a mimeograph to make copies, and filed in clothbound register books.

And how to explain the critical importance of this—not just for the earthquake survivors, but for the role seva played in my life? No, no one else could send this fax, and, yes, I would stand there all night if I had to until someone in the donor's office picked up and responded to my request for a fax tone. It was rare in India for a fax machine to have its own dedicated phone line. The telephone would be answered by a secretary or another office worker, who would, or wouldn't, be able to activate the fax machine and get a tone so my fax could be transmitted. I would do this patiently and exuberantly until the fax went through—no, sleep was not more important.

I spent fifteen years doing service from that perspective. Whatever, whenever, however—not out of compulsion or because I had no choice. If I'd said to Pujya Swamiji, "I'm exhausted. I just landed in LA after thirty hours of travel. I have to go to sleep," he would have said, "No problem. Health is first. You can do it tomorrow."

So, while he exhorts us to give, give, and give as a fundamental motto of life, he is also always one to remind us, "Take care of your body. Health is first. Work will never be finished, so be sure to take care of your health." My fervency for service was not due to fear of reproach. To serve had simply become my life.

I'd spent my first twenty-five years wrapped up in me—my drama, my history, my wants. Each ache, pain, sniffle, or sleepless night was cause for concern. Now, service—work for others, whether a letter of blessings or encouragement or condolences from Pujya Swamiji, whether schools or sweaters for children, whether a free medical camp or relief supplies—whatever it was, it was my life. To serve had become my modus operandi. That night in LA and countless nights in Rishikesh, under no one's instructions other than my own, I stayed awake all night to finish something. The next day, while certainly sleepy, I was exhilarated.

Then, after fifteen years, I hit a wall.

I had finished editing the *Encyclopedia of Hinduism* in early 2012. We were planning Pujya Swamiji's sixtieth birthday celebration that November. His birthday is in June, but it's too hot then to host an event with VIPs from all over the world. Our state government had erected a huge permanent platform that rose above the river in front of our ashram, a crescent shape in the center of which we had placed an enormous statue of Lord Shiva. The stage was filled with four rows of leaders—religious, social, national, political, and business leaders.

We themed the event "Environmental Protection for World Peace." "Our definition of peace has to expand," I explained in my welcome talk at the event. "For centuries, religious leaders have come together at parliaments and summits in the name of peace. But today, more people are suffering and dying from lack of clean water than from all forms of violence combined. Today, it is no longer enough to say, 'Thou shalt not kill.' Today, we must join hands to realize that if children of any race or religion suffer and perish due to our actions or inaction, their blood is on our hands. We are gathered here today in the name of a new, expanded definition of peace."

We released Pujya Swamiji's biography that day as well: *By God's Grace*, a book I had written with a beautiful foreword and introduction by His Holiness the Dalai Lama and Chief Rabbi David Rosen, a renowned Jewish leader. Mandala published it gorgeously as a large-format coffee-table book. The event was a great success, and it wasn't until two weeks later that I realized I'd hit a wall. At first, I thought I was just tired, and I slept—a lot.

I hadn't stopped working with urgency in years. Of course I was tired. I even thought about it neurologically. I was in parasympathetic nervous system backlash. When one stays fired up with stress—even just the "good" stress of hectic, exciting work, when that ends, in order to return to homeostasis, the body switches from sympathetic fight-or-flight arousal into the parasympathetic nervous system mode, which slows the heart rate, slows the blood pressure, and so on. I was simply, I figured, suffering the physiological and mental repercussions of a parasympathetic nervous system working overtime to balance years of intensity.

But it didn't go away. I couldn't even seem to generate enthusiasm, let alone urgency, for anything. Where had I gone? "I'm done," was about all I could say. I didn't even know what I was done with. Myself, it seemed.

The hot flashes didn't help. They had started earlier that spring, and although

I wasn't paying much attention to them yet, they were beginning to rattle me from the inside. As I looked at a paper or a file or an email, a physical agitation rose within me, and I began to shudder and had to look away. Hard work had felt so right for more than fifteen years. What was happening?

One day in mid-November, I said to Swamiji, "I need a vacation."

"OK—plan it," he said, looking up and chuckling.

Wow. I must be in horrible shape, I thought. *Vacation* is a four-letter word here, and those who need one are clearly not serious about their spiritual practice or their service. And now, without a question or hesitation, he had said yes.

Every single time I thought I could second-guess him, every time I had prepared conversations in my mind of what I'd say and what he'd say, he invariably surprised me. "You're not quite so smart," he seemed to be saying. "You still haven't figured this thing out yet." Vacations. Bad. OK, got it. A vacation? Sure. *What?*

But I didn't want to hex it, lest he change his mind. A few weeks later, we had a trip planned to Japan for programs and meetings. I remembered that Swamiji has close devotees with a home on the Big Island of Hawaii. He had stayed there once, years earlier, en route from a meeting with the publishers of *Hinduism Today* magazine on Kauai. I remembered him saying how beautiful and peaceful it was.

I contacted them. Could we spend four or five days there in December? Would they be there? They were, of course, beyond excited. People beg Pujya Swamiji to come visit them. He usually stays a night or two in cities around the world. Four or five days was unheard of. Of course they'd be there.

So I scheduled our flights to go to Hawaii first and then to Tokyo for our programs. Whatever spell Swamiji was under to approve my vacation plan seemed to have a long half-life. He OK'd the itinerary and didn't, at any point, say, "What are you doing? That was just a test." I was embarrassed, but desperate and immensely grateful.

I watched a Sherlock Holmes movie on the plane. I had never watched movies on flights after moving to India. I had grown to believe doing so was a waste of time. There was so much work to do, there was no justification for time-wasting indulgence. And if I wasn't going to work, I'd rather meditate, or read something inspiring, like a commentary on the Upanishads. Frivolous movies were out of the question. Yet here I was, headphones on, gripped by Sherlock Holmes's adventures. Swamiji sat next to me, working and meditating. When he saw my screen on his way to the bathroom, he said nothing. He didn't even make a face. I watched him carefully, ashamed for my transgression, yet feeling helpless to do anything else. I couldn't work. I couldn't meditate. Nothing about me seemed to function anymore. I just wanted to watch Sherlock Holmes.

We had to change planes in Honolulu. In the airport gift shop, I picked up a DVD about Father Damien, a Belgian priest who had moved to the Hawaiian island of Molokai in 1873 to minister—spiritually, medically, and logistically—to the thousands of lepers quarantined there by the government of Hawaii. I stuck the DVD in my bag. I'd had a morbid fascination with leprosy since seeing lepers sitting on the bridge across Ganga in Rishikesh, deformed hands outstretched for spare change. *What must that feel like,* I wondered, *to have your limbs fall off?* I was disgusted and intrigued, but it was too intense to watch now.

On the plane to Kona, I read the airline magazine about all the activities to do on all the islands. I didn't need activity, though. I just wanted to melt into comfort, ease, and pleasure. I wanted to feel myself again.

The next morning, comfortable in my plush bed at the devotees' home, I woke early and then went back to sleep. "I'm on vacation," I told myself, and laughed before falling back into slumber. It was midmorning by the time I woke again, and I went outside into the bright sunshine. Swamiji was seated at a round patio table on a huge covered porch overlooking the Pacific Ocean. The outline of the island of Maui could be seen across a deep, blue channel. He had a placemat in front of him and seven or eight of his small spiral notepads on the table. He was writing intently in one of them.

"Did you rest well?" he asked. Shouldn't I have been the one asking him?

"Mmmm," I said, unable to put in words the joy I felt looking out over the ocean. "How did you sleep?"

"Oh, wonderful," he said, and returned his attention to the notepads.

"What are you doing?" I asked incredulously. Here he sat in picture-book paradise, and he was writing notes in pads.

"Oh, I'm planning for the toilets and clean water in the Kumbha Mela," he said with a huge smile. I stared at him. I don't know why I was surprised. I was the one who needed a vacation, not him. Still, I couldn't believe it. Seriously? Here? Toilets?

"See," he said, opening one of the other notepads that lay on the placemat. "I already did all the plans for where we'll put the toilets on the Char Dham route between Haridwar and Badrinath. I did that before breakfast."

Page after page of his tiny pad was filled with his impeccably neat Devanagari script. I looked at all the bullet points he'd drawn—perfect black pinpoint circles, neatly lined up on the left-hand side of the minipage—and next to each bullet point was a word in Hindi, each one of the locations of future toilets. He flipped page after page with glee.

"And now," he said, putting that pad down and picking up the one he'd been writing in, "now, I am planning for the upcoming Kumbha Mela. It is so wonderful. We will have *Ganga tat pe Ganga jal* [clean water from Ganga, on the banks of Ganga] with this new filtration system. I am planning the locations for that and where our biodigester toilets can go."

During his sixtieth-birthday celebration, the Indian government's Defense Research and Development Organisation (DRDO), the Federation of Indian Chambers of Commerce & Industry (FICCI), and our organization had signed a memorandum of understanding to work together to bring into common usage the DRDO's biodigester toilet, invented for soldiers deployed at high altitude—a high-end engineering feat using enzymes to turn fecal matter into gray water. FICCI would help, through its corporate social-responsibility schemes, to put these toilets, which don't require elaborate sewage systems or treatment plants, at locations we would identify.

The Kumbha Mela was due to take place in January and February 2013 in Allahabad, in eastern Uttar Pradesh at the confluence of the Ganga, Yamuna, and invisible Saraswati rivers. It is said that the Saraswati River goes underground at Mana, a tiny town high in the Himalayas, past the holy temple of Badrinath, just before the India-China border. You can see the river dive under the flowing Alakananda River at what's known as Bhima Pul, a large rock bridging the Saraswati River and said to have been pushed there by Bhima, one of the heroes of the Mahabharata War, the setting of the Bhagavad Gita. It is believed that the Saraswati River appears again only at the confluence of the sacred three rivers in Allahabad, or Prayag Raj, the majestic confluence. More than 120 million people would flock to the Kumbha Mela over the main eight weeks; on the most auspicious days, 30 million people would bathe in the Triveni Sangam, the confluence.

In addition to the ceremonies, prayers, rites, and discourses, our main agenda was environmental protection. How could we make use of tens of millions of people in one place, full of devotion, sponges ready to broadcast the messages and teachings, for a mass awareness-raising campaign? Our slogan was "Green Kumbha. Clean Kumbha. Green India. Clean India." At the bare minimum, we wanted to work with local authorities to ensure that the riverbed of the sacred rivers did not become polluted by the waste of tens of millions of people. "A mela with a message!" Swamiji had said. "Not just inspiration, but also sanitation!" "Sanitation and meditation must go hand in hand!" "We must turn our focus from temples to toilets!" The slogans rolled from his heart and off his tongue.

And now, overlooking the Pacific Ocean, with the sun rising behind us, not yet overhead, a humpback whale breaching in the distance, he was planning toilets.

"I can't believe it," I said.

"This is the problem," he replied, taking off his reading glasses. "To you, it is work. To me, it is ecstasy. You see yourself as the doer of work, so you feel tired. If it doesn't go your way, you feel frustrated. If it goes your way, you feel proud. I do not think like that. I am not the doer." He looked far off, sort of up and sort of just out toward the ocean. "He is the doer—God is the doer. I am just His instrument. If I can be used every minute and every moment, for me, that is ecstasy. It is not work. I love it."

I had loved it too, I realized, squinting my eye as I walked toward the edge of their porch, no longer covered by the awning. I sat on the rough cement edge with flower pots hanging below and looked out. Other than the homes down the hill, all I could see was ocean, vast ocean.

Yes, I had also loved the work, passionately. But he was right. Even in my love for it, I was still the doer. I loved it because it made me feel useful. I was accomplishing beneficial tasks. I loved finishing what I'd been given, especially if I could do so faster and better than Swamiji had anticipated. And now, the doer had burned out.

After finishing the *Encyclopedia of Hinduism*, a task that in my wildest dreams I had not imagined could be done, after writing his biography, a project I'd wanted to do since my first month at the ashram, and having it turned into a gorgeous coffee-table book, after organizing the biggest event our state had ever seen in honor of his sixtieth birthday, after all this, there was nowhere to go. Nothing else I did felt meaningful.

The dominoes of my mind had begun to tumble. Swamiji had pushed the first one, saying, "You think you are the doer," and the rest toppled down one at a time. As the doer, it was all about me: What I could do. What I could accomplish. How good it was. How big it was. How fast it was. How many children or women or disaster survivors could be helped. Rather than me being an instrument for them, they had been tools for me, pieces in the game of my life. I arranged them in a way that I felt accomplished, worthy. How many sweaters or schools or computers would it take until I felt deserving of existence?

Swamiji was not building toilets to feel worthy. He was building toilets because toilets were meant to be built, and he was the vehicle God had chosen. He was building them the same way he planted trees, the same way he did everything—as an available tool. If God wanted the work done, Swamiji was ready. If God did not want the work done, if insurmountable obstacles presented themselves, so be it. As a tool, he was sure he'd be picked up and used for something else. It was never about what he wanted or thought.

I identified with the children, with the abandoned women, with the sick patients. If I could treat enough of them, provide for enough of them, maybe I could assuage the women, children, and patients in me. If I could hand back enough empty file folders to Swamiji—do everything faster, better, bigger than he'd imagined—maybe I would feel worthy of his blessings and the Grace that had been bestowed on me. And if I couldn't, I was not worthy and might be sent away—abandoned again. "Oh, wow," I whispered aloud as I watched sailboats and surfers far below. "Wow." Orange robes or white robes, there was so much to heal inside.

I pulled out a white patio chair with a floral cushion from the round table where Swamiji was listing locations for toilets in a makeshift city at the confluence of sacred rivers. I sat across from him and asked, "How to fix this?"

"Focus on realizing that you are not the doer. Focus on the real doer. Remember, you are serving your own higher self in others. It is not about you, the capable you, the intelligent you, or the dedicated you. It is about one part of the greater Divine Self serving another part, like my stomach serves the body by digesting food, my lungs serve the body by breathing. The lungs never say, 'You know, I'm the one keeping you alive. It's all because of me.' And they never get tired of breathing, because there is no sense of doership. They are just lungs. And so they breathe. The stomach is just a stomach, and so it digests. When you realize that you're not separate from this existence, not separate from the Creator, you will just serve without a sense of doership. Then the fatigue and frustration will be gone."

The next evening, after I spent the day snorkeling with sea turtles, flapping my finned feet in crystal-clear aquamarine water, we watched the DVD about Father

Damien. Ultimately, he contracts leprosy and dies, but not before transforming the leper colony into a place where people, even in impending death, sing together, pray together, and chant God's holy name together. He brought them the gift of life, even in the face of death. He knew he would probably contract the disease and die. It was part of the package, and he was prepared for it. Not because he knew that he'd build a hospital and school and proper housing before he died, not because he knew that a hundred years later, a DVD would be made about him and sold in airport gift shops as part of a plan to increase tourism to Molokai, not even because he knew that eventually he would be canonized by Pope Benedict XVI and immortalized as Saint Damien. He was prepared for it because to serve those people was his work—for as long as and as much as, and in whatever way, God wanted to use him. As the lungs breathe because they are lungs, as the stomach digests because it's a stomach, he served and died there because that was how the tool of his life was meant to be used.

Tears poured down my face. By the time the movie ended with a cutaway long shot of the colony he'd built and died in, flanked by some of the highest coastal cliffs in the world, floating as its own world in the middle of the green ocean, I had to rush into my room. I lay on my bed and sobbed, wordlessly and thoughtlessly. I did not sob for Father Damien's death or for the thousands of lepers who had died there. I did not sob for the unknown millions who have perished from leprosy around the world. I sobbed for the act of service. Yes. Yes. Yes. To be used like that. To be chosen to be used that way, to have the will of God flow though you in a way that death also becomes life. This is what I want.

I gasped in my tears and felt Father Damien begin to breathe inside me. At first, our breaths were disparate, mine fast and shallow, his deep and slow. Slowly, we began to breathe together, and in my breath now there was life. Yes, the lungs breathe because they are lungs. The nose has mucus because it's the nose, the tear ducts send rivers of salty water down my cheeks because that's what they do. And we serve not as separate doers, not to prove a point—even of our own worthiness—not to earn the right to occupy our place on Earth, but simply because, with each breath, that is what we do. Our joint breath extinguished the fire that had burned me out.

In the months and years that have followed, I find and lose and find again Father Damien's breath in mine. When I find it, I feel this saint breathing within me, and I cry. The gift, the fullness, of being used in such a way.

I serve, trying simply to feel the flow of the universe through me. How does the universe need me now? Whenever it starts to be about me, whenever frustration or fatigue starts to arise, I remember my guru ecstatically planning toilets while on a Hawaii vacation, because that's who he is. I find Father Damien within me and allow our breaths to align. I sit in the evening fire ceremony, where the priests chant at the end of each mantra, "*Idam namam, idam namam*" (Not for me, for you. Not for me, for you. Not for me, and not from me. For you, from you, through me who is also You).

CHAPTER 44

A Door Closes

DECEMBER 2012

Living in India is a phase, an adventure I'm on. I can go back to real life whenever I want.

I always viewed my life at the ashram this way, yet every time I sat on the banks of Ganga, I knew beyond a doubt, this is where I'm from and where I'm meant to be. My love for India was deep; the immersion of my being felt nearly complete here. Almost every night, I'd lose myself in Pujya Swamiji's singing in the aarti, merging my awareness with the sound of his voice punctuated by the crashing and breaking of the river's waters on the marble steps. And after the night's final offering, I became one with the cracking of the logs in the yagna fire.

I can always go back to America, I assured myself. *It's beautiful here but difficult—ecstatic, yet a nonstop struggle.* My ego bounced up and down like an inflatable punching bag: No matter how hard you punch it, it bounces back, smiling and ready to take another hit.

"This is not the Indian way of thinking," Pujya Swamiji told me every time I insisted or complained. "You Americans will never understand," he said. Being born in well-lit, sterile hospitals, held by nurses and doctors first and only later by our mothers, we seemed to have an internal compass drawn irresistibly to the pole of What I Want When I Want and How I Want It, a honed tool of self-righteousness. Whenever my ego became especially unsettled, I'd tell myself, *It's OK. We can go back to real life whenever we want. If it stops feeling right, we can leave and return to a normal life.*

The ego's strife waxed and waned for years, then appeared to settle into a faithful comfort in the choice of staying. As alluring as "normal" seemed, the call in my heart was to Ganga, to India, to the way the earth smelled in the rains, to losing myself in the sound of Pujya Swamiji's voice. And I was being invited worldwide to address events on themes ranging from spirituality to women's upliftment to entrepreneurship. I was being recognized as a spiritual leader, loving the travel, the events, and the satsang I led every evening, with crowds growing daily. It wasn't time for this phase of my life to end. There was plenty of time to return to normal later, whenever I wanted. For now, Ganga called and I responded, and it was profoundly resonant.

Then the hot flashes started. I was forty-one and hadn't paid much attention to the unpredictability of my menstrual cycles. They weren't hugely erratic, I thought, just five or six weeks between periods, then a second period two weeks after the first. "That's odd," I thought, then forgot about it. The heat began gently early in 2012. Suddenly, my body temperature—which always ran hot—felt like I was being cooked alive from the inside, as though someone had lit a Bunsen burner inside me on low heat, and slowly, slowly was turning the knob till every organ in my body seemed to be liquefying, and if I didn't tear my skin off, I'd burn from within.

Ayurvedically, I'm *pitta* (heat), with some *vata* (wind), so an airy movement of heat through the body, ayurvedically speaking, was just my pitta and vata being aggravated. It was, after all, springtime turning into summer. But something was really off with my pitta, I self-diagnosed, and I went to get medicine from the Ayurvedic doctor.

"I'm so hot," I told him, "out of the blue." He gave me his usual black pills and brown powder. The sizes and shapes of the pills varied from ailment to ailment, as did the intricate mixture of powder. To me, it all looked and tasted like dirt, and this time, it didn't work. This doctor had been able to cure me of everything from constipation to acne to bronchitis to gallstones during my years in India, but he was unable to do anything for the heat. I sprayed myself with bottle after bottle of cooling rose water, avoided anything spicy, ate yogurt by the bowlful, and kept taking his pills and powders.

For the rest of the year, the flashes of heat came and went. Days and weeks would go by without them, and then they'd appear out of nowhere. I attributed it to stress exacerbating my already aggravated pitta. I was in the midst of organizing Swamiji's sixtieth birthday, the largest event Rishikesh (or even Uttarakhand, our state) had ever seen. Leaders from around the world were coming for the three-day gathering, and I was frantically trying to make sure Swamiji's biography would be completed, printed, and shipped from California on time. Of course I was stressed and of course my pitta was aggravated. So I thought nothing more about it.

The book was finished beautifully and launched with great pomp and splendor. The event went off fantastically, the only hitch being a last-minute change of timing due to the hot midday sun and our reluctance to put a tent over the glorious stage in the middle of Ganga. I spent nearly a week after the celebration just relaxing—sleeping and catching up on pending items. I should have been completely cured, except for the emotional burnout. But the hot flashes continued.

In mid December, Pujya Swamiji and I returned from Hawaii and Japan to India. Airplanes are always cold, and the flight from Tokyo to Delhi was freezing. We sat with blankets over our legs, drinking hot water with lemon as we worked. Suddenly, as if cranked up by an invisible hand, the knob of fire that seemed to have been surgically implanted in my sternum grew unbearably hot.

To be hot sitting in the sun, or stepping into a car that's been sitting in a sunny parking lot, is one thing. This was different. It began from within, from the very blood nourishing my organs, muscles, bones, and, eventually, my skin. My blood was being boiled from the inside. Rather than flowing imperceptibly through arteries, veins, and capillaries, it began to bubble inside my veins like molten lava melting the walls of the vessels. When it finally reached the surface with a frenzy of volcanic steam, the heat had built up such pressure that it erupted through my face, my neck, the top of my head, my chest, and my arms, and out my eyeballs. I seemed to be crying, but I was simply melting.

And as the frenetic river of boiling blood flowed through my body, the intensity of my other physical systems was amplified as well. My heart was racing, and my mind dashing feverishly about, up and down every possible pathway. I threw the blanket off my knees, turned on the overhead fan, and asked the flight attendant for a glass of ice water. As the cool air blew over me, the heat subsided and the internal knob was gently turned down. My heart rate slowed and my mind calmed. I could breathe and focus again. I turned off the overhead air, placed the blanket back over my knees, asked the flight attendant for a cup of hot water and lemon, and continued to work.

Thirty minutes later, the cycle began again. Off with the blanket, on with the fan, and I panted for ice water as my heart beat furiously. After three or four more cycles of this, Pujya Swamiji looked up from his papers and asked, "*Ho kya raha hai tum ko?*" (What in the world is happening to you?) He'd been silently witnessing, perhaps assuming that as an indecisive, impulsive American, I just couldn't decide between ice water and hot water, blanket and fan. Finally, the oddity of my behavior caught his attention.

"I think I have a tumor in my hypothalamus," I told him.

"Your what?" he asked.

"My hypothalamus, the part of the brain that regulates temperature. Something is really wrong, and it's getting worse. I think I have a tumor."

"You must get that checked out," he said. "It is not normal."

So, as soon as we landed, I made an appointment at the internationally renowned Medanta Medicity Hospital, near the Delhi Airport, a multispecialty, top-of-the-line hospital where one of the chief cardiac surgeons is a close friend.

"I need a brain MRI," I told my surgeon friend as soon as I arrived at the hospital.

"Oh, no, why?" he asked.

"I have a tumor in my hypothalamus. I am sure of it. Everything is getting disrupted. My body temperature, my heart rate—it's getting worse."

"Come on in," he said, and he referred me to the proper specialist.

After I explained my symptoms to the neurologist and before he ran the MRI, he asked me, "Have you noticed any change in your menstrual cycle?" Hadn't he heard what I said? My brain has a tumor! I should've gone to Cedars-Sinai in Los Angeles. But I was polite. After all, I was a spiritual leader, and my cardiologist friend had pulled strings to get me this appointment.

"My menstrual cycle is fine," I replied calmly. "Thank you for asking."

He smiled a bit. "Are you sure? No changes at all? Any missed periods or other irregularities?" God, this guy was unbearable. I had a tumor in my brain that was expanding by the second, and he was asking about periods. Be nice, I reminded myself. You can fly to LA and go to Cedars after you leave here. Just be nice—you're a spiritual person.

"It has been slightly irregular, I guess. I used to have pretty regular four-week cycles—now, it's closer to five or six weeks, although a few times, only two weeks."

"Out of the last twelve months, how many periods have you had?"

I thought back. "Maybe nine or ten," I said.

He made some notes, then looked up at me gently.

"Have you heard of menopause?" he asked.

I'm forty-one, I thought. No one goes into menopause at forty-one.

"It's not menopause," I told him. "I'm too young. It can't be that."

"We'll run some blood tests, and we can take it from there. I don't think you'll need an MRI of the hypothalamus, though."

Idiot, I thought. Of course it isn't menopause. The doors of my life are wide open. I could walk out of India, back into a normal life in America, anytime. I could get married and have a family if I wanted. Of course, my vows would have to be rescinded, but Swamiji always said I was welcome to renounce being a sanyasi if I really wanted to. No one would hold it against me. The idea that those of us from the West are confused, shallow, and cultureless is ubiquitous in India, so it wouldn't surprise anyone if I gave up being a sanyasi and went back to have a family. "I knew she wouldn't make it," many would say. "I could see from the beginning," others would pronounce. Everyone would have predicted it.

So, that part never worried me, especially since Swamiji reiterated that all doors were open to me. Granted, I'd have to relinquish wearing orange robes and using the title of sadhvi, but that was OK. Still, every time the idea of marriage and a family flowed through my heart and brain, I knew it wasn't what I wanted. But I loved having options. I wanted all the doors to stay open. When I grow up, I thought, I'll decide what I want to be and do. For now, I'm still on an ecstatic Indian adventure. And I *am not* in menopause.

But I was. The blood tests at Medanta were conclusive, as were the ones I had at medical facilities throughout the US over the next few years. There was nothing wrong with me. I was, however, no longer a kid on an adventure. I was a woman in menopause.

At first, I laughed, thinking it can't be true—the way I laughed at eight, when my father said he never wanted to see me again. Fathers don't say that; it had to be a joke. It was the way I laughed at fifteen when Jimmy told me he'd found another girlfriend. He was kidding, of course. We were soulmates. I went to school the next day and announced to my tenth-grade classmates, "Jimmy has a new girlfriend. Isn't that funny?" It was ludicrous till I realized it was true.

I'm in menopause. Isn't it funny? Teenage me, in menopause. Young, unsure me, with every door in the world open, including the door of a family. Menopause. What a joke. Until, of course, it wasn't. Until I sat down to meditate, something I'd conveniently avoided most of the past year. My excuse was needing more sleep, having been awakened during the night by hot flashes. But that wasn't it. I hadn't wanted to meditate, because I hadn't wanted to face the truth. *A door had closed.* And when I finally sat still, I realized many doors had closed, some a long time ago.

Life isn't a buffet. We don't get to decide, "I'd like a bit of this, a heaping portion of that." It's more like a fixed menu where the chef is kind enough to let you make substitutions and changes—up to a point:

"American Jewish student becoming Hindu sanyasi?"

"OK—we can do that."

But, "Forty-one-year-old celibate renunciant spiritual leader simultaneously a wife and mother?"

"No—sorry, ma'am, can't make that dish for you. The two don't go together. I've given you the adopted child and a heaping portion of purpose and meaning. But I'm sorry, there's just no way to get wife and mother onto the same plate. Please look—your plate is already full. That should be enough to satisfy you."

Many doors are open to us, but some aren't. I never could have walked through the door of professional basketball player or ballerina or opera singer. And some doors are open but not forever, and others are not open simultaneously. One can't simultaneously be a full-time celibate nun and spiritual teacher, and a wife and mother. They just don't go together.

Yes, we're free. Yes, the world is at our fingertips. But each door we walk through determines which new doors open on the path ahead. We can't rewind, or live parallel lives simultaneously. We can't be a nun here and a mother there.

A message in so many inspirational books focuses on the ideas "You can have it all. You can do it all. You are all-powerful." This, I believe, is a disservice. We can't have or do it all. We make choices, and some choices preclude other ones. Living in New York precludes living in New Zealand. Being a full-time surgeon precludes being a full-time bassist in a rock band. This doesn't mean we can't take vacations, have hobbies, or change our minds and take up something new. But the idea that right here, right now, we can have it all is delusional. We can't simultaneously live two lives, have two careers, and make two choices with the fullness of our being. The idea that we can only leads to disappointment.

Yes, many doors of my life were still open. Yes, I could still choose a different path. But I could no longer pretend that being a sanyasi in India was a phase, a stage, or a temporary adventure. This was a door I'd walked through fully and consciously seventeen years ago, and the choice had repercussions, some of which were irrevocable: spiritual exaltation, personal transformation, and a lifetime in which I would not give birth to a child.

CHAPTER 45

Being a Woman in Spiritual India

JANUARY 2013

India has a complex relationship with women, and religious India's relationship with women is even more complex. Hindu tradition *worships* the Divine Feminine reverentially. Eighteen days a year are dedicated to worship of the Mother Goddess in her different forms. There are temples exclusively dedicated to the Mother Goddess—and even in others dedicated, for example, to Lord Krishna or Lord Shiva, you're likely to find an elaborately decorated image of Ma Durga or Ma Kali or Ma Lakshmi.

Among the many high-court judges and political figures who have served India, Indira Gandhi was prime minister for fifteen years and Pratibha Patil, a gentle, motherly figure, was president for five. On the religious and the practical and political levels, India is quite progressive in honoring women's rights and empowerment. At the same time, sexual harassment is far too common, as are domestic violence, rapes, and murders.

More and more organizations are forming to drag this monster out of the closet of denial and into the daylight of awareness and action. Women's-empowerment training programs in villages and cities are growing to provide not only sewing and handicrafts but also karate. This is one of the reasons our Global Interfaith WASH Alliance is working so ardently for the provision and use of toilets. When millions of girls and women in the rural villages don't have a toilet at home and have to go into fields and forests to heed the call of nature, they are easy prey for not only wild animals but also for men. Toilets in their homes provide safety and security along with obvious health and hygiene benefits.

But that lack of safety—whether on the streets of Delhi or in the rural villages, while trying to defecate in a field—is not something I've personally experienced in India. I have never felt unsafe on any street or dirt pathway of the country. Granted, of course, I am never out alone. I live in a cocoon of which I am acutely aware, a safe, protected, tightly woven existence of care, love, and respect. And yet the undercurrent of misogyny exists, only in a different way.

As the tradition of sanyas is seen as the highest level of religious leadership, and as the vows of sanyas include nonnegotiable vows of celibacy, and as the overwhelming majority of sanyasis are men, there is a mostly unspoken denigration of all things female. "I never travel with women" and "I never have women around me" are commonly used statements to impress listeners with the strength of the speaker's religious convictions, purity, and integrity. Conversely, "He is always surrounded by women" implies that "he" is corrupt and impure, and of a lower caliber.

Segregating men from women during worship is common in orthodox traditions around the world. My mother grew up attending an Orthodox Jewish synagogue where the men sat separately from the women, but after the service, my mom, her brothers, my grandmother, and my grandfather all walked home together. My mom and grandma were not expected to walk behind the men, nor were they expected to travel in separate cars. In India, though, there is an implicitly accepted understanding that the mere presence of a woman, even if that woman is also a sanyasi and therefore has also taken vows of celibacy, brings impurity. The holier the place, the higher level of religious leaders present, the less likely that a woman will be onstage.

The first time I was subjected to this tradition was in the Kumbha Mela in 2013. Prior to that, as my years in India went by and as I did more and more public speaking, I found myself on more and more stages, shared by both women and men—but in the religious world, mostly with men. I hadn't thought about my presence as a woman other than to notice that I was frequently the only woman onstage. I began accepting invitations to speak because I knew that if I didn't go, there would be no woman on the stage. I went so any girl or woman who wanted to take to a path of spirituality would see that there is also room for women. The doorway to God and to religious leadership is open to all.

The Kumbha Mela is seen as the holiest of holy times and the place where it takes place the holiest of holy lands. We were visiting the Kumbh camp of one of the most revered saints, a man I knew well, revered immeasurably, and loved dearly, someone I had spent a great deal of time with over the years at his ashram, at our ashram, and in many other places. The stage was filled with fifty or sixty of India's most respected religious leaders, all men, seated according to seniority. As Swamiji and I entered, the ushers took him reverently onto the center of the stage and he sat in the front with the saint whose event it was and the other most senior leaders. The ushers lovingly walked me up the stage and showed me where to sit—in the second row, off to the side.

As I settled into my seat and crossed my legs, one of the most respected saints, who I also knew well and loved dearly, rose from his seat and motioned for me to follow him. I jumped up immediately. "I am so sorry to have to say this, but I've been sent by [the saint whose event it was] to tell you that this is just a mahatma [great soul] stage." (The word *mahatma* is used colloquially to mean male religious leaders or saints.) He looked at me lovingly and said, "I am sorry, but there are no women allowed." My eyes filled with tears, and he clearly felt awful to have to tell me.

I flopped my head left and right as respectfully as I could—I'd become expert at the Indian head signal that means, "No problem—sure." I then bent down to touch the ground in front of his feet. I was afraid that if I spoke, my voice would crack, so I just turned to walk down the stairs. "They are putting a chair for you in front," he said. But instead of walking to the chair, I exited from backstage onto the mela grounds. It was the heat of the afternoon, after lunch and before dinner, a time when most people were either napping or sitting in one of the hundreds of makeshift tented halls.

I walked and walked until I got to the banks of the river, where it was thankfully quiet. I sat on a log with my back to the sun and cried. I hadn't felt that alone since elementary school, when the girls in my class would form "We hate so-and-so" clubs, each day dedicated to a different victim. One day, I had walked into school to discover that no one would talk to me—they only pointed at me and giggled. I must have been the so-and-so that day, and I experienced a sense of loneliness that day I'd never felt before or after.

As I child, I loved being alone. Whether doing art projects, photography, reading, playing handball against the garage door, or swimming and lying in the sun, I was always happy alone. But rejection was entirely different. *There must be something wrong with me to be "it" today*, I had thought on that day of fifth grade. To this day, I can still tap into the pangs of isolation I felt. As I took my walk of shame out the back of the Kumbha tent and down to the riverbed, I felt those pangs again. *It's just your ego, I told myself. So what if you can't sit on the stage? You think you deserve to sit on the stage with India's holiest saints? Get over it. Who do you think you are?* I berated myself for a while, and I vowed to work harder on my ego.

But something wasn't right. Rather than the clear spaciousness I feel when truth has been revealed, rather than the stillness I feel when I let go of another layer of false identity and sink deeper into true self, rather than that spaciousness and stillness, I felt a tug. Something in my heart tugged on me to listen. *This is not about you. This is not about being on that stage. It's about being female.* Being male or female is one of the most fundamental aspects of who we are in this finite, time-bound body, much deeper than our identification as our professions, our relationships, or our financial or social status.

To be pushed away due to something over which I had no control, something I could not meditate away or pray away or puja away, something I could not renounce away or serve away, to be unworthy of presence due to something that fundamental, and which I loved and never wanted to change, filled me with despair, indignation, and gratitude simultaneously—despair that I would be forever rejected, indignation that I should be rejected on the basis of gender, and gratitude because I realized in that moment, hunched over a log on the banks of the confluence of the sacred Ganga, Yamuna, and Saraswati, three female goddesses, holy, sacred, divine rivers that, despite (or because of) their femininity were not only pure themselves but were also the bestowers of purity on others, I realized as I scooped water up to wash my face with their waters that I was being pushed to a deeper level of anchoring.

I was being pushed into an inner expansion that had to make room for the simultaneous embrace of my femininity and of the world that rejected it, to be grounded not in having a place on the stage but in having a place in my own self. There would be stages where I'd be welcome, and there'd be stages I was not permitted on. My task was to understand that lack of acceptance on a stage does not undermine the presence of spirit, that females not being permitted somewhere does not undermine the power and purity of the Divine Feminine. People travel from across the world to bathe in the female rivers of India in order to attain purity.

I could send the paradox into my brain, where it would eat away at me, or I could send it into my heart. The heart can create space enough to embrace a world where they pray to the Goddess but don't believe that women's souls are great enough to be a mahatma, a world where we are taught that there is nothing but God, and where the teachers of this truth see women and men as separate. I have not yet fully resolved this paradox. But I work to expand the space within me until there is room for all sides of the paradox, in which I revere and adore these leaders, and feel deeply grateful for the opportunity to be with them.

And at the same time, if I were in charge of the rules, I would declare that women's souls are also *maha*, that the presence of female energy certainly does not defile and in fact uplifts male energy. And in that ever-growing spaciousness, I worship the goddess in the form of Mother Ganga, Maha Lakshmi, Kali, and Durga, in the form of Radha and *Mirabai* and Sita Ma, and in the very female body I was given. In that spaciousness, I can worship the Feminine while still worshipping the saints who would have her kicked off a mahatma stage. This is the spaciousness I seek in my heart. This is the expansion of consciousness I meditate on. There's room for it all. There is nothing but God.

CHAPTER 46

The Puzzle Is Not Complete— Or Is It?

FEBRUARY 28, 2018

I landed in New Delhi the day before the annual International Yoga Festival was to begin in Rishikesh at our ashram. As director of the festival, I had to be there; it was going to be huge. I was on my way home from Vienna, where I'd attended a conference of faith-based organizations, "United Against Violence in the Name of Religion," organized by the King Abdullah bin Abdulaziz International Centre for Interreligious and Intercultural Dialogue (KAICIID)—an intergovernmental organization that promotes interfaith dialogue to prevent and resolve conflict— the United Nations, Saudi Arabia, Spain, Austria, and other countries and religious institutions.

Amazingly, I had been in Vienna two weeks earlier as well to attend another conference, one devoted to the UN Plan of Action for Religious Leaders to Prevent Incitement to Violence That Could Lead to Atrocity Crimes (genocide, war crimes, and crimes against humanity). For two years, I'd been engaged with the Plan of Action, attending and speaking at the conferences around the world, including the Plan of Action launch in July 2017 in New York with the UN secretary-general. This was one of the numerous UN programs, events, and campaigns that I'd been invited to participate in over the last many years on behalf of India, Hinduism, and our Global Interfaith WASH Alliance.

Why me? I wondered to myself and to Pujya Swamiji.

"See?" he said. "I told you that you would play a major role in touching and inspiring people around the world. This is only the beginning." I love this work, the people at these organizations who are doing these projects, and the people in countries all around the world who will be touched by the impact of these efforts. Although two trips to Vienna in less than a month was not easy, it was worth it. These conferences were giving me a chance to have a part in something huge and impactful. And, as a dear, dear friend and hero at the UN reminds me, "Your voice is unique and adds value."

Our weeklong International Yoga Festival, a major annual event we had hosted since 1999, would be starting early the next day. I showered at the Delhi Airport—600 rupees (about $8) for a clean bathroom with individually wrapped soap, shampoo, cotton, and Q-tips (why cotton and Q-tips?)—before heading to the "domestic" terminal to fly to Rishikesh. In Vienna, it had been minus nine degrees Fahrenheit; I had watched people ice skating outside my hotel window. Here in Delhi, the heat beat down through the smog and was already sizzling the city.

As soon as I arrived at the ashram, one of the men in seva told me, "Pujya Swamiji is waiting for you. There is a press conference. Come." Shortly, I was smack in the middle of a news conference with local, state, and national media. Swamiji and I answered questions about the festival from a few dozen media representatives with nearly as many cameras and mics in front of us. "More than 1,000 people from 92 countries are registered, and we are sure it will grow as the week goes by." In fact, 2,000 people from more than 100 countries ended up attending.

Swamiji continued, "The vice president of India will inaugurate the festival on March 3. His Holiness the Dalai Lama is coming to bless us with his presence and inaugurate our Buddha garden and statue. He will stay with us on the third and fourth of March. We have two of India's most renowned musicians—Sivamani and Kailash Kher—coming to perform. And more than eighty presenters from twenty countries, including some of India's most renowned religious leaders and experts of dozens of streams of yoga—from Iyengar and Ashtanga to Jivamukti and Sufi meditation. There will be 150 classes over seven days, then an International Women's Day program on March 8."

The hours between the afternoon press conference and evening blurred in an unbroken flurry of meetings and conversations. The festival was run entirely by volunteers—devotees from around the world under the leadership of our resident seva team. Registration teams, catering teams, accommodation teams, scheduling teams, production teams, and media teams met throughout the afternoon, overlapping groups pouring into and out of my office. Anyone who has ever organized a mega-festival knows what the day before the event looks like.

At the welcome gathering for presenters, I was able to stay awake only by sheer willpower and the joy of seeing so many people I consider friends. Afterward, I just wanted to go to sleep. "Eat a little something," Pujya Swamiji said. For someone who left home at age eight and has never lived anywhere except the jungle and this ashram, he has a remarkably instinctive grasp of motherhood. So, I asked the guys to bring a cup of soup and some chapati to my desk.

While I was eating, I decided to check pending emails. I sipped the soup and folded the chapati between bites to be able to eat it more quickly. As I looked at my inbox to see if there was anything important, a new email arrived. The subject was "Manny." My breath stopped. It was from my stepbrother, Tony, son of Ellen, the woman my biological father had married. Tony and I had loved each other in childhood, and when Manny reached out and reestablished contact with me, seeing Tony again was an unequivocal bonus.

After almost ten years without contact, since our ill-fated meeting and my subsequent hospitalizations, Manny had flown to Detroit in the summer of 1999, where Pujya Swamiji and I were giving spiritual lectures and programs as part of the annual Dharma Yatra, and had taken me out to dinner. Swamiji had sat with him for a few minutes before we went out. "Yes?" Swamiji opened space for Manny to speak, as though, obviously, there was something to be said. Manny had fidgeted and fumbled and cracked a few jokes, and had looked relieved when the meeting was over.

Over dinner at a vegan restaurant he'd proudly found, Manny had begun as he'd begun ten years earlier, during my visit to Denver in spring of my freshman year at Stanford, but either the tone in his voice had changed, or the tone in my ears had. Now, even though he spoke words of empty explanation ("Your mother was too difficult"), I heard the repentance of a haunted man.

"He's haunted," I had said to Swamiji after I got back from dinner.

At Manny's request, I had gone to visit him and Ellen the following year, in May 2000, at his large home in Franktown, Colorado. It was before he was diagnosed with multiple myeloma, or at least before he told me about it. I was no longer looking for anything from him. Rather, I was looking for what I could give him. I hadn't really known him when I was a child, not in a way that I remember his personality. So I don't know if he had always been this haunted and nervous or if this had been triggered by meeting me again. But I had felt his anxiety, the whirling of his thoughts, and the pumping of his heart. I wanted to offer some relief, but I didn't want to talk about our history, as he had made his position clear. There would be no apology or repentance. He had said it twice, unequivocally, ten years apart. I didn't need to hear it again.

And there was nothing specific I felt a need to say to him then. The only unfinished business for me had been, *Could you at least say you're sorry? Could you at least acknowledge the damage done to me, who, despite decades of believing the opposite with my head in a toilet, did not actually cause your behavior? Could you at least, maybe, acknowledge that?* That conversation would have been my unfinished business, but it was palpably obvious that any conversation regarding what he had done wrong, any insinuation that he was not fully, completely justified in everything he did, was out of the question.

But that night, I had been able to feel his repentance in his pulse, in the jittery way he pulled the pizza from the oven and with great flair sliced it with a professional wheel-thing. I could feel it in the sound of his voice when he said, "And the no-cheese vegan variety for you. Extra veggies." I had stayed overnight that visit and found myself rising from bed in the night to lock the door of my room. At that moment, I had realized that, going forward, I would make only daytime visits. No need to put myself through this again.

Over the next years, I had visited him a few times. I had forgiven him. I had done what I needed to for myself and, I thought, for him. But I couldn't pretend the first twenty-five years of my life hadn't happened. Forgiveness, as

I emphasize in satsang, doesn't mean that what the other person did is OK. It isn't condoning the act. You're not expected to marry the person who hurt you or become their best friend or play the role of loving daughter. It simply means setting yourself free.

I was choosing to play the role of his daughter to feel better about myself as a person, helping assuage his guilt and alleviate his pain. *I'm OK*, I thought. *Even without your presence, your love, your care, or even your money, I've turned out fine. Even without the apology or repentance you keep reminding me I'll never get, I'm still OK, and I still absolve you to the extent I'm able.* The karmic fruit people get for the seeds they've sown does not depend on our forgiveness.

I forgave Manny because I needed to be free. I forgave him because, as Pujya Swamiji reminded me that day in September 1996, no one else could draw that line for me. I had to do it. I forgave him because the only other option was to stay identified as a victim, ensconced in my drama. But I cannot uproot the tree he planted in his karmic garden. I had gotten back in contact, as he had requested. I had maintained the contact lovingly and unconditionally. My visits were not dependent on him apologizing.

But I also had to honor myself. Loving-kindness has to include ourselves. When we send loving-kindness and compassion to all of Creation, it has to go inward as well as outward. I extend my arms inward and embrace myself—not just my divine, higher Self, but also my individual, impacted self who is doing her best. Compassion begins in the depth of my heart, the depth of my being, and includes all the parts of me, not just the most awake. Only when I can embrace myself in loving compassion will I be able to embrace the world.

I'm not just a bestower of compassion. I'm also a deserving recipient of compassion. To be there with Manny, pretending that those decades hadn't happened, would not have worked. I had to be there consciously, as that consciousness enabled me to know—to absolutely know beyond any vestigial doubt my intellectual mind might still have had—that something magical had happened to me in India. Being there with him, laughing and eating pizza without rushing into the bathroom to throw up my pain and anger, was a miracle. But I did not need to continue putting myself in that situation just to prove what a beatific giver I was now that Mother Ganga had taken my pain. I was still very human and very much in need of self-compassion.

So, I had continued to visit, but only sporadically, stopping occasionally on layovers between flights. Once, Swamiji and I had dinner at Manny and Ellen's before they drove us to the airport for our flight. One year, we met in the airport itself, as my layover was just a few hours.

Tony, Ellen's son, and I reconnected with love. He joined us on one of our pilgrimages to Tibet and spent time at the ashram. He flew out to Los Angeles with his wife and son during one of my visits to get together. We emailed regularly.

"Do you remember everything?" I had asked him one time as he drove me to the airport in Denver.

"Yes, I think so," he had said. "How did you forgive?"

I had spoken with him gently, not sure exactly how much he remembered and not wanting to make things worse for him. I shared the ritual of giving my pain to Ganga. I shared what I had learned about forgiveness, and I shared the freedom I had found in it.

Manny's multiple myeloma stayed in remission for sixteen years. His diagnosis in 2002 had predicted a life expectancy of a few years. But he was a doctor and a smart man. He researched and researched, developed and developed, volunteered for new trial after new trial. When I saw him in 2015, he looked older and a bit weaker but relatively healthy.

I had stopped going through Denver for many years. Itineraries got busier and other things took over. I noticed also that until he got an email from me, I never heard from him. When I reached out, he was gracious, happy, and eager to see me. But unless I did, years went by without so much as a "Happy Birthday." Finally, I thought to myself, "Reach out to him. He's in pain. And when he passes, you don't want to feel like you missed an opportunity." So I emailed in June 2015 after being out of touch for a few years. He came to see me while I was visiting LA that summer, making up a story about a medical convention he had to attend. I was touched by the lie. He couldn't bring himself to say, "I'm flying here to see you," but clearly, he wanted to see me and made up an excuse. We met for lunch between meetings of his "medical conference."

In 2017, he had driven up to Boulder, Colorado, to see me for a few hours during a program Pujya Swamiji and I had there. "Do I really have to do this?" I asked Swamiji. "I feel so done with him."

"It's just for a few hours," Swamiji had comforted me. "He's sick. And he is the reason you're on this planet, remember?"

So, we spent a couple of hours sitting in a sunlit den making small talk. Manny told me the details of the treatment he was undergoing, but he didn't say he was dying. At one point in the conversation, he said, "I should stop talking about my life and ask about yours. I've been talking the whole time." I smiled and said I was happy to listen to him.

"No, no, you talk," he said. "Tell me about your life."

I told him about the work we're doing, shared about the new programs for water, sanitation, and hygiene. I told him about being at the UN. I told him about my menopausal hot flashes. He listened attentively, commented thoughtfully, and made jokes that I don't remember now. I laughed, not just to be polite but because he was genuinely funny. After a few hours, he had to get back for treatment. We hugged goodbye, and he walked out.

Tony's email a year later was short and simple: Manny had died the night before, on February 26, 2018, in Denver. There would be no funeral. He wanted to be cremated. There also would be no memorial. He had not wanted one.

I went and sat with Pujya Swamiji for a few minutes and cried—tears of loss, tears of separation. But I was, surprisingly, OK. I felt really done. Although I never got the apology I'd yearned for, his demeanor had felt like an apology. He was clearly haunted by guilt. Who opens conversations with "If you're looking for apologies or repentance, you're looking in the wrong place"? I was at peace with my relationship with Manny, because I was at peace with myself.

That inextinguishable peace lasted a matter of weeks.

At the end of March, I received an email from his wife, Ellen, with a letter she said Manny had left for me. It took some maneuvering to download the attachment; my operating system couldn't recognize it. She told me Manny had written it before he died and had asked her to send it to me.

The letter was dated October 2010. It was four and a half single-spaced, typed pages explaining why he was not leaving me anything in his will, how first my mother, then Frank, and then I had hurt him, insulted him. With each page, my eyes got drier and drier from staring without blinking. What was he talking about? Who was he writing to? What history was he describing? He had taken the chronology of our life, the chronology of my life, and rewritten it.

He was hurt that once I was out of my mother's house and in college, I hadn't bothered to contact him. What? We had corresponded regularly from the first week I arrived at Stanford until I traveled to Colorado to visit him during my spring break. That was when he had announced I should not expect any apologies or repentance. A week later, I was in the hospital, vomiting blood and with a blood pressure of 80/40. He had known about the hospitalizations. He had known I was out of school. My doctors had written to him. I had spoken to him on the phone from a line of payphones in my second hospital, the summer between my first and second years at Stanford, five months after we'd been together in Denver.

Manny's only concern had been that because, at that point, I wasn't registered as a full-time student, because I'd broken the stipulation in the divorce agreement to remain continuously enrolled, because I was in a hospital instead of in school, he was absolved from his financial responsibility. *What did he mean, I hadn't contacted him?*

He was insulted that I hadn't told him about my wedding? Three years after he paid an agreed-on lump sum to cover the rest of my college education and then made me sign a document that I had no right to expect anything more from him? After not reaching out to ask how I was after the hospitalizations, to find out if I was even alive? And he was insulted not to be invited to my wedding? My heart was pounding so strongly, it felt like a huge mallet striking a heavy gong in my chest. I was suffocating and choking. *What is he talking about?* I asked my empty office.

He claimed he had tried to contact me during those ten years between the age of eight and eighteen but that my mother had intercepted the mail. In those years, my mother had worked full- time. I had brought in the mail every day. And my mother's not a liar; I was certain of that. There was no way she would have watched me sob and pine for my father while withholding his letters or efforts at communication. I know her too deeply to believe that Also, Manny had told me numerous times that he'd been "unable to reach out to me" during those years of my childhood, and now, suddenly he's claiming that he *had* reached out? How dare he rewrite history—especially after he was dead?

He also shared how he'd been abused by his own father and how painful that had been for him. He did not acknowledge that he carried that imprint into his own fathering, how the cycle of abuse continued from him to me.

Also, this letter was dated 2010. I'd seen him at least twice since then, and both times, he had gone out of his way to see me—once in Los Angeles, once in Boulder—and both times, the meetings had been sweet. Never very deep, as per his explicit and implicit instructions, but sweet, soft, and what felt to me complete. He had been sorry. I could feel it even if he wouldn't say it. I had forgiven him. I had told him that explicitly, as gently and lovingly as I could, and I had hoped my actions and my nonverbal, energetic communication had showed him that. No, we were not going to rewind history and start over now that I was in my forties. I have a dad, Frank, from whom love comes unencumbered by fear, anger, or hate, a dad I know will always, in any and every way, be there for me and with me, not dependent on my sending the first email. I didn't need another dad in my middle age. But it had seemed to me that Manny and I were both at peace with what our relationship had come to include—connection, understanding, forgiveness, and even love.

If he was that hurt, angry, and insulted, why hadn't he told me during the eight years between writing the letter and dying? Why had he sat across the table from me for hours talking about everything except his feelings? And why had he not seemed at all angry, hurt, or insulted? He had seemed anxious. He had seemed guilty. He had seemed haunted, restless, and awkward. But he had never, at any point, seemed angry or hurt. Why had he waited until he was dead to get the letter to me, ensuring that we would never have a conversation to discuss any of this?

"The letter is your stepmother's way of making sure you don't try to get any money," a close friend told me. "It's not even signed, just a computer document that she sent you a month after his death."

Oh, God, I thought. *Did she not realize that I'd signed off all rights at the age of nineteen, that I'd been legally adopted by Frank and so wasn't even legally Manny's daughter anymore? Did she not realize that there was no way I ever would imagine trying to fight for Manny's money?* I'd let go of trying to get anything from him decades ago. I will never know who wrote the letter, when it was written, or any of the other mysteries surrounding it. There are places even Hercule Poirot and Sherlock Holmes can't go. There are depths in the heart and mind of people that don't follow the laws of nature and can't be figured out.

There are jigsaw puzzles that remain unfinished, with pieces missing forever. I could reenter the world of "Who did what to whom, and when?" I could use my intelligence—not the spiritual intelligence discovered in India, but the Stanford-groomed academic intelligence—to scour the pathways of my past to find some of the missing pieces of the jigsaw puzzle.

Or I could look at the puzzle with its empty pieces and make room within me for the reality that it's unfinished and always will be. I can open those empty places to the Grace of Ganga and let Her wash through them and in them, filling them not with answers, facts, or reasons, but with a stillness and a presence of being in which questions don't need answers and mysteries don't need to be solved—a place that just is.

The time after I received the letter purportedly from Manny has been a time of sitting with a fullness that includes the holes, a fullness that doesn't require answers. In this fullness, emptiness blossoms.

On Ganga Dussehra, the festival celebrating the day that Mother Goddess Ganga descended to Earth from heaven, on that day eighteen years earlier, I was bathed in my sanyas initiation ceremony and became Sadhvi Bhagawati. On that day, Pujya Swami Gurusharananandji and Pujya Swamiji's hands channeled light and energy into my brain, into every cell of my body, and into the depths of my nonphysical being. And on that day in 2018, I burned Manny's letter in the sacred yagna fire with ghee and camphor as purification, and with the traditional mix of sesame seeds and rice as offering. (The seeds represent our ego.)

"O God, take my false ego self. Free me from identifying with this story. Fill me not with answers, facts, reasons, or details, but with the fullness of Your Grace, and bring Manny peace, wherever he is. He has suffered enough. Mother Goddess, as you have washed over me, wash over him wherever he is and in whatever form he may now be, bathe him with your healing Grace. Free him from the cycle of suffering.

"O God, help me continue to grow and expand into these empty spaces. Help the love in my heart flow through the parts of my life that are interwoven with his. Help me feel how OK it all is. I may not be ready to see the absolute perfection in it, but for now, help me see the fullness and OK ness."

After the yagna, I bathed in Ganga. "O Mother Goddess, purify these karmic bonds, the chains that hold us to each other, the chains that hold us to our identification with this relationship. O Mother Goddess Ganga, liberate me and bring me ultimate peace."

From the moment Pujya Swamiji told me all he wanted from me was to get closer to God, serve humanity, and be happy, I have found they are not three things, but one. It is through service I feel closest to God, and through being close to God, I am happiest.

Hanuman is what we call in India my *Ishta Devta*, the form of the divine closest to my heart. Hanuman embodies the *miracle of love*. He embodies miraculous power and strength, the ability to accomplish the impossible, the essence of surrender to the word and the will of his beloved Lord Rama. And at the core of it all is his *love* for Rama. Love, I have found, is that divine power at the core of all possibility. It's what compels me to serve, *and* it's the fruit of service. On days I feel frustrated or overburdened by work, I turn inward and ask, *Where's the love? What has made it dry up? What distraction or inner pattern has pulled me out of love and made service feel like a burden?*

Pujya Swamiji's pronouncement that I would touch many has turned out to be true. It seems he knew, as he beheld the lump of clay of the twenty-five-year-old me, what he would shape the clay into. Or perhaps, like a meteorologist, he was able to forecast the weather and direction of my life force going forward. However he knew, I've had the opportunity to be of service to many.

The seva has expanded, as he also anticipated, branching into creation of the Divine Shakti Foundation, which provides education, vocational-skill training, and empowerment for women, girls, and schoolchildren, and our Global Interfaith WASH Alliance, the world's first major association of interfaith religious leaders for water, sanitation, and hygiene. The seva has expanded into many other significant programs at Parmarth Niketan as well, including our International Yoga Festival, which has been uniting people from all across the globe for more than twenty years. Through no merit of my own, my cup runneth over with love and an eagerness to share, and I've served as president, secretary-general, and other positions of authority for all these organizations and programs.

Twenty-five years has not dulled the astonishment with which I behold each day. When I find myself walking into the UN and speaking to or with world leaders about women's empowerment, gender equality, and the human right to water, sanitation, and hygiene, I chuckle a bit inside and whisper to God, "So funny you are. Me? Really? Here?" It's at moments like these that I return to Hanuman and remember, "It's not about me. It's not about this event, function, project, or partnership. It's about You. These are all ways for You to flow into and through me, allowing me to express my love for You."

My favorite is satsang, the spiritual lectures both with and without questions and answers. When I close my eyes—whether there are 10 or 10,000 people in the room—and simply get out of the way, remembering that it's not me, it happens. I rest in the awareness that I don't have the wisdom or know the answer, and if I can just get out of the way and create internal space, free from any sense of strengths or shortcomings, Grace flows—as wisdom, as truth, and as offerings of service to those in need.

Through the many aspects of service, I've been blessed to experience my Self in others—in those sitting before me in satsang; in the children, the girls, and the women in our free schools and training centers; in the survivors of natural disasters we've been blessed to provide with new homes, schools, and more. Recommitting myself each day to the promises I made to Pujya Swamiji, I find both God and my own Self in the eyes of those we serve.

CHAPTER 47

Life Choices

One of the most common ways I hear myself introduced at public gatherings is as "someone who has left everything to live her life in India," or "someone who has left everything for spirituality." As the form of my day-to-day seva shifted from secretarial and administrative to teaching, leading, and bigger-picture planning, I found myself on more and more stages. Despite the availability of my biographical information in a variety of places on the internet, emcees tend to emphasize the sacrificial nature of the choices I've made.

Audiences, even before I give my address, clap loudly at the idea that "someone who had it all voluntarily gave it up" *just* for spirituality and service. I appreciate the importance of this dramatic story and the deep impact it has on people, especially those running after more and more. By seeing me as someone who "had it," then "gave it up," it may awaken in them an awareness that perhaps money, prestige, and possessions are not what's most important. And even though I love the idea of people getting that lesson, when I hear this story being told by an emcee, I feel a knot in my stomach.

At first, I thought it was false humility. But over the years, I've come to realize that the knot in my stomach is my truth compass. It forms because the story isn't true. The facts are true. I grew up in Hollywood and come from privilege. But I did not make the decision to live as a renunciant at an ashram in India as a sacrifice. I did not push away a life of material possessions or sacrifice a life as a professional or a wife or an academic in America, or anywhere. I grabbed onto a life that offered, and has provided, a happiness I never knew before and most likely would not have found had I not listened to the call of Ganga and the voice I heard telling me to stay.

In a series of moments in September 1996, I chose to stay back at the ashram when Jim went to the mountains, to come back to the ashram from Mussoorie when he went to Lucknow, to be here in Rishikesh rather than anywhere else in India, and then in the world. I chose this not as a sacrifice, but because it offered me true happiness. And, although the initial years were difficult for him, this decision actually ended up offering Jim true happiness as well. He has married a wonderful woman and has a beautiful family and life that fulfill him deeply. We have reconnected as friends over the years, and his friendship is a true blessing.

As I think about my life and the lives of everyone I know and those I observe but don't know, I see that everything we do is, ultimately, to make us happy. Sometimes we choose immediate gratification. Sometimes we are able to put off the immediate for the long term. We grin and bear it through school because we need a good education to get the job we want, and we believe that job will make us happy. Or we tolerate a job we don't like because we need it to make money, and we believe money, or the things money can provide us and our families, will make us happy.

There are infinite possibilities, but what we all do, ultimately, is what we think will make us happy. We diet to lose weight so we'll look better and feel happy. We go through pregnancy, childbirth, and child-rearing because we believe our children will make us happy. We sacrifice for our spouses, children, and family members because a) feeling like a good husband or wife, father or mother, makes us happy and b) because when our loved ones are happy, it gives us happiness.

Even the social service or volunteer work we do, which seems so selfless, is still, ultimately, for our own happiness. To be of service to others, to feel my life is meaningful and beneficial to others, makes me happy. Hence, I serve. So, even the most "selfless" decision we make is still, ultimately, one we make for our own happiness.

We've been indoctrinated to believe that doing something for our own happiness is selfish (and bad). It isn't. Happiness is our birthright. We get to choose how we'll go about it. We get to choose whether we want our happiness on a superficial level, constantly fluctuating between eating chocolate ice cream or buying a new handbag; whether we're looking for a deeper happiness through choices that bring about a more consistent joy; or whether we yearn for an even deeper level of happiness through embarking on a spiritual path, doing yoga, meditating, praying, connecting with the Divine. We can also choose all three; they're not mutually exclusive. We can enjoy chocolate and long-term life choices *and* be steeped in spiritual truth.

We also get to choose the way we interact with our own happiness. For me, living the life I do in India is the choice that has brought me the greatest happiness. It's a sacrifice of some things, sure. But we always have to do that. In order to enjoy an Indian meal, you have to sacrifice enjoying Thai food that night. In order to enjoy being a parent, you have to sacrifice enjoying the freedom of being unencumbered by children. For me, in order to enjoy my life in India, I had to sacrifice enjoying life in America. But it's a choice I made and continue to make every day—not from a place of sacrifice, but from embrace of a life I deeply believe is the best choice for me, for my own happiness. Life offers us different "packages" from which we can choose to cocreate our best, most open, engaged, connected, fulfilling, meaningful life possible.

There are no right or wrong choices. Every option can be a right option, depending on how you interact with it. The only wrong decision is to assume you can have it all. I chose the package of being a sanyasi in India, a package that doesn't include a husband or children or a nuclear family. But it's a choice that brings me deep happiness and the awareness that happiness is a choice, not only in big-picture decisions but in every moment of every day.

This book is about the presence of Grace, how Grace entered my life. It may enter your life in an entirely different way, but Grace is available to all. Grace does not discriminate.

Grace flows into us *not* because of what we have done, *just because*—because it is Grace. Grace is what flows into and through our hearts and washes through us. It fills us more fully than any food, intoxicant, or material object. Grace doesn't care whether we have status, whether we meditate, whether we've stuck to our diet, whether we're married or divorced, rich or poor, white or black or brown, overweight or skinny. Grace requires only that there be space in us in which it can flow.

There is a story of the young man who goes to a faraway land in order to become enlightened. He asks everyone where the most enlightened teacher is, and they all point to the guru on the mountaintop. So the young man walks for days, fords a river, climbs to the peak, and finally walks into the cave where the guru is meditating.

He bows at the guru's feet and explains that he has come for enlightenment. He tells the guru all that he's learned, everything he's practiced, the many books he's read, the multitude of his experiences, including his struggles and challenges. When he finishes, the guru invites him to have a cup of tea.

The guru goes to the back of the cave and returns with a teapot and two cups. He begins pouring tea into one of the cups and keeps pouring as the cup gets more and more full and eventually starts to overflow. And the guru continues to pour.

"Stop!" the young man exclaims. "What are you doing? The cup can't hold any more."

"Ah," the guru says quietly and puts down the teapot. "The cup is like your mind, so full of who you think you are, what you've done and learned, what you need, and there's no room for me to offer you anything. As the cup cannot hold any more tea, your mind cannot receive until you ingest what you already have, until you empty your cup."

This is a book about emptying, letting go of who we think we are so we can experience who we really are. Letting go of our stories, our identification with this or that aspect of ourselves, those things that are agreed on by others, and those that are not true. When we let go of all we are not, we can step into the truth of who we are—which is expansive love, Divine consciousness, spirit, truth, oneness, and perfection. For true healing, we need to dwell in presence and in love with the *fullness* of our experience.

Many spiritual biographies, especially those from Eastern traditions, are about men born into pious families who knew from an early age that their son was special. These boys came out of the womb enlightened, or at least already on a well-trodden spiritual path.

This is not my story. First, I am not a man. When I was thirteen and writing my Bat Mitzvah speech, Frank, my dad of the heart, suggested an opening line. In traditional Bar Mitzvah ceremonies, a thirteen-year-old Jewish boy solemnly declares, "Today, I am a man." Frank, always ready with a joke, gave me a perfect beginning: "Today, I am not a man."

The opening line brought laughter and applause at my Bat Mitzvah and still feels poignant, although not as funny today. I am not a man, and there was no indication in my infancy or childhood that I was spiritually awake or even inclined toward spirituality. I enjoyed school and sports and parties with my friends. I took art classes, built a darkroom to print black-and-white photos, and got a black belt in karate. I spent summers at a camp where we rowed and went waterskiing and snuck into the boys' cabins at night.

The goal of spiritual practice is freedom—freedom from ignorance and illusion, freedom to know and be who we really are. Through opening to the Divine in India, through "giving it all" to Mother Ganga, through receiving and offering satsang, I have found freedom from all the ways I had identified, the ways I thought I was unworthy, not enough, tainted, impure, or deficient. And I know now that this freedom is available to all. I hope this book is an opening for you—that it helps you realize there are alternatives to feeling depressed, stressed, jealous, and frustrated and that it encourages you to find alternatives, to tune in to your own inner Divinity, or inner voice, and feel the resonance of speaking and acting from the truth of who you are. It's possible to reboot, to be free of the ideas and identities that keep you stuck. Changing the filter and seeing ourselves anew can change everything.

I still get angry and frustrated and afraid, and find myself yearning for something or dreading something, and in those moments I've learned to *stay present with the feeling*, the experience, and not push it away. I see what I can, when I can. I have learned to be interested in my anger, my frustration, and embrace it as an opportunity to go deeper. This, too, is the voice of God. And sometimes it's enough to just let the emotions or feeling states blow across my awareness like a wispy cloud on a windy day.

At the end of *The Wizard of Oz*, Toto, Dorothy's dog, pulls back the curtain and exposes that the terrifying, dominating wizard is just a small man with a great projector. (Like a film, DVD, or PowerPoint projector.) Behind the screen with his projector, he pretends to be huge and powerful, but face-to-face, without his screen or projector, he is a manageable, not-very-large man.

Much of what causes us to suffer is like that. If we run from it or turn our back or try to deny it, it stays behind the curtain of unconsciousness and feels like a monster. But when we muster the courage to face it, pull back the curtain, stare it in the face, and say, "OK, show me," most of the pain and anxiety dissipate immediately.

This is a teaching in the Upanishads:

Om Purnamadah Purnamidam Purnat Purnamudacyate

Purnasya Purnamadaya Purnamevavasisyate

It says that everything in the universe is pervaded by the Divine. There is nothing, no one, no place that is not pervaded by the Divine. That includes me, and it includes you.

Spirituality does not take us away from the world; it brings us closer to it. Spirituality is awakening from the illusion that who we are is based on what we earn or achieve into the reality that we already embody the Divine. I hope this book opens the space in your heart and mind for your own awakening. That is my prayer and my intention.

CHAPTER 48

Om Brahm

Om Brahm, Om Brahm, Om Brahm. My toes sink into the sand with each step. Om Brahm. Pujya Swamiji has taught me, as his guru taught him, to chant this mantra with each breath, each movement, each step—right, left. Om Brahm. Om Brahm. All is Brahm. All is One. All is God. The Creator and the Creation are one.

I walk up and down the beach as the warm ocean laps at my ankles, the sun setting behind me, dropping into the tops of the palm trees and behind the reef to the west of us. The sun is low enough that even when I walk toward it, I don't need to squint. In a few minutes, it will dip into the ocean.

Om Brahm, Om Brahm. I continue to walk slowly at the water's edge. It's our last night in Hawaii, and I didn't want to miss the sunset. All the others are indoors or watching the sunset from benches at the edge of a cove next to the house. I'm a few hundred yards east of the home at a small, sandy beach, so I can have my sunset in solitude, with my toes in the ocean. *Om Brahm. Om Brahm.* My thoughts are as still as the water of the sea, barely a ripple, and a poem emerges from the gently shifting tide:

> *We build castles in the sand,*
>
> *And pay little heed to the maker of the sea.*
>
> *We use rivers for electricity,*
>
> *And pay little heed to the maker of the rain.*
>
> *We linger over lavish meals,*
>
> *And pay little heed to the maker of the seed.*
>
> *We raise glasses in a toast,*
>
> *And forget to toast the maker of the vine.*

I stop at the far end of the beach in the remaining patch of sunlit sand to face the last rays of the sun. My feet are held by the wet sand as the tide gently comes in and out, splashing softly across my ankles and shins on the way in and gently pulling the sand beneath my feet on the way out. The tide in, the tide out, legs in the ocean, legs not in the ocean. It's a gentle shift. The water is warm, as is the evening air, and the sea is calm. But gentle though the movement is, it is distinguishable. Now, I'm in the ocean; now, I'm not. Now, I'm in. Now, I'm not, as the tide moves in and back out to sea.

As the tide flows in, immersing my legs, I imagine the individual soul approaching like a small wave coming out of the sea and entering a body. Then, in the ebb as the water recedes, returning to where it came. There's a slight tug on the body, a tug on the impressions and connections made during its expression in form, but the tug is gentle and fleeting. The wave has gone back to the sea, and the body, merely matter now, is left on the shore to disintegrate, while the I, the Self, the content, has pulled back into the Ocean.

I close my eyes into the setting sun and drop into oneness with the waves at my feet. The tide is in, my legs are in the water, and the soul is in my body. I feel the dhoti tied at my waist, the heat of the setting sun on my face, the breath in my lungs, and the fine sand between my toes. The tide pulls out, exposing my legs and feet to the air, and my consciousness goes with it, leaving just flesh and bones on the shore. And I feel not the cloth around my waist or the sand between my toes, but the infinite expansiveness of the ocean itself; the wave that was me has merged back into its source. The wave that was me has merged back not only into the ocean, but also back into the sky, into the sun that is setting. It is all the source from which that wave, which is now no longer a wave, had come.

A moment later, the water is again lapping at my legs. Its warmth bathes me, and my feet sink deeper into the sand. The soul has come again into the body. I draw my awareness back into the finite form. I feel the wind against my bare arms, notice the water rising almost to my knees. Again, I'm aware of the breath in my lungs. Then, as the tide recedes again and the current pulls the water and the sand, my awareness is pulled back out to sea. Oneness is the only word my brain can offer, as I have again melted back into wholeness, into that one inseparable, into the Creator itself.

I stand there motionless for many moments, allowing my consciousness to ebb and flow with the tide—now in the body, in the individual, now in the ocean and sky, in the indivisible. The waves of the ocean, coming in and going out, coming in and going out, each real for a moment, seemingly separate for an instant, truly present as it bathes my form, and then a breath later, back out again, back into the waveless whole. My consciousness in and out with the water:

I am body, I am ocean

I am individual, I am infinite

I am form, I am formless.

The tide recedes, pulling more forcibly now at the sand around my legs. As I merge again, carried by the ebbing water into the formless, into the ocean, another wave, a separate stream, flows onto my legs from the other side. It came around and behind me from a slight bend at the end of the beach to wash over my now bare legs. And I realize in the darkening sky that I am *both*—the water that just washed up on me and the expansive ocean into which the other wave returned. I am *here* and I am *there*. I am this individual *and* that expansiveness. It's not either/or. It's both, simultaneously.

I open my eyes. The sun has set outside and has risen within me. *Om Brahm.*

BLESSINGS

When Sadhviji first came to the ashram, I knew she was different. Her purity of heart and the depth of her inner quest were extraordinary. She had had divine experiences on the banks of Mother Ganga that can be understood only as Grace, but her container for experiencing, understanding, and sharing the grace was very unique. From day one she has been completely surrendered to *seva*. She always asks, "What through me?" rather than "What for me?" Her life has been focused on giving more, sharing more, serving more rather than on having more. Now she is a great inspiration to so many, touching and inspiring people all over the world in so many capacities.

I remember when she first came, she used to say that she should have been born in India. But I believe it is truly by God's Grace that she was born in the West because so many more people can relate to her, and her wisdom is applicable to so many more people as she has had the same experiences they go through.

When Sadhviji told me that she was writing this book, I was so happy, as I have always known that her reach and impact will expand throughout the world, touching so many. She has come "From Hollywood to the holy woods of the Himalayas"; however, in this book she has shared more than a journey from Los Angeles to Rishikesh, more than a journey from comfort and luxury in the West to sadhana in the East. She has shared the full depth of her internal journey as well, including even the parts that most people would leave out.

For a respected and renowned spiritual leader in a country like India to share openly about a history of trauma and suffering takes a vast amount of courage. These are things that most people in the East implicitly agree not to talk about. We don't talk about things that might lower us in people's eyes or that would lower the image of our family. When Sadhviji spoke to me about this, she said, "If I removed those parts which could make anyone think less of me, I wouldn't even know myself." In fifty years, she's never done something, or not done something, based on what people will think. It is difficult to convey to those not versed in the cultural traditions of India how deeply courageous and unusual this is.

I am so proud of her for having this courage to share, with an open heart, her full journey and life experiences. She has shown in her life and in her book the power of Truth—that truth matters, and truth should come first! For someone of her caliber to share her truth so openly will have far-reaching ripples and will, I am sure, touch, heal, and inspire so many others to know that they too can be free. Many others will know that they too can forgive, let go, and move forward into freedom. Sadhviji's journey and her raw openness about it will bring the teaching, the touch, and the transformation to those stuck in shame.

Sadhviji is blessed to have been carried to India and India is blessed to have her.

H.H. PUJYA SWAMI CHIDANAND SARASWATIJI
PRESIDENT, PARMARTH NIKETAN, RISHIKESH
FOUNDER, GLOBAL INTERFAITH WASH ALLIANCE

ACKNOWLEDGMENTS

This book is about the blessing of transformation with which I have been gifted. A twenty-five-year-old Jewish Stanford grad from Los Angeles with a history of sexual abuse and bulimia sees God on the banks of a sacred river in India, moves there, becomes a disciple of one of India's most revered saints, is initiated into the sacred Hindu order of sanyas, and becomes a spiritual leader, sharing platforms with luminaries ranging from the Dalai Lama to Prince Charles! Even though I've lived it, it still seems unbelievable. The sheer number of people whose love, wisdom, and abundant generosity of time, energy, and spirit have gone into these fifty years of my life and into this book has been uncountable.

I must begin with gratitude to my parents: my mom and dad (Frank) for raising a young woman so deeply rooted in her commitment to Truth that she took the outrageous step of moving to India at twenty-five after having a spiritual awakening. The courage they gave me to believe in myself is what permitted me to take that step and follow my heart and soul. Their support all these years has been a great blessing.

Love and gratitude to Dr. Ronald Gershman and Suzanne McLellan-Goewy for seeing in nineteen-year-old me a woman who was not actually sick and provided an unconditional love-filled space for me to find my own wisdom and experience my own truth.

Deepest gratitude and love to Greg Schelkun, my amazing "magic healer." Kim Chernin introduced me to Greg when I was twenty-four and said she couldn't quite describe what he did other than "he makes the unbearable bearable." He did that for me then, and for more than twenty-five years has been my go-to psychic diagnostician as well as healer for any ailments of the body or mind.

So much love for Jim and the deep, turbulent, transformative beauty of a marriage we shared, for always being more curious and more fascinated by my suffering than judging it, pushing it away, or trying to "cure" me. And unbounded gratitude for bringing me to India and, ironically, creating a situation where I was alone at the ashram in the soil where transformation and healing blossomed. If I had a magic wand to re-create those years, the only thing I'd change is the pain you experienced. I am so deeply grateful for your continued presence and friendship in my life.

There would be no book in your hands if it weren't for Arielle Ford and Marci Shimoff. For years they pushed me to write my story, helping me realize that, no it's not just a fascinating story, but actually something that will inspire and transform others in a profound way. And well beyond their initial inspiration, they have guided, helped, led, and manifested every aspect of the production, publication, marketing, and more. I've joked that Arielle is the sperm donor, midwife, and milkmaid of this entire book. I grew it inside of me and I pushed it out, but she's done the rest. Arielle is the embodiment of brilliance, experience, expertise, wisdom, boundless energy, and the unparalleled ability to manifest what she sets her mind to; her personality is rooted in the mantra of "yes." Her active lead on this project from the first page helped in every possible way turn this idea into reality.

Jack Kornfield, Jack Canfield, Trudy Goodman, Rev. Michael Beckwith, Bruce Lipton, Barnet Bain, Seane Corn, Rinaldo Brutoco, Dr. Azza Karam, Jonathan Granoff, Prince Ea, Bharat Mitra, Adil Kassam, Barbara Fields, Victor Kazanjian, Janine Firpo, and so many more dear, dear friends have provided deep support, love, and wisdom throughout the writing of the book, and especially around making the choice not to remove the writing about my biological father's sexual abuse (which had been suggested to me, lest I not lose respect in the world of religion). I am so deeply grateful that all of you are in my life.

Extra thanks also to Prince Ea for gifting this book, and me, with such a brilliant Foreword and for your enthusiastic "Yeah!!" when I asked if you would do it.

Great thanks go to Linda Sparrow for her support and assistance with the book proposal and much more, and to Gareth Esersky, my wonderful agent who believed in this book so deeply and has championed it throughout this process.

The team at Insight Editions led by Raoul Goff and Roger Shaw has been so fantastic since the beginning. They really "got" the book, including the vast global impact of its core message. They have put such love into creating a publication that is truly beautiful and also into getting this book into the hands of as many people as possible so that people can realize the possibility of their own healing, their own opening, and their own transformation, and ultimately so that our global family can open themselves to the incredible power of Grace. Much gratitude to Matt Wise and James Faccinto for their commitment and love of this project and their crucial roles in bringing it to such a successful fruition.

My wonderful editor Arnie Kotler was recommended and introduced to me by Jack Kornfield, who gave me loving, generous kudos on the first edition of this book but told me I'd have to be Tolstoy to hold people's attention for the nearly 400 pages. He suggested that Arnie was my answer, and he was! What a joy to work with such a wonderful wordsmith who understood and appreciated the subject so deeply.

Thanks so much to Ganga Nandiniji and the whole seva team of Parmarth Niketan, Global Interfaith WASH Alliance, and and Divine Shakti Foundation for your beautiful presence in my life, and for taking up so much more additional seva while I worked to finish, managing it all so beautifully and perfectly as always, and for being such incredible beings of light, devotion, and service. It's an honor and joy to share this path, and my life, with you.

This book is dedicated to Kim Chernin, PhD, a woman whose role in my life, healing, and transformation cannot be expressed in words, even by one who loves words as much as I do. I met Kim when I was twenty-five, a few months before heading off to India, the universe providing me with a woman equally able to journey with me into my deepest darkness as she was able to later weep with me in ecstasy as we loved God together. There was no thought, feeling, or experience I had that Kim wasn't able to know and feel immediately, deeply, and personally in her own self and then, from that place of knowing, hold my hand as I discovered that I, too, knew. In addition to being my everything for the last twenty-five years—therapist, best friend, and mentor—she was also the first editor of this book, encouraging me page after page to "tell less and show more," to dive deeply into my felt sense of the teachings, and to take the reader along with me on the journey. The tragedy of the Covid pandemic stabbed through my heart as it took her life. Her beautiful body is no longer with us, but I feel her presence nearly constantly, and almost every day I can hear her exclaim with love and wonderment, "Oh, Bhagawati."

Lastly, and most importantly, to my Guru Pujya Swami Chidanand Saraswatiji I offer all the gratitude, all the devotion, and all the love that I have. In Sanskrit the word *Guru* literally means the one who dispels darkness and brings light. A true Guru is one who shines the light not on himself or herself, but who shines the light on you. From the beginning Pujya Swamiji has held that metaphoric superpowered flashlight, and even when at times I was attached to the story of my darkness, he has stood there calmly, quietly, steadfastly until I had no choice but to look into the light and see what he had seen from day one when he told me I could be free. I thank him so deeply for his words "Welcome Home" and opening his home to me, and to so many others from every corner of the earth. I also have such deep gratitude for the way that he has nourished, nurtured, guided, directed, and graced my path. To have a Western woman as a core disciple and to put her onto platforms typically occupied only by Indian men is no small feat. It has not been easy for him, I know that. But his anchoring in divine, genderless (or genderful) truth has made him emphatic and resolute about the role women *must* play in the world, including the world of religion.

GLOSSARY

Aarti: A Hindu religious ceremony offered to one or more deities, frequently made with flowers and incense.

Abhyanga: An Ayurvedic massage that uses warm oil.

Achamana: A purificatory and cleansing preparatory rite of sipping water in Hindu rituals; it is performed at the commencement of such acts as having meals, washing the feet of guests, or any sacred ritual, etc.

Ashram: A hermitage in which a spiritual seeker in the ancient Indian society is supposed to give up the comforts of family life and stay in seclusion under the supervision of an experienced teacher.

Ayurveda: A completely natural, traditional Indian system of medicine that not only concentrates on the disease but seeks to eliminate all toxic imbalances from the body so that the power of resistance to disease is increased.

Badokanasana (Baddha Konasana): A yoga pose (also known as Butterfly Pose) created when sitting by pressing the bottom of one's feet together and letting the knees drop to the side, stretching the inner thighs and groin.

Bhagawan: The exalted one, God; the Supreme Being who is the object of love, knowledge, and worship of all beings; the Absolute that creates, sustains, and dissolves the universe; a term used for Krishna in the *Bhagavad Gita.*

Bhandara: A sacred meal, typically enjoyed by sitting in long rows on the floor, surrounded by dozens, hundreds or thousands of others, and typically partaken of by saints, sadhus, brahmacharis and other spiritual renunciants.

Bindi: From the Sanskrit word *bindu* meaning a small particle, dot, or point, it is the colored dot that lies in the center of a woman's forehead, on the point of the third eye or ajna chakra.

Bolo: Speak, in Hindi.

Brahman: That which is all things, but for some acharyas, it is a term that denotes the Supreme Deity; the all-pervasive manifestation of God.

Chaiwallah: A merchant who sells chai.

Chakra: Meaning "wheel", the energy centers in your body that correspond to major organs, nerves, or areas of the body, starting at the base of one's spine and rising towards the crown of one's head in a straight line.

Chapati: Indian flatbread made from wheat flour, salt, and water.

Darshan: Derived from dṛś, meaning 'to see,' meaning to behold a divine being.

Deva: A deity; a term that can be applied either to the one Supreme Deity or any of the divine beings.

Devanagari: Literally, the script of the gods, almost universally employed for writing Sanskrit; it has influenced the growth and development of many other Indic scripts.

Dhanyavaad: An expression of thanks; the spirit of gratefulness/ obligation in Hindu tradition.

Dharma: Right action; in the *Bhagavad Gita* it means "acting properly in accordance with preordained rules or in relation to virtue." It also refers to the core essence/purpose of anyone or anything (e.g. the dharma of fire is to burn).

Dhyana: Meditation; controlling the mind and turning the vision inwards in order to gain direct perception of the *atman* or soul.

Ghat: A platform leading down to a river, typically a flight of steps.

Gobar: A traditional Indian mix of straw and cow dung.

Gopl: A milkmaid or cowherd woman referring typically to the devotees of Krishna.

Grihastha: Grha means home and *stha* an occupant; *grihastha* is one who has a family, or a householder who maintains functioning of a household through prescribed duties and privileges; the second stage of life.

Guru: A teacher or spiritual guide; "literally, the remover of darkness.

Ishta Devta: The Supreme Deity. The term is sometimes used for the atman.

Jai: Victory or glory.

Jalebi: A treat that consists of sugary batter dipped into boiling oil and deep-fried in overlapping circles, like figure eights.

Japa: Quiet or silent recitation of a prayer or *mantra,* frequently on a string of beads called a mala.

Juta: Literally meaning shoe; also colloquially used to mean unfit or soiled.

Karma: Action that brings future reactions as destiny unfolds.

Katori: A bowl.

Kichari: An Indian meal that consists of mung beans and rice cooked together.

Kumkum: A red-colored powder signifying auspiciousness; made from vermillion powder with turmeric and applied on the forehead of the pious or at the parting of hair of married women.

Kurta: A loose, collarless shirt or upper garment worn by men in South Asia.

Lila: Amorous, playful sport, appearance, or disguise; its philosophical significance refers to a spontaneous creativity of Brahman; a fluxional principle of creation and contraction of the manifest forms of the world. Colloquially it refers to the play of God.

Loki: A zucchini-like squash.

Lota: A large, wide, vessel for water, used frequently for bathing.

Mala: A string of beads, frequently rudraksh or tulsi, upon which one chants a mantra, or japa.

Mantra: A hymn, prayer, or sacred sound; often used in meditation.

Mudra: A symbolic hand gesture used in Hindu ceremonies, yoga, or meditation.

Muni: A hermit; a holy person; a devotee; an ascetic; one who has taken a vow of silence.

Namaste: A simple greeting of hello; in the Vedas, it is a salutation to a divinity.

Om: The sacred sound of the Universe; the sound made during meditation to release healing vibrations deep in the body.

Pakora: Deep-fried potato fritters.

Pavitra: Purity.

Phalhara: "A diet of fruit"; the term used to describe food that is permitted during a fasting period in India.

Pitta: According to Ayurvedic tradition, the subtle energy of fire in the body relating to digestion and inflammation of the joints.

Punya: Piety, virtue; forms of action that lead to favorable karmic results.

Puja: Meaning "offerings", an object that is dedicated to a form of a Lord and used as a way of worship.

Puri: One of the four holiest places in India; it has been said that one who stays here for three days and nights will gain freedom from the cycle of births and rebirths.

Reiki: A healing technique whereby the healer channels energy by means of touch to restore the energy centers, or *chakras,* in the patient's body.

Rishi: A sage or holy man; the *rishis* were the original recipients or "hearers" of the Vedas.

Rishikumar: A name that indicates one as diligent, empathetic, and hardworking.

Rudraksh mala: Rudra refers to a form of Shiva and *aksh* means the "eye"—Shiva's eye; *rudraksh mala* refers to the rosary made from the reddish-brown seeds of the bead tree (*Eleocarpus ganitrus*), believed to represent Lord Shiva.

Sadhana: The means of attaining a result; regulated spiritual practice.

Salwar kameez: Denoting a traditional South Asian outfit: *Salwar* describes loose, pajama-like trousers that cinch at the ankle; *Kameez* describes a long shirt or tunic.

Sanyas: According to Indian tradition, the stage of full renunciation of material pleasures and dedication only to spiritual practice.

Saree: A traditional South Asian garment of cotton or silk, draped elaborately around the body and worn by women.

Satsang: Literally, company of the good that sustains spiritual life.

Seva: Selfless voluntary service to a *guru* and humanity; usually translated as "service" and is related to a job or work paid for, but this does not convey the meaning in the context of Indian spiritual traditions.

Shavasana: A posture in yoga in which all the muscles of the body are in a relaxed condition, resembling that of a dead body.

Swaha: A propitiatory word used in sacrificial rites that are offered as obligations through the medium of fire.

Swami: A name denoting a spiritual leader.

Swamiji: An affectionate term for a spiritual mentor.

Tilak: Religious mark on the forehead and other parts of the body, usually lines drawn with white or colored material; women have only forehead marks, while men have marks on other parts of the body like the arms and the chest.

Vanaprastha: Dwelling in the forest as the third stage of life; one who resorts to the forest alone or with his wife living a frugal lifestyle.

Vata: According to Ayurvedic tradition, the subtle energy of movement associated with wind.

Vedic: Of or relating to the Vedas, the most ancient Hindu scriptures.

Yagna: The ancient ritual prescribed in the Vedas whereby offerings to the gods are made into the sacred fire.

Yatra: An auspicious time for setting out on a journey for specific purposes, including pilgrimages.

Yoga: The practice of mental restraint and inward meditation through controlled breathing and physical movement.

ABOUT THE AUTHOR

American-born Sadhvi Bhagawati Saraswati, PhD, moved to India in 1996. A graduate of Stanford University, she was ordained by Pujya Swamiji, founder of one of the largest interfaith institutions in India, into the tradition of *sanyas* and lives at the Parmarth Niketan ashram in Rishikesh, where she serves Pujya Swamiji's humanitarian projects, teaches meditation, lectures, and counsels individuals and families. One of the world's preeminent spiritual leaders, Saraswati is the author of four previous books on spirituality, and is also well known as a writer, speaker, and activist. She serves on several committees (including in the UN) for international charity and economic development and is a member of the Transformational Leadership Council as well as the Director of the International Yoga Festival. She lives in Rishikesh, India.

MANDALA

An imprint of MandalaEarth

PO Box 3088 San Rafael, CA 94912

www.MandalaEarth.com

Find us on Facebook: www.Facebook.com/MandalaEarth

Follow us on Twitter: @MandalaEarth

Text © 2021 Sadhvi Bhagawati Saraswati

Library of Congress Cataloging-in-Publication Data available.

Trade Edition ISBN: 978-1-64722-365-6

Export Edition ISBN: 978-1-64722-535-3

PUBLISHER: Raoul Goff

ASSOCIATE PUBLISHER: Phillip Jones

CREATIVE DIRECTOR: Chrissy Kwasnik

ASSOCIATE ART DIRECTOR: Ashley Quackenbush

DESIGN SUPPORT: Brooke McCullum

EDITORIAL DIRECTOR: Katie Killebrew

MANAGING EDITOR: Matt Wise

EDITORIAL ASSISTANT: Sophia Wright

SENIOR PRODUCTION MANAGER: Greg Steffen

ROOTS of PEACE REPLANTED PAPER

Earth Aware Editions, in association with Roots of Peace, will plant two trees for each tree used in the manufacturing of this book. Roots of Peace is an internationally renowned humanitarian organization dedicated to eradicating land mines worldwide and converting war-torn lands into productive farms and wildlife habitats. Roots of Peace will plant two million fruit and nut trees in Afghanistan and provide farmers there with the skills and support necessary for sustainable land use.

Manufactured in Turkey by Insight Editions

10 9 8 7 6 5 4 3 2 1

TOP LEFT: On a whale watching trip to Catalina Island with dad (Frank).

TOP RIGHT: Sadhviji's bat-mitzvah, 1984.

BOTTOM: With mom and dad—early to mid-1980s.

TOP: With mom, sometime in the early 1990s.

BOTTOM LEFT: On a backpacking trip in the Tetons, summer 1988.

BOTTOM RIGHT: Stanford graduation, June 1993.

TOP: Crossing from Nepal into Tibet on trip to Kailash Mansarovar, June 1998. Left to right: Sadhvi, Pujya Swamiji, Pujya Sant Shri Rameshbhai Oza (Bhaishri), Pujya Swami Gurusharananandji Maharaj (Maharajji).

BOTTOM LEFT: In the tent camp on the banks of Lake Mansarovar, June 1998.

BOTTOM RIGHT: During a special event at Parmarth Niketan, mid-1997 or 1998.

OPPOSITE TOP: Being blessed by Pujya Swamiji—early 2000s.

OPPOSITE BOTTOM: On the banks of Ganga in the early days.

TOP: With Swami Ramdevji at the Kumbha Mela in Prayag Raj.

BOTTOM: Speaking with His Excellency Ram Nath Kovind, the President of India, at President House.

OPPOSITE TOP LEFT: With a young mentally and physically challenged girl who had come for a free medical camp at Parmarth Niketan.

TOP RIGHT: Love during a Hindu-Muslim interfaith celebration of India's Independence Day, August 2018.

MIDDLE RIGHT: Sharing love, and the gift of reading, with a child at one of Divine Shakti Foundation's free schools.

BOTTOM: Meditating on the banks of Ganga with the rishikumars of the gurukul/orphanage at Parmarth Niketan.

TOP: Launch of the *Encyclopedia of Hinduism* in London by the Prime Minister of Great Britain, Mr. David Cameron, with many dignitaries at the Queen Elizabeth II Centre.

CENTER LEFT: Panel event on women's religious leadership at UNFPA headquarters, New York, during the United Nations Commission on the Status of Women, March 2019.

BOTTOM LEFT: With friends Prince EA and Dr. Bruce Lipton in Colorado.

BOTTOM RIGHT: Giving a TEDx talk at the University of San Francisco.

TOP LEFT: Love with Sister Rev. Sr. Agatha Ogochukwu Chikelue.

TOP RIGHT: Sharing about the work of Global Interfaith WASH Alliance with Secretary-General of the United Nations, António Guterres.

BOTTOM: Interfaith peace prayer ceremony and mega event at the international Peace Palace, the Hague.

TOP: At Governor House, Mumbai, October 2019. Left: Anil Kapoor, Bollywood actor.
Center left: Pujya Swamiji, Hon'ble Governor of Maharashtra.

BOTTOM: Launch of Sadhvi's book *Come Home to Yourself* in India with HH Dalai Lama, 2019.

OPPOSITE TOP: With Jane Goodall at the Parliament of the World's Religions, 2015.

OPPOSITE BOTTOM: With Pope Francis in Rome.

TOP: With Sting and his wife, Trudie Styler, at their home in New York.

BOTTOM: At the NDTV Cleanathon with famous actor Amitabh Bachchan, offering him a rudraksha sapling.

OPPOSITE TOP: Prince Charles and Duchess Camilla perform Ganga Aarti at Parmarth Niketan.

OPPOSITE BOTTOM: Sadhvi speaks about the importance of protecting water at an interfaith gathering hosted by HH the Dalai Lama in Bodhgaya, India.

TOP: Special interfaith worship to WASH event hosted by Global Interfaith WASH Alliance with UNICEF in Ladakh, uniting hands for clean water and sanitation.

BOTTOM: Leading meditation at Maharishi Ashram (Beatles Ashram) in Rishikesh, during the International Yoga Festival.

OPPOSITE TOP: Meditating under the trees.

OPPOSITE BOTTOM: International Women's Day celebration at Parmarth Niketan.

ABOVE: Being showered with flower petals on her birthday by
devotees, friends and the children of the gurukul.